Praise for *You Know*

'Heron's descriptions of life in 195... winningly dour Ivor Cutler-ish air . . . Greig has a knack for refracted memoir, viewing his own life . . . with elegaic wisdom'

Peter Ross, *Guardian*

'Mike Heron and Robin Williamson, the Edinburgh band's two leaders, threw open the doors of possibility, as musical liberation and philosophy entwined . . . It is the vision of the joyful player that this co-written memoir celebrates . . . Exceptionally beautiful'

Wesley Stace, *Times Literary Supplement*

'Heron's turn of phrase and eye for detail extend . . . to every aspect of Edinburgh's mid-sixties beatnik life, realised in beguiling sensory images . . . Heron *has* to write a second volume, but at least this first instalment might help to secure the recognition the band so transparently deserve'

Mark Ellen, *New Statesman*

'With his characteristic modesty and self-deprecating humour, Mike Heron recalls the beginnings of the British folk revival and, though he would never admit as much, the part he played in bringing folk to a new audience'

John Burnside

'Charming and oddly moving . . . His account of growing up in Edinburgh in the late 1950s and 60s has all the excitement of a good rock biopic. We share in the thrills . . . Heartwarming, charismatic mix of self-effacing charm and wistful empathic engagement with the world'

Matt Milton, *Songlines*

'Warm, meditative, evocative . . . Much more than a conventional music biography'

Graeme Thomson, *Herald*

'From travelling in an open-sided military helicopter with a terrified Ravi Shankar and catching Jimi Hendrix's closing set at Woodstock, this book is a must-read for anyone looking for an insider's view of the psychedelic sixties'

M Magazine

Praised by Paul McCartney and Robert Plant, Mike Heron, born in Edinburgh, was a founder member of the Incredible String Band. As a solo artist he has worked with John Cale, Pete Townshend and Keith Moon. He is still writing and performing music, touring regularly with a host of musicians including his daughter Georgia and Trembling Bells.

Andrew Greig is the author of six books of poetry, two mountaineering books; two non-fiction books and six novels. He won the Saltire and the Scottish Book of the Year awards, and has been shortlisted for the Walter Scott Prize. He lives in Orkney and Edinburgh with his wife, the novelist Lesley Glaister.

By Andrew Greig

FICTION

Electric Brae • *The Return of John MacNab*
When They Lay Bare • *That Summer*
Romanno Bridge • *In Another Light* • *Fair Helen*

NON-FICTION

Summit Fever • *Kingdoms of Experience*
At the Loch of the Green Corrie • *Preferred Lies*

POETRY

This Life, This Life: New and Selected Poems
As Though We Were Flying
Getting Higher: The Complete Mountain Poems
Found At Sea

YOU KNOW
WHAT YOU COULD BE

Tuning into the 1960s

Mike Heron & Andrew Greig

riverrun

First published in Great Britain in 2017 by riverrun
This paperback edition published in Great Britain in 2018 by

riverrun

An imprint of

Quercus Publishing Ltd
Carmelite House
50 Victoria Embankment
London EC4Y 0DZ

An Hachette UK company

A CIP catalogue record for this book is available
from the British Library

PB ISBN 978 0 85705 4 876

10 9 8 7 6 5 4 3 2 1

Typeset by CC Book Production

Printed and bound in Great Britain by Clays Ltd, St Ives plc

Contents

PART I:

YOU KNOW WHAT YOU COULD BE

PART II:
IN THE FOOTSTEPS OF THE HERON

Part I

You Know What You Could Be

MIKE HERON

Dedicated to Corrina and Georgia. Always.

Atty Watson

It's 1957 and I'm standing in a corner of the vast playground of George Heriot's School in the shadow of Edinburgh Castle. I'm fifteen, it's my first day at a new school and I don't know anyone here. I've started to wonder how I'll ever fit in when at the edge of my vision I see a small boy approaching, carrying a huge guitar. At close range I see the guitar only looks so big because he is very small indeed. Slightly out of breath he leans on his guitar case and holds out a hesitant hand: 'Allan Coventry.' He has sticking-up black hair, thick glasses and a toothy smile.

Allan's heard I play guitar and wonders how many chord shapes I've learnt. Chatting away about tutor books we discover we both favour the Bert Weedon method, 'Play in a Day'. It's the lunch break and we're part of a sea of school uniforms. As soon as we move on to discussing what music we like, a boy of about our age comes over to join us. He's of athletic build and dressed in a naval cadet's uniform, which doesn't fit brilliantly but gives him an important jaunty look.

He's in the same class as Allan so we're introduced: 'Atty Watson.' Assuming he's joined the boys' navy I admire his outfit. 'I'm a flyer not a floater,' says Atty vehemently.

Heriot's encourages cadet membership, resulting in a playground awash with scaled-down sailors, soldiers and airmen. Unfortunately when Atty enrolled in the trainee air force there was only a sailor's outfit available. He explains he isn't even interested in the navy, but like us is interested in and excited about guitars, chords, tutor books and the repertoire we hope to have the day *after* reading Bert. We're still talking when the bell rings, and the three of us agree to meet after school.

Allan's father plays double bass in a prominent Scottish country-dance band, he's also a thriving landlord with a family home large enough to house three guitar-thrashing novices in an enormous unused room. Allan, of course, has a brand new Gibson. Luckily, after surfing the wave of the '57 skiffle craze, cheap and nasty guitars landed in music shops. Atty and I manage to get one each.

It's Sunday afternoon and we're standing outside Allan's large detached stone house on opulent Napier Terrace, clutching our cardboard triangles. A brief greeting later and we are perched on chairs (two of us have yet to get guitar straps) following Bert's 'how to tune your guitar' instructions (on page two). It has taken longer than expected to learn the three chords required for our first attempt at a song, but we now feel ready for Atty to count in 'That'll Be the Day'. My local newsagent stocks a monthly booklet called *Favourite Chart Hits*. This month's edition features Buddy Holly, Fats Domino and the Everly Brothers. It has the words of hit songs with the chord names written above, which is all we need – we already know all the tunes. We haven't got to single note melodies yet (that's on page 108), so I have to 'dah dah dah diddley dah' the solos. We are strumming the three chords: they sound right, and we're doing our best to coordinate. Atty and I are singing the words in unison and it's completely different to our solitary bedroom versions. Feet are tapping, half-suppressed smiles are exchanged, and everything slots together as we'd hoped. The door opens and Allan's little sister Diane arrives and starts skipping and bopping around – our first audience.

Elated and slightly dazed, we go our separate ways, but dream the same dream. Hordes of girls are dancing and screaming in a constantly changing sequence of concerts at famous venues. We are on a raised stage amid stacks of expensive equipment, playing dozens of chord shapes with ease. We all have guitar straps, supporting our top-of-the-range electric guitars. And really cool outfits. Banners are everywhere, shrieking out the name we came up with after hours of heated discussion: we are the one and only RAMJETS. Unfortunately though, despite the fame, Monday arrives.

At 6.30 a.m. in the kitchen at Sydney Terrace, the coffee percolator is already gurgling and wheezing on the stove. In the corner of the room between two chairs, a muslin jelly bag suspended by a walking stick is slowly dripping its contents into an enamel bowl. It could be any morning in term time; the variations are minor. Across the table the *Scotsman*'s pages rustle. I look up and see my father's thin and anxious face taking in the births and deaths; a distant acquaintance has died, which just serves to point out the sameness otherwise. My father has time for his daily bowl of porridge, having prepared everything the night before. Shoes polished, briefcase stuffed with marked homework, umbrella and hat waiting by the door. He fills his Thermos flask and lights up a Capstan Full Strength. He is a serious smoker; his nickname at school is Kipper. Unlike my father, I haven't prepared anything at all. After I transferred to Heriot's, where he is head of the English department, the morning routine has been disturbed, and he has to tolerate my frantic five minutes of scrabbling and gathering before we hurriedly set off together.

It's well into autumn, so our collars are up as we wait together at the bus stop. It's a regular service and, since he makes the journey every weekday, my father's timing is impeccable. There is barely a minute to nod to our daily fellow travellers before our bus arrives and we climb upstairs. We always use the top deck as it's 'No Smoking' downstairs. My father, of course, lights up immediately and unfurls his paper, sighing with the satisfaction of familiarity. I, on the other hand, immediately feel a bit sick; one smoker early in the morning on the top of a bus is bad enough – today there are four puffing with determination.

It's a two-bus journey. One takes us all the way up Regent Road and halfway along Princes Street; the other up The Mound to The Meadows. From there it's a half-mile walk to school. We started out at 7.30 and it's taken an hour: perfect timing. Fifteen hundred pupils need to be in the senior hall by 8.50. As we walk we become more and more engulfed by the blue, white and grey of school uniforms converging from all compass points for morning assembly. Although there's a podium from which the headmaster will deliver his pep talk after the obligatory hymn, the entire tedious carry-on revolves around one man – head of the music department Dr Eric Smith.

The teachers are not required to attend assembly, so when I head for the senior hall, my father climbs up to his large turret-top room. The coal fire there has been lit by the janitor at 6 a.m., and stoked at regular intervals, so that when he opens the door it's a welcoming temperature. The fire is blazing and the scuttle full. He unscrews his Thermos, lights up, and, before there are any boys to see him, puts his feet up on a desk and plans the day's lessons.

By contrast, I am clinging to a lukewarm radiator in the freezing assembly hall, still feeling sick and hoping Dr Smith will choose a mellow, comforting piece of music to start the school day, and not go for anything too rumbustious. Every day he selects a suitable piece to begin the service with, and another for the boys to file out to twenty minutes later. Being the kind of person he is, 'suitable' tends to mean highlighting his prowess. Arms flailing, feet pounding, organ stops being pulled out like chicken feathers.

Eric Smith is an imposing figure. In his fifties, slightly plump, today he is crammed into a maroon three-piece suit. His spiky black hair is combed back and he has just a hint of a moustache. Atty is three seats to my left and we catch each other's eye. We are fascinated by Doc Smith. He's a gifted musician and knows it. Atty and I have compiled a top ten of our 'most feared exhibition pieces'. These are not evil in themselves, but become so in the context of being played in front of hundreds of cold, half-awake boys in a huge damp echo chamber. The Doc's flamboyant delivery doesn't help. Widor's Symphony for Organ No. 5 is at number one.

He raises his hands above the keyboard. We can't look. Very gradually, though, it dawns on us that there is a sweet melody warming the chilly air. It's a tune that sheep could safely graze to, meaning that we can slide the backs of our hands across our brows in relief. We do exactly that while standing for 'We Plough the Fields and Scatter'. The sprint at service end, as the sound swells, is expected; the first class of the day starts in ten minutes. As Widor's storm is brewing, Atty and I escape – bobbing on the blue sea of schoolboys, all with the same idea.

'Have you thought about what you want to do in life, Michael?' It's the voice of Mr Campbell, the careers master. It's a full-time post, though you would never guess it from his level of expertise. A burly man with unruly salt-and-pepper hair, he has gone for the smart-casual look, possibly to hint at the fun that lies ahead by making a good career choice. He's wearing a pale-green Viyella shirt, sports jacket, slacks and suede shoes, and makes a funny crunchy noise with his knuckles while awaiting my reply.

My response is a long time coming. I will not be mentioning the Ramjets: I know that I won't be able to talk to him about the three fifteen-year-olds who are barely able to strum three chords in the right order, so I stop my lips from forming the word 'music'. (Doc's music is a serious, exam-orientated, adult kind of thing, always classical, save for a burst of Jimmy Shand on Burns Night. Preferably it involves performances of works by dead composers and should lead to a proper job with a salary.)

Mr Campbell's usual role is to console pupils who have failed their leaving exams and offer them an alternative route to their chosen career. In this instance, however, as I've been dumped from chemistry in the third year without a hope of passing even the lowliest of exams, I've been sent to see Mr Campbell to decide which subject will eventually enhance my leaving qualifications. Looking at his beefy expressionless face, I summon up my reply: 'Sir, I think I need more time to find which profession most suits me. Would it be possible to have some free periods in the library for study?' I didn't have the slightest intention of ending up in a profession, of course, but he didn't care. I had at least come up with something, and a look of relief crept across his face as he saw me move towards the door.

There are turrets at each of the four corners of the school, and in the centre, a large cobbled square – the quadrangle. There are cloisters under the arches on two sides. One leads to the dining room; beyond the one opposite is the cloakroom.

With a new young cook offering a quiet revolution in the lunch hall, Atty, noticing the crowd swelling daily, sees it not so much a queue as an audience. He has mustered his puny troops and picked his day. It's pelting down, but it's dry under the arches and no one wants to lose their place. A captive audience.

As the pupils begin to snake through the cloisters, from the clock tower comes the bell for the lunch break. In the cloakroom, Atty plays as much of a 'powerchord' as he can manage on his acoustic guitar, and all three of us sing 'That'll Be the Day', frantically strumming the chord of A. When we finish the song, the cheers are thunderous. This is partly due to sheer numbers in the echoing arches, but mostly because it's boys doing something for boys; three of the third year choosing to use their lunchtime to entertain them. The Ramjets have had their first ovation, and it feels great.

Although we hadn't done a lot to deserve it, the roar of appreciation that day spurred us on through hours and hours of practice, after school, at weekends and in the holidays. We taped pick-ups onto our guitars, and shared ownership of some of the most abused and feeble amplifiers in existence. A five-watt Elpico, a tatty old second-hand Selmer covered with Fablon and a triangular Watkins Dominator well past any domination. Allan and Diane put on parties at their house where we could listen to records and hopefully impress girls with our versions of chart hits. We recruited a classmate, Bart Faccenda, to swell the band repertoire with Elvis vocals, his speci-ality. The popularity of dances, mostly in church halls, was steadily increasing as rock 'n' roll tightened its grip on the youth. We felt a drummer could help us get those kinds of gigs and decided to ask Mervyn Smith to join us. Another thing in his favour was that his father owned The American Man's shop, in Edinburgh's East Side, which specialised in college campus-style 'preppie' clothes: loafers, desert-sand-coloured slacks, powder-puff-blue shirts and strangely embossed pullovers, all of which we thought pretty cool. He had an expensive drum kit and could play the drum break in the Ventures' 'Walk Don't Run', an instrumental that we liked a lot. Mervyn was small, round-faced and cuddly-looking, and when dressed from head to toe in a preppie outfit (which he usually was), looked like a little neat teddy bear.

We persuaded the organiser of the Trinity Scout Hall dance night that he needed us to do a set when the main band took a break. Mervyn cut out a card circle that was big enough to fit his bass drum and scrawled RAMJETS on it. The banners would have to wait. I sang 'Peggy Sue' and 'Oh, Boy!', and Bart, who was the same age as us but looked a good deal older, did 'Are You Lonesome Tonight?' and 'It's Now or Never', with a bit of hip movement and a slightly worrying Latin lover's sneer. The organising boy scout liked it and spread the word. Once we were on the other halls' booking lists, the gigs kept coming: Corstorphine, Portobello, Oxgangs and, for a glimpse of life outside the circuit, the Lotus Club in Musselburgh. The audiences did contain girls. Laconic, aloof, detached sort of girls, standing around looking as if they were there by mistake. They were not the enthusiastic hormone-charged screaming girls that we had fantasised, wildly dancing their inhibitions away. A spark of hope for our future remained though, when Allan spotted a poster announcing auditions for singers and bands at the Palladium Theatre. We were there in a flash.

When we got to the audition we found that eight girls of assorted shapes and sizes had independently decided that 'Sailor' by Petula Clark was the song for them. As each one stepped up to the mic the band in the pit played exactly the same intro in exactly the same key, followed by voices in a variety of timings and pitches. Then it was the turn of the groups. Three guitars, drums and a singer seemed a very popular line-up; most of them feeling 'Lonesome Tonight', so that by the time it got to our turn, the judges were fading fast. Bart, deciding an up-tempo number might cut through the lethargy, had launched into 'Twenty Flight Rock', rather than the well-rehearsed

Elvis balladry we expected, leaving the band lagging a bar behind him all the way through.

'*Next!*'

Licking our wounds in the wings, we watched silently while stack after stack of gleaming equipment was wheeled past us onto the stage. On the bass drum painted in silver, black and red was 'SILVER DUKES'. The band followed, (surprisingly only four of them) all wearing matching tartan suits. With synchronised high kicks and fancy footwork they leapt into 'Please Don't Touch (I Shake Too Much)' the lead singer vibrating violently. With the judges still out of their chairs clapping wildly, we mutually agreed to disband the Ramjets.

The snow falls, each flake in its appropriate place

I'm leaning into the sleety wind as I make slow progress up the Bridges from Princes Street. I feel like a man on a mission. I'm playing most nights with a band I'm chuffed to be in, but I've replaced a really talented jazz guitarist, (whose group it was originally), and I am clueless in the genre. I do, however, like the oddball bunch that is left: Atty on bass, Vic the drummer (no, that's not maracas you hear, he just takes a lot of pills), lead singer Russell Fallon (bricklayer by day) and electric banjo player Andy Turner, (window-dresser by day). Andy looks like Toulouse-Lautrec and boasts a lot about his sexual activities with his circus trapeze-artist girlfriend. Atty and I are impressed. Andy Hampton, the sax player and band leader, just puts on his world-weary look and counts in with a '1-2-3-4 "Hallelujah I Love Her So" . . .' We have a residency at a small but popular club, the Gamp, much to the annoyance of the Screaming Citizens, our greatest rivals. We are . . . ROCK BOTTOM AND THE DEADBEATS.

I have press-ganged Atty into joining this expedition (he's used to my random obsessions). As the sleet turns to snow we pass the Central School of Dance, and the memory of one of our worst ideas is stirred. Our combined pace slows noticeably.

A couple of years earlier, to our surprise, in spite of our band appearances and general social skills, we'd experienced a scarcity of 'girl action'. We misguidedly thought that ballroom dancing might fill the emptiness. Taking the initiative, Atty found the Edina School of Dance, and we turned up in sports jackets and brothel creepers, our hair neatly parted. Reggie (pronounced with a hard 'g') Harkins, an enormous Doberman at his heels, demonstrated the quickstep and foxtrot for a shilling, while Karl gazed at our fleshy legs, slobbering in anticipation. We completely failed to learn anything (fear having played its part), but our shilling had run out, and we were sent to another of his establishments, not a hundred yards away – the Central School of Dance. There, we were to practise ballroom dancing with two twenty-year-olds who were about to sit their teaching exams. Paying another two shillings enabled us to judder around the room, dancing quickstep with the girls to the ringing tones of 'Side Saddle' by Russ Conway.

We did finally take our dancing to the Palais, only to find the whole place was under the spell of the Twist.

It's great fun with the Deadbeats. Andy Hampton is older than us and, outwardly at least, more respectable, which seems to attract a good class of gig – graduations, twenty-firsts and weddings. Also his charm has earned us gigs of some diversity and calibre, including

Burntisland Palais, the Edinburgh University Nigerian Union and Kirkconnel Miners' Welfare Club. Our favourite though is the American Air Force logistics base at Kirknewton. An all-male affair in the 'other ranks' mess, it's a drinking, chatting audience, but they're appreciative of cover versions of songs by American artists. We're able to offer our Jerry Lee Lewis, Chuck Berry, Buddy Holly and Ray Charles, ensuring our popularity and repeat bookings. This is important as, though we don't know it, we won't be able to taste burgers as good as theirs again in Scotland for about thirty years. The quality coffee and imported beers are welcome too, but the things that really make us desperate to return are the cocktails, which are only a shilling each: Moscow Mules, Manhattans, Whisky Sours and Vodka Gimlets.

The band provides a lot of satisfaction; what it doesn't do is allow for the inclusion of original songs. It's 1962, and if people like the way we play familiar stuff, they dance. If they don't, they talk. I'm increasingly interested in writing songs and have noticed that, when it comes to folk music, attention seems to be paid to the overall quality of a song – familiar or not.

I have begun subscribing to an American folk audio-tape service, which, in return for a postal order, sends home-compiled reel-to-reel tapes of an obscure and sometimes downright arcane nature. Woody Guthrie describes features of the American landscape while casually playing a rustic fiddle tune. Next comes a recording of tapdancers' clogs in Tennessee, followed by a Midwestern stockman playing a waltz on a horseshoe using a cow's jawbone. You get the idea.

All this is marrow to my bones. Here I am living with my parents in a stifling, middle-class part of Edinburgh and every month an alien and strangely stamped package travels halfway round the world to clunk through the letterbox. I grab it and rush to the Grundig: cowboys, dusty vistas, secret pickings and tunings, coyotes, yodelling hobos, shady groves and, above all, weirdness. I want in.

There are treasures among the trivia, some of them still glittering for me today. Rediscovered guitarists coaxed out of obscurity: Reverend Gary Davis, Snooks Eaglin and Sleepy John Estes. Artists that weren't well known at that time: the Carter Family, Doc Watson and Robert Johnson. And then there's a feature that particularly gets my attention – about a guitar-playing nanny called Elizabeth Cotten.

When Appalachian guitarist Ralph Rinzler accompanied Ewan MacColl's singing at a Glasgow show in 1958, a bug-eyed Archie Fisher listened with amazement and begged him for the secrets of a particular technique he had used. Credited to Elizabeth Cotten, who wrote 'Freight Train', it's familiar to us now through Blind Boy Fuller, Taj Mahal, Ralph McTell and countless folk floor singers. It made a lone guitar sound like a trio – walking bass line, rhythm in the middle and a melody on the treble strings. Nobody else knew how to do it then, and it made Archie the go-to guitar teacher.

Snow-covered and numb, we're almost there. Up Chambers Street, behind the university's courtyard – here it is – the Crown Bar. In Gordon Simpson's music shop, when I asked about the folk music scene, they had directed me here, to Archie's 'Night at the Crown'.

Phase One of the mission is complete. Inside now, we take in our surroundings – crowded, bright, noisy and hot. Noticing that no one is drinking anything other than beer, Atty shuffles through bodies to the counter, bringing back two pints. The steam rising from us mingles with the fug of tobacco smoke on its way up to the yellow flaking ceiling. The central herd is conservatively dressed and exclusively male, but around the fringes are little clumps of would-be bohemians of both sexes, slouched at tables and looking exotic and alluring. Without a word we surreptitiously edge outwards. That's when we see the open door and a girl at a table taking admission money for the folk club. We advance, holding two shillings. And we're in! It's full but we find a table at the back to lean against. At the front of the room is a wide strip of clear space serving as a stage. On it are two microphone stands, two wooden kitchen chairs and a bar stool. There is no stage lighting, but the ceiling lights are angled to focus on that part of the room. From our table, even though it's dim around us, we can see that the audience is the reverse of those out in the bar. Apart from a sprinkling of Aran sweaters, sports jackets and pipes (uniform of the strict traditionalists), all is bohemian. Some are folkniks by night, some are deeply rooted in beatness, but none is as genuine-looking as the young man now clambering onto the stool. He's the real deal.

Lanky, thin and pale with an orange–yellow mane flowing over his grey flannel shirt, his outfit has been carefully selected from second-hand shop rails: herringbone tweed waistcoat, orange-and-black kipper tie and baggy olive-green cords. His legs end in brown moccasins that he's obviously made himself. He is a tall man, but a bit stooped and lopsided with an awkward gait. Wearing a look of someone wise beyond their years, he perches on the stool, his banjo nestled so fondly in his lap that it seems part of him. Tilting his head a little, a dreamy expression on his face, with a half-wink he casts a knowing look around the rapt audience and launches into 'The Spaniard that Blighted My Life'.

'Ladies and Gentlemen, that was his first performance at The Crown, let's hear it for . . . Clive Palmer.'

Forgetting my urgent clawhammer instruction needs, I sidle through the wildly applauding throng, acutely aware that my white office shirt, cavalry twills and school raincoat can't even touch the hem of flamboyance. Nonetheless I'm determined to meet this otherworldly troubadour. I want to tell him how his performance has catapulted me out of my folk comfort zone, how I always hated banjos until I heard his, and how I will never miss an opportunity to see him play again. What I secretly want to ask him is what made him so charismatic and could he please be my friend and provide me with a passport to the beatnik underworld? I don't quite reach him though before the next performer moves towards the stage. Introduced as Robin, he is obviously a regular, and requests reverberate when he reaches the microphone. He has slightly long fair hair, a pink complexion and the beginnings of a pointy beard. He looks more poet than minstrel in his tweed jacket, jeans and black waistcoat. Singing with a Scots burr and a serious expression, he plays skilful guitar accompaniments to English and Irish songs. He ends with jigs and reels played on the whistle. I leave him and Clive in mutual appreciation and rejoin Atty, who looks as if he's rather enjoyed his brief folk sojourn.

I never did miss the opportunity to see Clive play; but it wasn't enough. His charisma remained a mystery. We became close friends, and the passport was delivered . . .

Billy

Clive's friend Billy is a drug-dealer. He sells hashish and there are only a few that do in early-sixties Edinburgh, but to bundle him in with them would be misleading. What he deals in is the gratification of the senses; no shabby backstreet exchanges for him. Just gaining entry to his flat is not a given. I climb the stairs. Thanks, Clive.

A record of Dylan Thomas reading *A Child's Christmas in Wales* is resonating deeply. The room is all cushions and Persian carpets dominated by a central hookah. The walls are totally covered with collages made from Sunday supplements, rare posters, Chinese calligraphy, Japanese ink-sketched scrolls, album covers and mosaics. There is not a cushion unlittered by beautiful people. Espresso is sipped, Turkish delight and baklava nibbled. In the corner sits a decadent-looking Clive.

Through flat-sharing in Glasgow, London, Paris and St Ives over the years, Clive and Billy couldn't know each other any better. They know what the other is going to say before it registers as a thought on his face. But with this closeness comes a certain tension: they've quietly slipped away from each other many times, and quietly returned.

One Dylan is replaced by another when Billy's girlfriend Maggie arrives with Bob's first album and puts it on the turntable. I've already choked on my first ever joint and am stoned out of my muffin, rather like the whole room, which is held by this music, astonished and silenced: transfixed . . . When the record ends Billy decides to become master of ceremonies. He's imposing, tall and muscular with long thick black hair. Wearing the leader's uniform – which is a cross between a poncho and a magician's cloak – he organises a game that involves everyone sitting in a circle and facing inward with their eyes closed. Everyone of course but Billy, who paces round the circle slowly and menacingly for what seems like ages till finally he taps the chosen one's head with a rolled-up newspaper. We all shriek nervously with paranoia coursing through our veins. It still seems to beat parental Ludo hands down. Everything is brought to a close by Clive singing 'Blues My Naughty Sweetie Gives to Me'. It seems oddly normal.

I'm back at the drug emporium two days later. I don't want to appear too eager or addicted. It's not so packed this time: there are only a couple of freaky blokes and two pretty girls with long dark hair, enormous black eyes and Bulgarian embroidered blouses. Clive is in a corner doing macramé. At his feet are little bits of thonged leatherwork, tiny Japanese boxes woven from bamboo and whittled wind-instrument reeds. I'm just about to remark on how good he is with his hands when he picks up his new construction and produces a wailing noise. It's a set of bagpipes made out of pyjamas and hollowed-out bones he's found in the woods. They sound okay. They sound amazing, considering.

Clive introduces me to Eddie, a very thin chap with a fertile waist-length dark red beard. He's wearing a homemade version of seventeenth-century Highland dress, and his sporran is stuffed with the wherewithal for joint-making, which is exactly what he is currently doing. As I'm leaving two or three hours later, I realise it is not just lack of people that has made the flat more spacious: it has also been the subject of extreme tidying and cleaning. Gone is the hookah as are most of the cushions, and in their place are a dozen bales of expensive-looking tweed. I've learned enough about this place to know not to ask.

I wait a whole week before my next visit, just to show that I see it as no big thing to have been accepted as one of them (it is!). This has allowed enough time for the transformation of the front room into a bespoke tailors' salon. In the centre is Clive, tape measure draped around his neck, pencil in clenched teeth, scissors in hand. He is flanked by his assistants – Eddie (in full regalia) and Billy. They are fluttering around a light-brown houndstooth tweed suit (which is being tried on by a stiff-looking city gent) making last-minute adjustments. The penny drops. The arrival of a lot of Harris Tweed from God-knows-where has triggered entrepreneurial thoughts in the trio. Clive's 'good with his hands' skills can be put to use by making it known that his made-to-measure suits and quality of cloth are second to none and available at a reasonable price. So, last-minute tweaks are done, much money is paid and hands are shaken. We run to the window and listen to his descending footsteps on the stair, restraining our whoops. Now the main door opens and he walks pompously off down the street where first a penny-sized circle appears on his backside, then a broad band of white, then no trousers and . . . behold, a Y-fronted city gent. Time to pull the curtains and lock the door.

In the dark and battened-down room, there is no escape from the dominating presence of the tweed money. After ten tense minutes Billy pockets it blatantly. He morphs into a military commander in a crisis. On the turntable, at low volume, is Ravi Shankar. Deep bending growling notes are squeezed out as, from a still place, he steels himself for the emotions of the developing raga, providing us with a temporary shelter from the storm. Billy comes to a decision: he dispatches Clive to a safe house in Kirkcaldy, Eddie to friends in Skye, and beckons me to the back room.

He wants to let me know he's worried about my artistic progress and concerned that I'm not playing to consciousness-awakened beatnik types, but to lushes in bars who are numbing out the world. I have found this to be a common theme, the smokers versus the drinkers. Billy comes up with a plan that will expand my audience among the like-minded. We could go down to Brighton he says, and busk on the beach, 'Why not bring your friend Mike Smith (drinking buddy of mine, music fanatic and recent hash convert) along?' Noticing I looked slightly hesitant he continued: 'C'mon, man, only two or three days, you could do with an adventure.'

It occurs to me that he needs to get away from the house, do something to make the tailoring money disappear, and maybe buy drugs to sell on. Although slightly nervous, I am feeling ready for some expansion and Mike had just left his job at the bank. So off we hitch.

The solo busking on the beach goes surprisingly well, though I can't imagine how these people have any money to spare – they're all roll-ups, patches and sleeping bags – but they're generous, enter into the spirit of things and the coins keep chinking in. There's not a lot of competition as there are only two others: a girl with a tambourine, singing and soft-shoe shuffling on the shingle, and an older guy in a suit playing a twelve-string. I form an impromptu trio with them and briefly discuss repertoire. Beginning with 'Jug of Punch' and 'Wild Rover', we are soon across the pond doing 'Blueberry Hill' and 'My Blue Heaven'.

The sun goes down. Billy, Mike and I are sitting on a wall eating fish and chips in the moonlight. Unfolding a hand-drawn map, Billy shows us the way to his friend Rob's cottage, which is where we can stay the night. It's a complicated route, and an hour later, burdened by backpacks, sleeping bags and a guitar, we are still climbing over fences, stepping in puddles, and trudging through ploughed fields. As we get within sight of the railway station, Billy triumphantly points to a red-and-brown railway carriage in a siding. 'There, that's where we're staying. We've found it.' Mike and I look incredulously at each other. 'We thought you said cottage,' we say weakly in one voice. 'No – I definitely said carriage.'

Once inside the carriage, Mike and I immediately discover that the moon can't penetrate the gloom, neither can the Woolworths torch we've remembered to bring with us. With no food, water, heat or experience, we are the definition of hopeless. Also, Billy is looking restless and we are sure he'll abandon us in the night and head for the money-laundering opportunities that surely teemed in the backstreets of London.

What keeps us both awake all night though is our upbringing. We've been taught to be terrified not only of the dark and the unknown, but also the unlawful. To add to our fear we quickly realise that this is not an abandoned carriage, it's just parked up in a siding and could be hooked to a moving train as we sleep.

As the sun rises, we see that Billy has indeed slipped away. Mike and I scramble to the nearest main road. Shabby, tired and hungry, we are nonetheless hopeful of a lift. We review our weekend. It has certainly been different – part uncomfortable, part gratifying, part challenging, part rewarding, part initiation. Well, on second thoughts, maybe all initiation.

Mike suggests it may have brought us closer to the circle of interesting druggie friends who have Billy at their centre. We are trying to persuade ourselves that this is a good thing when a lorry pulls up.

It's 5 a.m. on Monday morning when I get back to my parents' house. There are three bottles of milk on the doorstep; I take them into the kitchen and find the cornflakes. I look around but nothing feels, looks or sounds as familiar as I was expecting. I wonder if the path of my life has shifted – or if I simply haven't arrived back yet. I'm not standing at the crossroads, but there is a change in how I see things moving and what they might be moving towards. As I pull the not-entirely-familiar sheets back on my bed I remember I'm due at the office in four hours, and then I wonder where I told my parents I was going for the weekend. Then sleep intervenes.

Climbing Up These Figures

As my last teenage year began slipping away, the answer to Mr Campbell's question 'Have you thought about what you want to do in life, Michael?' was still 'no'. My father's position as head of the English department had helped me to hide away in the library for longer than would usually have been possible. I managed to keep a low profile at school in the daytime, while playing in assorted bands at night. I hadn't stacked up enough grades for a university place, and, although thirsty for knowledge, had failed to organise my subjects along any kind of career path. I was beginning to notice, with dismay, that everyone around me at school seemed to know what they wanted to do in life, and had taken steps towards achieving it. With the possible exception of Atty. We had remained unlikely friends ever since his rescue mission in the school playground; sporty, confident, practical and popular, Atty was everything I wasn't. Even tall. What we shared however were passions for rock 'n' roll, and girls. Being able to turn his hand to most things, Atty had more choice about his future than I did – my plans were limited to avoiding any responsibility (including a proper job) and being in a band. I wasn't travelling the path to a respectable career in music or achieving anything that would satisfy my increasingly frustrated parents, but it was only when we discovered we were the oldest boys still at school that Atty and I knew it really was time for serious decisions. Instead, we secretly clubbed together and bought a wreck of a Morris Ten with the idea of using it to pile our rickety gear into and get ourselves to gigs. To break it in we decided to drive 350 miles down the A1 and watch the motor racing at Silverstone. We took turns driving, and on the way back, by the time we reached Scotch Corner found ourselves discussing the finer details of our exhausted hallucinations. Arriving in Edinburgh very late on Sunday Atty dropped me off at Sydney Terrace, where I was surprised to find a real rectangle of white paper on my pillow.

> *Dear Michael,*
>
> *Your father has formally notified the school that you have left. Together, we have selected an accountancy firm where you will start your new job tomorrow.*
>
> *Love Mum*
>
> *PS More details at breakfast.*

To say this was unexpected would fall short of the impact it had on me.

I had been indentured in my absence to an office for five years at a salary of twenty-five pounds a month. Having no aptitude for either maths or business, accountancy seemed a puzzling choice.

From 42 Castle Street the view is spectacular, dipping out over Edinburgh's New Town, past Goldenacre and Leith to the Firth of Forth and the Kingdom of Fife beyond. This is the address of William Home Cook and Co., where, along with my fellow accountancy apprentices, Derek and Dave, I inhabit the junior loft. It's a large room stretching under the eaves, painted a municipal green, with three tables facing into the centre. There's not a lot of window light but, if you squeeze into the east-facing bay and squint, you can catch the sparkle of the Forth. There is a constant acrid smell, a mixture of overheated Bakelite fittings and unsafe gas-fire fumes. In the corner, on the brown cracked lino, is a green metal filing cabinet. On top are twodozen identical green cups and saucers waiting to be filled with stewed tea. We only cater for the male staff. Women meet in the basement. Eleven o'clock and I'm making tea instead of learning the mysteries of accountancy.

Gerry Ellis was my boss, or at least I think he was – he certainly acted that way. Nobody explained the office pecking order, so I just went along with it. He was one of the mid-rankers, not a chartered accountant, but with the equivalent Irish qualification. This didn't sit well with some of the old-school-tie brigade, who called him Gerry, not Mister like his peers. Big, broad and brash, he resembled a jolly but humourless farmer. He would often make personal remarks that even if they had been intended as jokes would have only been marginally acceptable. They weren't, and you would look in vain for a smile. When we heard his brogues slowly clumping up the four flights to our eyrie, we knew we had time to prepare ourselves for the expected onslaught. His heavy voice would boom out: 'Heron, you can do nothing right!' Plastered-down grey hair, red face, bulging veins – no smile. Had he only been referring to the cup of tea I was handing him, he would have had a point, but, of course, he wasn't.

When Gerry wasn't being my boss, Mr Millar was. In my five years at the office, I never once saw them in conversation, and can't imagine what shared interest they could have had. Mr Millar was slight, with wispy, dull, thinning ginger hair. His skin was pale, with freckles on his face and arms. He was a product of the RAF. He was so much a product of the RAF that, as he stood meekly in the office, wearing his ill-fitting suit, dangling his briefcase, he looked so out of place that it made you want to hand him a spanner, dust off his blue dungarees, and send him back in time twenty years to the Air Force engineering unit. An innate tinkerer, he always looked as if he'd just emerged from under a car bonnet, oil-sprinkled and stained, with his pipe clamped in his mouth. It never seemed to be lit and most of the time was being fiddled with either in or out of his mouth. It had its own maintenance kit, which meant that working alongside Mr Millar involved a great deal of time observing his tapping, polishing and grinding activities. Tiny screwdrivers, pincers, rasps and pipe cleaners were scattered on his desk among the receipts, cheque stubs and staples.

Mr Millar had been using RAF slang for decades and it had welded itself to his core. We juniors began gently imitating him. Then Gerry joined in with a cruel slant. It soon stretched from the typist pool in the basement to the partners on the third floor and gradually became habit, rather than mimicry, engulfing the firm from bottom to top.

We juniors really liked Mr Millar – he didn't shout at us, humiliate or patronise us, and was generally patient and friendly. There was a hint of a 'generation gap', but what kept us from being close was his strange personal world. It seemed to contain tinkering, Air Force slang, a hatred of accountancy and not a lot more. Derek, Dave and I persisted in trying to find topics that would lead to a conversation, but we couldn't get Mr Millar going, and he would never talk about his past or family life. He did have a stab at breaking the ice on a number of occasions, but his opening gambit always came from so deep inside his personal world that it just hung in the air while we struggled to relate to it, let alone respond.

In our loft, behind a peeling shutter, was an already-peeled Brigitte Bardot. A faded poster of a pose by the seashore, reminding us that previous batches of apprentices had amused themselves while waiting to serve up the tea. Sometimes one of the seniors, arriving for his break, would playfully flick open the shutter while we laughed dutifully. On one such occasion Mr Millar looked at us three and said in a matter of fact tone: 'My wife's dumphies are like two fried eggs.' Those words, unreplied to, remained suspended above the teacups and digestive biscuits until the day I left William Home Cook and Co.

Comptometers were an essential part of office life in the sixties. They looked like oversized typewriters, but had a numerical keyboard. The majority of trainees were typists who emerged from their courses as comptometer operators able to skilfully add, subtract, multiply and divide large figures. William Home Cook and Co. had two comps – Pat and Helen. Pat came in on the SMT bus every morning from a small village outside Edinburgh, and was greeted by Gerry in a gentlemanly and chivalrous manner, which only appeared smarmy next to his usual rough demeanour. Pat was small, thin and frail-looking, with straw-coloured hair and little round spectacles. She was maybe twenty, but looked younger, and seemed happy to have an office father figure in Mr Ellis.

We never got to know Helen's age: she kept it securely in a deposit box, along with her lack of confidence, vulnerability and self doubt. For day-to-day convenience, we juniors assumed thirty-two, but would never have said so publicly. She would breeze in an hour late, unkempt, and tottering through a cloud of stale perfume, cigarettes and gin, and not an eyebrow would be raised. The more accomplished of the comps, the time she saved was of such value to the firm that she could get away with murder, and even the partners, unused to uninhibited women at work, were a bit scared of her.

Helen tirelessly promoted her femme fatale image. Her out-of-office world was populated with stories of glamorous millionaires, gangsters and princes, gambling and dancing till dawn. Thankfully, however, being ten years younger than her, we were spared intimate details of her relationships. Of course, we only ever met the 'morning after the night before' Helen, talking incessantly, spilling out of her low-cut blouse as she clanked away at the comp machine, charm bracelet swinging in time. Her hair, various shades of orange and ginger, was severely scrunched into a bun on top of her head – a marmalade kitten in a net. Her small, heavily made-up eyes blinked out from a white shiny face, its skin stretched tight by the bun.

Our main loft activity was adding up columns of figures, which, in the era before calculators, was really tedious. Comps obviously could have done our loft assignments, but the seniors were always at the front of the queue with more sophisticated calculations and we were kept busy with the dross. Sheets of numbers would arrive for us to tot up, until we were deemed responsible enough to compile the columns ourselves from piles of receipts. The process was completed when we had ticked the column and stamped the receipt. This was the bread and butter of William Home Cook and Co. and was so important it had its own name: 'Stamp and Vouch'. It even got taken on the road.

External audits fell into two categories for us. There were companies within striking distance of Edinburgh, which for me usually meant travelling there and back on the same day in Mr Millar's sputtering Morris Minor. But there were also the seemingly more exciting jaunts by train to the station hotels in Inverness, Dingwall and Dundee. These didn't come my way till my fourth year, and I quickly learned that plusses came with minuses.

My interest in hashish had been reawakened by the Brighton episode, and was nurtured by the Edinburgh folk scene, where it was prevalent. On one of my visits to Billy I found the front room was dominated by a large Heath-Robinson-type water pipe that he had constructed from laboratory equipment. At its centre was a huge glass flagon filled with water; plastic tubing sprouted out of its neck along with a clay pipe-bowl filled with a tobacco and hash mixture. Clamps and clips held it all together and it worked fine. Billy was pleased with it, as were the four other people in the room, and he casually remarked that he had made a small portable version which could be assembled and dismantled in minutes. It worked well too he said, and only needed a milk bottle, tubing and silver foil. I tucked this information away.

One long Friday afternoon, Dave Clyne, Helen and I were told by Gerry that the following week we would all travel by train to Perth for a five-day audit of the Hydroelectric Board.

We had gathered at Waverley station, Dave and I out of breath from taking turns carrying the comp machine the mile from the office. We both always managed to look shambolic, even when suited and combed, but Mr Ellis looked smart in a countrified way, as if ready for a day at the races. Helen, in a purple figure-hugging suit, had things that looked like chopsticks sticking out of her bun, jangling gold-coloured jewellery and a pink overnight bag. I would have liked to bring my guitar to play in my room after long days at the Hydroelectric Board. (I'd wavered in my early resolve to attempt to take the office seriously by this time, and was musically moon-lighting like mad.) Dave, though, pointed out the likelihood of an apoplectic Gerry if I rolled up at the station carrying a guitar case covered with CND stickers. He had a point. However, I'd remem-bered Billy's pipe construction and rinsed out a milk bottle, which was now in my suitcase under my pyjamas, with a length of tubing and a roll of tin foil. On top of my pyjamas were the *I Ching* and a selection of Basho's haikus. Nestling amongst them was a necessary bundle of incense sticks. This'll pass the evenings, I thought, fin-gering the nugget of Lebanese in my pocket.

We chugged over the Forth Bridge in a fug (smoking was man-datory in the mid-sixties). Gerry was in one window seat reading the *Irish Times*, I was opposite, reading Jack Kerouac; Helen was in the corner of the compartment touching up her make-up; Dave nodding off. Holding up his newspaper, Gerry's huge fingers were discoloured butcher's sausages, blotchy red-and-purple-looking, as if made of some synthetic substance. Helen had added the Eiffel Tower to her charm bracelet. It was perched next to a swallow, and they jingled all the way to Perth as she filed and painted her nails. The two soldiers stuck between us sat bolt upright, stock-still and silent for the entire journey.

The first time Dave and I had been sent off on an external audit, we were delighted to be out in the world during office hours. Anticipating being welcomed into a different working environment (perhaps even with coffee and cake), we were looking forward to fresh new faces; some of them maybe girls' faces or those of blokes we could have a pint with. We naively imagined a world awaiting our whim and forgot that three clueless strangers poking around your workplace in the hope of finding errors, inadequacies or perhaps even embezzlement was more likely to qualify for 'worst nightmare' status.

We learned, though, to get used to being hated and so, as we gazed at the grey bulk of the Perth Hydroelectric offices, we were certain no comfort beckoned. It made no difference that we were a totally hopeless investigation team: me half-stoned, Dave on the lookout for girls, and the bumbling blustering Mr Ellis. No, that just made us a needless annoyance, intruding on well-rehearsed daily routines. All we did was stamp and vouch, and make an occasional fruitless enquiry. I dreamed of my milk bottle, Dave of girls in the typing pool (that he didn't have to walk home very far), and I'm happy to leave Gerry's dreams unruffled.

It was very different for Helen. Doors were thrown open and she trotted through them to a warm embrace, chocolates and flowers. The international league of comptometer operators welcomed one of their own. They were a powerful sisterhood, united by secrets. We were excluded. I imagined that after work they went for a meal, on to the cinema and then downed gin-and-orange and blue lagoons in bulk, while flirting haughtily through the night. However, even as the sisters sipped their cocktails they knew their days were numbered and couldn't last – computers were already planning a coup, But it looked like the high life from our three lonely rooms in the Station Hotel.

I found the boredom, noise and hostility that made up our working day stressful, and the sound of my hotel room door closing behind me had become something to look forward to. Alone and relaxed, though, I immediately missed my guitar. There was plenty of music in my head, but none in the air. Radio Luxembourg 208 metres medium wave on my transistor would have been nice, but the signal was dire. Instead, as the milk bottle gurgled and bubbled, I let the stillness engulf me, and I floated with the thin, blue curl of incense smoke. I opened *On the Road* at the dog-eared pages that marked my favourite chapter and waited for my surroundings to fade – as they always did. Yes, there was Jack in the bus station, there was Teresa; they were trembling towards their destiny.

> *Terry was a Mexican girl*
> *Movin' hips like a cheap sharp pachuco*
> *Giving me sidelong looks,*
> *Every mile down the loneliness of Route 66.*

And always those big blue eyes
Got space like an airman's dreams
Calling me close to her
Just to lay my head in her long black hair
Terry was a Mexican girl,
We got close as the airbrakes sighed
I knew she was my kinda girlsoul
Just to anchor my heart on the lonely sad American road
Let's hitch out to Bakersfield right now
Get stoned on wine and mambo rhythms
In a shack out in Mextown
We'll make wild love all night.

Transported – immersed in the give and take of emotions – the whole glorious unfolding. I had been in this place countless times before though, and sensed a change – the balance of loneliness to freedom had tipped in favour of loneliness, and I really missed Michelle. The angel face of Terry had been replaced by the angel face of Michelle.

I had seen Michelle around the Edinburgh coffee bar scene. She and her friend Nina hung out mostly with the hip 'Stafford crowd' in the West End. They were both small and pretty and swanned around together in identical outfits in the style of Juliette Gréco, whom I'd always imagined to be quite tall. Easy to spot in black polo-neck pullovers, tiny black skirts and black stockings, they styled their long black hair with a deep fringe that was cut straight across, just above the eyebrows. The sight of them together (which was how they always seemed to be), sashaying adroitly between coffee tables,

Cocktail Sobranies held aloft, was enough to wither any 'cool' that Atty and I could lay claim to. Cleverly we avoided them.

After work that pivotal Friday, when Gerry had made his Perth announcement I had been thinking of the week ahead as I ambled along Princes Street. Suddenly my daydream was nudged by a soft French accent with just a hint of huskiness, and there was Michelle. With a disarming smile and mild flattery, she recalled seeing me play at the Crown Bar. The assumptions I'd made about her being cold and aloof dissolved as she slipped her arm through mine and we strolled along slowly while I fell in love with her voice.

We left Princes Street, going down Regent Road and along Meadow-bank till we reached the greenness of Queen's Park. We told our stories as we walked – she was the same age as me, but had put her days to fuller use. I was beginning to feel very close to her, but had no idea what she was feeling – maybe the arm-linking was a polite Continental sort of thing (like kissing on the cheek), and didn't indicate romantic interest or even affection. Exploring what links we had in common, Billy came up in conversation, and by some secluded rocks she fished out a joint from her bag.

In that still, warm air that lingers at the end of a bright spring day, time did that stretching and widening thing it does when around marijuana. I explained how I'd ended up in the office, and she sketched her divorce, her little boy, her parents and the friends she had here in Edinburgh. We moved on to our shared taste in books, paintings and music, and I got to look into her eyes for what seemed like for ever – space like an airman's dreams.

Friday came at last and it was time for the jaded loft-dwellers to return to the office and prepare for the annual exams. I could hear my mother's voice saying the same thing she had before every exam approached, advising me just to get the letters after my name – and then do what I wanted. Maybe it was the quiet evenings alone in a hotel room, the hash pipe might have helped, but the lion of truth was suddenly there and rampant. I had taken five years to stop lying to myself and own up to something. What was the point of the final exam? I was never going to use that virtual badge: C.A.

My indenture was truly vanquished.

> *Climbing up these figures, the sun is tugging at my shoulder,*
> *And every step I take, I think my feet are getting older.*
> *Come dip into the cloud-cream lapping,*
>
> *I can't keep my hand on the plough because it's dying*
> *But I will lay me down*
> *With my arms around a rainbow*
> *Oh I will lay me down to dream.*

At Waverley station a deliciously unfamiliar lightness caressed me as I glided down the platform, a few strides behind my team members. I didn't have to report back to the office like them, I could just keep walking. Then I spotted Dave's Edinburgh girlfriend standing at the ticket barrier ahead. Next to her was the shadowy but instantly recognisable figure of Michelle under a wide-brimmed black hat. A radiant smile lit up her face, and the glow of the Gauloises tip in her waving hand melted my heart.

Young Communists

I walked Michelle home from the station, and continued strolling slowly round the gradually emptying Edinburgh streets. When I was sure that my parents had gone to bed, I slipped into the house and up to my room. I couldn't think of a comfortable way to tell them that I had decided to abandon the job, and how the letters after my name (those very ones that they'd seen in their mind's eye) had scattered in the wind.

In the morning, I could hear raised voices and the front door slamming. I waited for a few minutes before tiptoeing downstairs, holding my shoes.

My mother was in the hall looking up, her arms crossed like a stop sign, five feet of fury. 'Michael Heron,' she said, taking an ominous step towards me 'We had a phone call last night from Mr Ellis.' I knew what was coming. 'How could you do this, Michael, how could you leave, you were *almost an accountant*.' All her hopes for me had vanished and were replaced with an anger fuelled by anxiety for my future. Her warmth, kindness and love for me had reached breaking point and, with her voice settling in at ear-splitting volume, there was no escape from her disappointment. Needing to do something fast, I stupidly attempted to sweeten the air by relating the story of the lovely French girl I'd met and her little boy from a previous marriage. It didn't have quite the effect I'd hoped for: 'Well, I'll not have you sleeping under my roof without a proper job while you're off philandering with a French divorcée. Just go and live with her.'

'All right then, I will.'

I had deftly introduced an extra problem – Michelle and I hadn't even kissed yet. I stomped down the garden path and, instead of going to Michelle's, walked in the opposite direction. I had no way of knowing how open her arms might be. At Edinburgh's seaside suburb, Portobello, I plonked myself on a bench with a sea view. I was usually very comfortable here; Portobello had been my playground through layers of growing up. It had started with sandcastles, deckchairs and donkeys, moved up through arcades of slot machines leading to the full-blooded waltzer and dodgem funfair, complete with a rickety rollercoaster and high-volume distorted Eddie Cochrane records. That morning though, as I sat in the rain and wind, looking out at a grey turbulent sea, I felt deflated, weak and hopeless. Fighting against the temptation to feel too sorry for myself, I searched through my memories and experiences for something strong and reassuring, and came up with Owen Hand.

Owen was just four years my senior, but was worldly-wise and had lived a bit, while we youngster folkies were finding our feet. He'd been a miner, a boxer and a whaler, as we'd been learning to tune our guitars. With wrestler's shoulders, a Desperate Dan chin, a scar on his cheek and a broken nose, he looked the ultimate thug, but had sensitivity, patience and time for everyone. Owen had become part of the Edinburgh folk scene at the Howff in the High Street.*

Owen and Archie became friends there, and when I finally got round to asking Archie about clawhammer, it was Owen that he recommended. I asked around but kept missing him, so I didn't get a lesson for some time. How I got to hear him play is another story.

The Crown had become a folk meeting place. If anyone wanted to find a collaborator, book a performer, or set up guitar lessons, they would leave a note at the bar. Two folk clubs had become established there. Robin Williamson ran one on Thursdays, a sister to Archie's 'Tuesday Night at the Crown'. Robin, Clive and Bert Jansch shared a flat and were regulars at both. Robin's club was initially more introspective and cannabis-slanted – it was created with bohemians in mind – but no lines were drawn, and they were both always packed. When the club opened at lunchtime, folkies would shamble in to collect messages, socialise and find out what was going on. I longed to see if Owen was there, with his legendary shoulder to cry on, but it was still a couple of hours till opening time. More grey waves to watch.

While trying to think of anything but my current situation, the memory of the Young Communists' social gathering back in '62 revisited me. The poster had been pinned behind the bar at the Crown.

---

* The Howff was the predecessor of the Crown Bar and closed in 1961.

YOUNG COMMUNISTS' SOCIAL GATHERING
ALL FOLK SINGERS AND THEIR INSTRUMENTS WELCOME.
BEER PROVIDED.
There will be young people from all around the country
singing together celebrating the loosening grip of Capitalism.

Arriving at the gathering in what was usually a quiet street in Portobello, it was clear that celebrations were well under way. Although it was still early in the evening, the strains of a vigorous 'singalong' were coming from a large detached house, where camper vans and a coach covered with CND signs were already parked outside. Some folk enthusiasts recognised me from the Crown, and we approached together, wielding guitars and banjos. There were no obviously druggie beatnik weirdos among us though; the Young Communists were renowned for eschewing any drugs other than alcohol and tobacco.

We tumbled through the door, and avoided tripping over the sea of couples on cushions and mattresses, in sleeping bags, or just covered with sheets. 'The Tracks of My Tears' was playing, and two or three couples were managing to slow dance around the bodies. The majority, however, were cuddling, kissing, drinking and smoking – in no particular order.

We folkies had met many a YC at the Crown, and knew they were keen on folk music, so it wasn't a huge surprise when a tall man wearing a rust-coloured shirt stood up and announced: 'Quiet now, we've got some culture here, so hush for the folk singer.' Whatever people were doing, they obeyed. He had an authoritative, shop steward's sort of voice, and silence fell.

What followed, slotting into the silence, was that cascading, bell-like, rhythmic network of notes that I had come to recognise as top-grade clawhammer – the source was Owen Hand. I was bowled over by the close-range experience of something I'd only come across in a very diluted state, namely my hissy American tape deliveries. Owen was a mere arm's-length away, and, as a gravelly version of 'Goodnight, Irene' took shape, I had a strong feeling that this rough-looking diamond would become my friend as well as my guitar-picking teacher.

None of my acquaintances seemed to know the reason for this party. Perhaps there was a significant YC/CND-related date to remember, or an important birthday/anniversary to mark. Something had provided the excuse, and absolutely no one was complaining. Coaches had come from Glasgow, Birmingham and London, carrying YCs to a night of celebration, and then on to a protest in the morning. The atmosphere crackled with decadence and dwindling morals. To someone whose teenage years were all in the repressed fifties, it was as relaxing as a warm bath.

The hush that had been demanded ahead of Owen's performance had no chance of reigning over the entire house, which was beginning to jump. It was limited to the sleeping-bag room where Owen had sung; so while the rest of the house vibrated, I stayed there. Since half the coach travellers were closet folk singers, the entertainment had sunk to the level of a campfire sing-song, involving buckets with holes, hammers and little boxes. The 'quiet room' had become the surreal room, but there was a reason I had to stay there. I couldn't take my eyes off a girl who had sung 'The Queen of Hearts' earlier. She was with the London CND contingent, had green eyes that shone with a spine-tingling brightness and hair the colour of hazelnuts. I had a spectacularly long losing streak with girls at parties, never getting as far as a kind word, let alone a kiss, but she was so gorgeous that I resolved to win her with a song, and forget all my previous failures.

An emaciated adolescent Burl Ives, spruce in socks and sandals, had just given us his 'Big Rock Candy Mountain' when I got the nod. My turn. Clambering onto the communal stool, I knew where she was in the room without looking. I had decided that it was time for a bit of grit, and settled on songs from the first Bob Dylan album. 'In My Time of Dying', and 'Man of Constant Sorrow' were so much what the doctor ordered, that the room wanted one more. Halfway through the first verse of 'Baby, Let Me Follow You Down' I dared a glance in her direction, and a chat-up line took shape at the back of my mind. She had beautiful skin but a completely neutral expression, and I couldn't read what she was thinking at all. When the applause began to die, and I had just put my guitar down, she took my hand and I found myself being led upstairs. She took me into a bedroom, and sat me on the edge of the bed, telling me to stay there. I thought, 'I could have done with a drink, and I seem to have forgotten half the chat-up line.'

After about ten minutes, a toe gently nudged the door open, and a beautiful naked girl walked slowly towards me, smiling and holding a pint of beer in each hand. 'If this is real,' I thought, 'I might not need the chat-up line.' I guess it was an overload of the senses, and out of my control, but a voice took over my mind. Why was I born in 1942? And why not once, in all my teenage years, had a beautiful girl that I didn't know, walked towards me with beer in her hand and sex on her mind . . . ? She had reached the bed and, bending over, she placed the beer on the low bedside table. Hesitantly, tentatively, I reached out. She was real.

I blinked my eyes open and looked out at the sea again, wondering how long I'd been sitting there. My left leg had gone to sleep. I thought it surprising how vivid my memories of that night had been, how it had just unrolled like a film. The girl's role, though, that was different. I could play that back in full colour, any time, right from the day after it happened. I could feel the beat of her heart, her breath on my cheek, and the warmth of her touch. But all without a name, and I longed to speak that out softly into the air.

The Crown had become a kind of club for me now. It had more than its fair share of wide-eyed dreamers, trad-song collectors and obsessive guitar-pickers. It contained more eccentric Zen beatniks than you could shake a bamboo stick at, and the sawdust-strewn floor was awash with talent. The 'folk revival' permeated the place, and brought with it a new enthusiasm. Some were making a living from it, like Archie, Hamish and Alex, some just needed to be near it, and some, like me, were new to it and were just absorbing everything until we discovered what to do with it.

Every time that you came across Bert he was playing guitar, John Martyn was discussing and swapping records, Robin was playing Bulgarian fiddle tunes, Hamish was instigating group sea shanties and Clive was painting a Japanese landscape on parchment.

Amid mountains of high summer
I bowed respectfully before
the tall clogs of a statue
Asking a blessing on my journey.

I was enthralled by the buzz of inspired activity there and called it my second home. Actually, I realised (as I shook the circulation back into my leg and shuffled off the bench), at that moment it was my only home.

The 'Young Communists' recollections had occupied the morning and by the time I reached Chambers Street, lunchtime activities would be peaking; the Crown was tugging like a magnet. At the very least there would be like-minded company, and music to divert. If Owen were there, he would no doubt have the time and patience to hear my woes, reduce my anguish and map my escape.

One night I had rolled up at the CND bus stance at the coach station. It took Edinburgh members south for protest marches, but was happy to take more casual supporters if there were empty seats. I wanted to see Reverend Gary Davis at Les Cousins in Soho, and Owen wanted to rehearse with a London folk group that he'd signed up with. We sat together on the back seat in the dark with a bottle of whisky and talked folk and blues all night. We talked about those at the Crown who had been involved in the scene for longer than us. They were the heralds of the folk revival – Alex, Archie and Hamish. Then we moved on to the newcomers – Anne Briggs, John Martyn, Bert, Robin and Clive.

Robin Williamson had started out doing traditional ballads with the polite, smooth bits removed. Rough songs about being human, delivered without artifice. He met Clive Palmer one Tuesday at Archie's club night and, amazingly, their art forms meshed (I never quite knew how). Clive was an extraordinary person – a bohemian banjo player whose main musical interests at that time were Victorian music hall and vintage American jug bands. What emerged from their collaborations was like nothing else. Every time Owen and I had seen them play, their act was expanding in its scope and skills. We were both fans. We also agreed how much we liked Bert, but then everyone liked Bert – women formed a queue to mother him.

Bert was mostly interested in improving his guitar-playing but, if he wasn't already on the bill, had to be persuaded to perform. One night in the Crown, after Owen bought him a pint, Bert shambled up to the mic, borrowing a guitar on the way. He was wearing a little-boy-lost expression, and a dull green pullover many sizes too big. He put the full glass down, and slipped from tuning to playing without a join. With his foot now tapping, a jazz chord-sequence emerged. It was a happy, faintly familiar tune, but with so much happening around it that it wasn't until he sang 'she brings me coffee in my favourite cup' that we knew it was 'Hallelujah I Love Her So'. Likky was his girlfriend at the time, and it was easy to imagine them together in his flat, Bert playing in front of the one-bar electric fire. He had made the song his own, and was singing in his real, unaccented voice. Whenever Bert's name comes up, that's the performance that comes to mind.

Our words trailed off drowsily from time to time, starting up again when either of us woke. When we were dropped in harsh cold daylight on the outskirts of London we were closer, but wrecked.

I left Portobello and its seaside bench behind, and set off for Edinburgh and the Crown. I stopped short forty minutes later when I'd arrived at Lothian Street. I could see the Crown two hundred yards away, but I stalled. I had never been able to go there at lunchtime during the week as it was too far from the office for a quick pint, so it belonged to my evenings and weekends. The nine-to-five framework of my life had collapsed, like the relationship with my parents, and, just for a moment, I felt more empty than free.

When I pushed open the door, Celtic whistle tunes, banjo plonks, and unfeasibly hearty singing swept past me into the street. Bacon rolls, tobacco smoke, coffee, pie and beans and beer fought each other. It was the lunchbreak pie-and-a-pint for office and shop workers, bleary wake-up coffee for the late-night bohemians, and a bit of both for the folkies. Owen was at the bar with Hamish and Archie, so I took my pint to an out-of-the-way table, and pretty soon Owen joined me. He listened as I told my tale, and asked the sensible questions that I thought he might: 1. Do you think your mother might change her mind? 'Not a chance.' 2. How likely is it that Michelle will take you in? 'Not very.' Armed with this scanty information he advised: 1. Go to parents' house – pick up guitar. 2. Go to Michelle's place with guitar. 3. If you can't stay at Michelle's, meet me here at six. If you can stay, meet me here tomorrow at lunchtime.

Michelle came to the door of 12 East Thomas Street. Without a word, she took my guitar case into the flat, before throwing her arms around me. We sat on the faded brown velvet chaise longue listening to Sidney Bechet, with the rain beating on the window while dusk drew in. Mucha's posters of decorative women looked on, stuck in time to the wall. An embroidered fringed shawl and the LP covers of Edith Piaf, Georges Brassens, Juliette Gréco and Jacques Brel lay scattered on the floor. The lamps were draped with paisley silk scarves, giving a soft haze of light, hiding the everydayness. The room we were in doubled as the kitchen, and a coffee percolator was spilling black liquid onto the gas cooker.

The next day I arrived slightly late at the bustling Crown to meet Owen. He told me that I'd just missed Robin and Clive, who'd already been in, putting the word out that they were looking for a guitarist to join them. They hadn't heard me play, but knew me as a fixture in the audience, and Owen had put in a good word for me. I thanked Owen for everything he'd done and tried not to look too excited. Just yet.

Clive's Incredible Folk Club

Early in the sixties, there was a beatnik circuit of houses that you could travel to and unroll a sleeping bag. One such place was Society Buildings in Edinburgh's Chambers Street. A friend of Clive's with a private income rented an enormous room there, which had originally been a Quaker meeting hall. He welcomed a free-loading wastrel, whose beatnik ambition was to smoke as much dope as possible, and own only a sleeping bag, with as much generosity as he would a bohemian traveller seeking the meaning of life. Clive, whose lifestyle lay somewhere in the middle, set up camp in a small tent nailed to the floor. An island amidst a sea of bedding. A procession of tenement flat-shares with Robin and Bert Jansch around the low-rent segments of Edinburgh followed. After a couple of years though, Bert headed south to seek his fortune, and Robin and Likky moved in together. Unfortunately for Clive, by that time Society Buildings had been demolished.

Rehearsing my indifferent attitude I climbed up to Robin's top-floor flat in West Nicolson Street. I had heard through the Owen-instigated grapevine that Robin and Clive were 'up for a bit of a play – see how it goes, man.' I was about to be auditioned by the two musicians I most admired, and I didn't want to come over as embarrassingly eager. Clutching my guitar, I knocked on the door, trying to envisage the interior that was about to be revealed. I suppose my expectations had been stoked by Billy's pad – Turkish rugs in deep reds and blues perhaps, cushions everywhere, the smell of hashish mingling with coffee. Comfort and colour would be the theme.

When the door opened, I tried to look right past whoever was there, in the hope of a fantastic salon beyond. But there in a shimmering white light stood Robin. Automatically I shielded my eyes from the dazzle. The entire room was whitewashed. On an uncomfortable, worn-looking old leather couch sat Clive, holding a mug of tea and a digestive biscuit. 'Hi, man,' they chorused – Robin in a tentative, cool sort of way, Clive in a more open, smiling, crumb-showering sort of way. As my eyes grew accustomed to the glare, the room came into focus. An orange-crate table, a Van Gogh kitchen chair, three scratchy ink drawings pinned to walls, wayside flowers in a milk bottle and a string of garlic hanging at the window. On the crate were a pack of tarot cards, a tin whistle and a chess set. Leaning against the table ends, a banjo and a guitar.

I perched on the kitchen chair with my guitar, with Robin and Clive sitting on either end of the couch. Of course I knew their entire set from watching them at the Crown, I even knew the warm-up songs they did with guest singers. There, in the brightest of rooms, at eleven o'clock on an autumn morning, the three of us were about

to play together for the first time – there was no applause, and my
heart only skipped the smallest of beats.

> *My bark of life was tossing down*
> *The troubled stream of time,*
> *Since first I saw your smiling face,*
> *And youth was in its prime.*

It had always struck me as a great opening verse, right back to
when it jumped out from one of the American mail tapes, but when
I heard those two singing it, I almost missed the cue for the chorus.

It was so much fun harmonising that my cool went out of the
window. We did two more Carter Family songs – 'Wildwood Flower'
and 'Will the Circle Be Unbroken?' – then Robin, who could do a
pretty good Blind Willie Johnson bass growl, launched into

> *I know I've got religion and I ain't ashamed*
> *Let your light from the lighthouse shine on me*
> *Angels in heaven done wrote my name*
> *Let your light from the lighthouse shine on me.*

Driving banjo from Clive and blues harp from me picked it up
and we sailed into the chorus:

> *Shine on oh, let it shine on*
> *Let your light from the lighthouse shine on me*
> *Shine on, oh, let it shine on*
> *Let your light shine on me.*

Robin and Clive had been playing the clubs for three years, and had a very entertaining act worked out. The successful solo and duet pieces would remain, but they would be able to expand instrumentally in the group numbers with me holding the chord structure in place. This was the theory but, as they started a fiddle and banjo duet, I had no clue as to the success or otherwise of my audition. However, as Robin started to pack up, after exchanging a little nod with Clive, he suggested we meet at his flat on Thursday afternoon, work out a set together, and introduce the Crown audience to our new trio in the evening. I quietly put my guitar in its case.

As I fastened the catches, I became aware that someone had entered the flat. I looked up: tiny feet in ankle boots, ribbed dark grey stockings, a loose tweed skirt, herringbone riding jacket and a purple beret worn at no hint of an angle. Likky always looked as if she'd raided the dressing-up box with her eyes closed. She walked past me, holding some twigs and feathers in her fingerless-gloved hand; she didn't seem overly friendly, but then I was an unknown square interloper in her very hip home. Anyway, nothing could faze me at that moment. It looked like I'd just been handed my dream job.

When I turned up on Thursday, Likky seemed more relaxed and brought us a pot of jasmine tea with little blue-and-white cups on a black lacquered tray, before leaving us to it. The first thing to find out was which songs in the set would benefit most from me joining in. Their act featured British folk, bluegrass, Edwardian banjo, old-timey Americana, jug band music and vaudeville. We tried out everything we knew that we could play as a trio, and patched a set together around the ones that worked best. When we arrived at the

Crown the back room was packed, but it felt a bit like I was hitching a ride – 'Robin and Clive' already had an ardent following without me. Robin, though, introduced us as a trio: 'Sometime we'll think up a name, but for now it's Robin, Clive and Mike, we'll be the resident group here every Thursday, so bring your friends.' He pulled up a chair, picked up his guitar, and started:

Relax your mind, relax your mind
Ooh, it'll make you live a great long time
Sometimes you've got to relax your mind.

We chorused along together until Robin switched from Lead-belly to Blind Willie Johnson: 'I know I've got religion and I ain't ashamed.' And the whole thing took off – kazoo, harmonica and the audience singing 'let it shine on.'

Here we were in the middle of the folk revival, preaching to the converted, and I loved it. I'd forgotten about the creative energy and interplay that goes along with playing in a group when everything is working. With this set-up, each number came alive in different ways. Robin and Clive never clung to rigid structures and, starting that night, I quickly learned how to follow them when they veered off.

Weekly practices continued, and every Thursday at the Crown the crowd settled in at capacity. However, Clive was also in demand elsewhere on the emerging Scottish folk scene and was looking more exhausted every week. He was spotted asleep at the bus station, and seen heading west, hitching on the A8. It eventually became clear that he was living near Glasgow and making his way (commuting doesn't seem the right word somehow) through to Edinburgh for the gigs. Clive had found Temple Cottage.

In a house up a muddy track, twelve miles from Glasgow, lived Mary Stewart, her five children and many animals. It was a long low farmstead, with more space inside than seemed possible from the outside. Mary was a vet who commuted daily to Glasgow Veterinary College. American, but living in Scotland since her marriage had dis-integrated, she brought her warmth and enthusiasm for folk music with her and the house was well known as an after-concert watering hole. Archie and Hamish dropped into Mary's after a nearby gig one night, with Clive and his banjo. When they left in the morning, Clive and his banjo didn't. It was often a late-night sing-song gathering there, with a peaceful rural day to follow. There was nothing like the Society Building's open-house attitude, but from time to time, due to Mary's generosity, it did have a temporary sleeping-bag pop-ulation. Clive loved his early days there. Having run low on other options, he settled in happily as part caretaker, part impoverished musician; keen to entertain the children and feed the animals. Ini-tially he tried to keep it to himself, but, at the back of his mind, he always knew his secret temple would be discovered.

Clive knew he could trust his friend Ian Ferguson, though, so did confide in him. Ian wasn't a folk fan; he was, however, a Clive fan. He'd been promoting bands in Glasgow on a small scale, and running a modest club. They met when Clive first arrived in Edinburgh, and he knew right away that he'd never meet anyone remotely similar. Ian loved to listen to Clive's tales of travelling as a busker in Europe. The one-day hops over borders to avoid repatriation; the nights spent sleeping in cemeteries, under hedges and in industrial-size bins. The route had been well travelled and Ian treasured the stories involving fellow buskers – Davey Graham, Wizz Jones, Ralph McTell and Alex Campbell – and was astonished at how many people on the folk scene Clive knew and could count as his friends.

Ian lived in Glasgow, and sometimes put Clive up in his spare room during his journeys to and from Edinburgh. He hung on every word Clive spoke, every gesture he made, every obscure Victorian banjo piece he played, but it didn't prevent activity in the impresario sector of his brain: 'Look for a large, cheap space in the centre of town; no food or drink just put on folk music, so no licence required.'* He'd been to the Crown, seen the crowd, tasted the atmosphere and, as he listened to the music, that part of his brain had huge hopes.

After a month of being a trio without a name, at the next practice we decided to find one. I didn't contribute any suggestions as I still thought of myself as an apprentice proving his worth. Having luckily side-stepped the Superior String Band and the Fruit-jar Drinkers, Clive and Robin came up with the Incredible String Band. We were completely unaware that 'string band' meant a specific thing in America, especially in the South. If you called yourself a string band there, a strict tempo set of dance tunes with a caller was expected. It was many years later, in Tennessee, looking out from the stage onto a hall of expectant couples at a graduation dance in Memphis, that we found this out. Until then our name served us well.

---

* At that time in Glasgow there was a yawning gap in the entertainment market, licensing laws meaning there was nowhere to go after 10.30 on a Saturday night.

The next time that Clive rolled up, knocking on his door, Ian was able to report the discovery of the ideal all-night premises. He'd rented the whole fourth floor of a disused office space at 134 Sauchiehall Street, and had already painted the interior surfaces matt black. Including the windows. There were two hall-sized rooms with adjoining spaces, and two fire escapes. Access was via a small, open, cage-like lift, which was operated by a large brass lever. It only held five people. But so far he hadn't unearthed any further drawbacks.

When 'Clive's Incredible Folk Club' opened on Saturday, 26 March 1966, it was not only brimming with audience members, but also with performers. Clive and Hamish Imlach, nervous about not providing the seven hours of continuous music they'd advertised, had booked Wizz Jones and Pete Stanley, Davey Graham and Archie Fisher. And, just in case, they'd also engaged source singers Davey Stewart and Jimmy MacBeath. After midnight, all the folk acts playing in the south of Scotland turned up – Alex Campbell, John Martyn, Matt McGinn, and Owen Hand. The club held five hundred, but that night no one was counting.

Ian and Clive had foreseen problems without someone in charge of the night's entertainment, and had persuaded Hamish that he was the man for the job.

Hamish Imlach was not tall, he was rotund and very good-natured. He had a gift for reaching an audience that made him the most in-demand MC on the folk scene. A good organiser, he booked the guest artists, listed the floor singers, supervised the running order and MC'd everything. Sometimes his songs had to make way for his jokes, but he was a good guitarist with a lovely rich voice and a great repertoire: some coarse Glasgow street songs, the occasional sensitive gem and a ton of sing-along Leadbelly. When dawn arrived he was ready to unwind, which he did by taking all the performers to Mary's for an early-morning party. Astonishingly, Mary didn't seem to mind a bunch of carousing folk singers in her house. Clive, on the other hand, hated to see his Shangri-La overpopulated, but knew everyone would be gone by Tuesday.

I had usually left by Sunday afternoon, lured by the likelihood of French provincial cooking, a glass of Bordeaux and Michelle's smile. I spent my time at East Thomas Street making up for the time I had lost at William Home Cook and Co. Thanks to Michelle I was able to dwell in the possibilities of the life I had wanted all along. I read freely, played guitar endlessly, developed clawhammer variations, and listened to obscure folk LPs alongside the borrowed trickle of world music that was finding its way to Edinburgh in the early sixties. The freedom and happiness of those days shaped my early songwriting.

At the Glasgow club, over the course of seven hours, Robin, Clive and I did solo sets, duet combinations and a long trio set. In my solo set I often did my farewell to William Home Cook and Co., just to remind myself how good it felt to have escaped.

> *I'm going way over the wide skyline*
> *And I'll sing and be happy*
> *You can't keep me here, no how*
> *I'll sing and be happy and my world is my own*
> *And I'll do what I want to*
> *You can't keep me here, no how*
> *Hey baby, don't cry for me*
> *Hey baby, when the sun comes up, I'll be free.*

Clive's Incredible Folk Club was open for ten weekends, and with no other all-night folk clubs in existence in 1966, word spread fast. Soon we had built up an audience of enthusiasts committed enough to spend a long night absorbing folk music. Of course this made the best performers in the field keen to play there, and everything worked together, resulting in a great, if slightly strange, venue.

The Incredible String Band, sitting at the hub of all this creativity and appreciation, was bound to be affected. We were accustomed to being thought of as a beatnik sideshow, not a popular attraction, so we added an extra weekly practice day at Robin's (with only the slightest of objections from Clive). Always on the lookout for suitable trio songs, we also worked on making our solo and duet spots more interesting.

By now I had a collection of songs that I'd written, mainly at East Thomas Street. I kept them in my solo set, as the trio only did one original song, Clive's poignant 'Empty Pocket Blues'. I felt hopeful that I might be able to write a few songs specifically for the three of us, though, built around Robin and Clive's playing.

Having an all-night gig every weekend, and mingling with the guest artists led us to take the whole thing a bit more seriously. It certainly made us a better band, and word was spreading that record labels were expressing interest in us. Clive would have liked us to make a jug band record, Robin played so many different styles of music brilliantly that it was hard to imagine what sort of record he would have fancied making, and I would have been content with anything that didn't involve accountancy.

When not doing our trio set, we would tend to wander into one of the two larger rooms, both of which had stages. Most of the music happened there, alongside most of the marijuana intake. When one of us was doing a solo set the other two would be in the audience. As the weeks went by, our three solo slots began to attract distinctly different audiences. Clive pulled in the beatniks who liked anything left field – old-timey banjo, music hall, English folk or an international medley played on homemade bagpipes. My early Dylan, harmonica rack and bottle-neck stomping stuff attracted assorted blues enthusiasts. But Robin always had the largest crowd, made up of his staunch followers. With his instrumental and vocal scope, and his wide musical interests, Robin packed his allotted forty minutes; but it still felt too short.

At about 2 a.m. one Sunday morning I was standing with Clive in a particularly heavily scented corner of the main room, when I heard talk that Robin's set was going to be special. Clive gave me a knowing look, as if he knew something I didn't, but then he had that look a lot of the time. The room was beginning to fill up with drifters from the other rooms who were coming through to join the converted. It was overflowing by the time Robin shambled on with his guitar.

> *I'll sing you this October song*
> *There is no song before it*
> *The words and tune are none of my own*
> *For my joys and sorrows bore it.*
> *Beside the sea, the brambley briars*
> *In the still of evening*
> *Birds fly out behind the sun*
> *And with them I'll be leaving.*

Words and music had developed together, and merged easily: sweeps, slides and grace notes in the voice and guitar painted a shimmering, wide, hazy landscape.

> *The fallen leaves that jewel the ground*
> *They know the art of dying*
> *And leave with joy their glad gold hearts*
> *In the scarlet shadows lying.*

> *When hunger calls my footsteps home*
> *The morning follows after*
> *I swim the seas within my mind*
> *And the pine trees laugh green laughter.*

My attention turned to the sound coming from Robin's guitar, and a conversation I'd once had with Clive came to mind. He'd shared a flat with Robin and Bert in Rose Street. There was only one guitar between them, so Robin's Levin was shared around. Robin picked it up the day after Bert had used it for a gig and noticed it wasn't in normal tuning. It was a serviceable but slightly rickety instrument, and the strings, which had been slackened off to produce an open chord of D major, were buzzing randomly. Robin, liking the effect but not the unevenness, stuck a match between the bridge and strings, so that all the notes buzzed when sounded. It was as if a ghostly sitar was playing along next door. I looked in Clive's direction, but couldn't think how to mime 'D tuning? Matchstick?'

I used to search for happiness
And I used to follow pleasure
But I found a door behind my mind
And that's the greatest treasure.

For rulers like to lay down laws
And rebels like to break them
And the poor priests like to walk in chains
And God likes to forsake them.

The instrumental passage played out with the phantom sitar player keeping up, until they both finished with an arpeggio – prrrrrring! There followed a total silence. Then the room erupted. Robin wasn't known for songwriting, but that had seemed too revealing and personal to be a cover of anyone else's song. When it quietened down, Robin spoke, 'That's the first song I've written, it just formed itself.' I turned to Clive. 'You knew,' I said in light-hearted accusation. With an enigmatic characteristic smile, Clive said, 'Well, I just happened to be in the room, man.'

The Mormon Redeemer

On the last Saturday of May 1966, just before midnight, the people queuing outside Clive's Incredible Folk Club started drifting away. The padlock on the door and the five policemen mingling with the crowd had killed off any remaining hopes that it might open. Ian's main financial backer had to pull out suddenly and as a result the rent account had been frozen, so Ian was left with no choice but to close the club down.

Ian drove Clive, Robin and me back to Temple Cottage, and the four of us passed gradually from sadness, through regret, to amazement that Ian had managed to set it up in the first place, and that it had been such a success for the ten weeks of its life. By the time we arrived at Mary's, we were swapping our favourite moments.

Mary was a keen and experienced climber so there were often members of the climbing fraternity staying the night. They mingled easily with folkies, children, dogs, Mary's friends, and, on this occasion, two Buddhist monks who were on their way to Lockerbie to set up a Tibetan monastery. The most unlikely people always seemed to mix with enthusiasm at Temple Cottage. Things were already rollicking along when we arrived and, after picking our way through rucksacks, ropes, crampons, beads and prayer wheels, we were soon raising a glass to Clive's Incredible Folk Club.

Sunday mornings always got off to a slow start at Temple Cottage, but the disappointing thought of no more 'Clive's folk club nights' had me awake before noon. The sun was streaming through the bay windows, illuminating just as many sleeping bodies as empty wine glasses and full ashtrays. Out on the front grass, surrounded by barking dogs and running, laughing children, I could see the two monks pacing about, hoping to find a quiet spot. As my eyes grew accustomed to the sunlight, I could make out Clive sitting in the corner of the room where the furniture had been pushed aside to make way for sleeping bags, blankets, mattresses and quilts. He was in monosyllabic conversation with a young man in a grey mackintosh, whose briefcase sat beside him on the couch. Clive's understandable reluctance to talk freely with this stranger was due to him being dressed in a style somewhere between that of a plain-clothes cop and a Mormon. When Robin and I approached, stoked up with coffee, the syllable count increased rapidly, but still cautiously. We could hear an American accent, initially confirming our Mormon suspicions. The conventionally dressed young man then explained that he had come up to Glasgow to see the Incredible String Band play, but had found the venue was closed. Police and potential audience members were dotted outside, and among them was a plump, friendly man, Hamish Imlach, who had given him Mary's address and told him he would find us there. The grey-mackintosh guy then explained that he worked for Elektra Records in New York and was setting up their London office, and that he was looking for British bands to sign.

All over the room, small pockets of activity were breaking out. With grunts, stretching and an isolated cough, Temple Cottage was coming to life. Shuffling feet trod a path to the bathroom, the kitchen and, eventually, the outside meditation-cum-crèche area, leaving only me, Robin and Clive and the young American tucked away in the corner.

Because as yet we didn't know much about our stranger's background, and I was afraid of being labelled gullible, I kept quiet. Robin and Clive, true to their beatnik ethos, remained observant but silent, so Joe Boyd handing us his Elektra calling card had the stage to himself.

America was a far, distant, promised land to us. We knew you couldn't take three strides without tripping over a rural bluesman, every church had a gorgeous gospel choir and families sat round in the evening singing Carter Family songs. Static-free assorted American music wafted in the air coast-to-coast, regardless of state lines. When Joe started to relate stories about real people, who to us were only album sleeves, we edged forward in our seats. Joe told us that, aged twenty, when he'd enrolled there, he'd booked Lonnie Johnson for a gig at Harvard University. He followed that up with Sleepy John Estes and Joe Williams. We could see all three monochrome faces and hear the hissing vinyl as he spoke. We didn't notice the point at which Joe took off his raincoat; however, we did pay close attention as he told us about the summer of '64. That was the year, when, as tour manager, he'd taken the American Folk Blues and Gospel Caravan on the road through Europe and eventually onto the flickering TV set around which my friends and I had gathered.

When Sister Rosetta Tharpe, Muddy Waters, The Reverend Gary Davis, Brownie McGhee and Sonny Terry were filmed picking their way through artificial cotton bales spread round a disused railway station on the outskirts of Manchester, we saw the epitome of a show, moving and united. Joe saw gifted individuals, strangers to each other a month ago now brought together by him and the music they loved.

The cop and the Mormon had been sent packing, and slowly passing the joint Joe saw three men the same age as him, demolished by his credentials. Not only did he know the movers and shakers at the heart of blues and roots, but he loved the music with a passion.

We were soon playing our songs for Joe. A trio version of Clive's 'Empty Pocket Blues' was followed by a Carter Family-style arrangement of Robin's 'Dandelion Blues' and, finally, 'Maybe Someday', a song I'd written with Robin's Bulgarian-sounding fiddle part in mind. Then, in the moment between dusk and darkness, Robin played 'October Song', while Clive, Joe and I sat held by its beauty and potency.

When Joe left, Ian drove Robin, Clive and me back to Edinburgh. After about ten miles, he broke the silence, wondering where the meeting with Joe might lead us. His questions hung in the air unanswered. We'd been asked to record five or six of our songs, including 'October Song' and the 'Bulgarian-sounding ensemble piece'. The hope being that Elektra's founder Jac Holzman would find the tape interesting enough for his label, and Joe would then produce our LP. Elektra was well known to us as an adventurous independent; we'd passed Judy Collins, Tom Paxton and Tom Rush records around among us, and what Edinburgh band wouldn't have liked to be on a cool New York label? No one held their breath though as the marijuana hit and the city lights grew brighter.

Arriving back at East Thomas Street the ground was floating as I turned the key and prepared to tell Michelle the day's news. As soon as I was inside I knew something was wrong. The flat was surprisingly quiet and there were none of the usual comforting smells of cooking and Gauloises. I put my guitar down in the bright, too silent kitchen. Peering through the curtain into the adjoining bedroom I froze. I saw Michelle lying motionless on top of the bed. As I walked into the room, attempting to unstone myself with every movement, Michelle suddenly sat bolt upright and grabbed my arm. Shuddering, she managed a description of her last few terrifying hours. Having put a mug of tea on the floor by her side, she'd been lying on the velvet bedspread, quietly waiting for me to return when, as she reached out for the mug, her heart stopped. She felt something large, warm and hairy brush past her hand before seeing it disappear into the kitchen; her worst fears were realised. It was undoubtedly a rat. My relief at not having to confront an attacker and prove my worth resulted in a large, stoned smile. Breathing heavily, with an unusual steely calm creeping into her voice, she instructed me to open every cupboard, look under every pile of discarded clothes, every drawer and crevice, or she would never get out of the fucking bed again. Comforting myself with the thought that it was probably next door's cat, and realising a lack of choice, I obeyed. Looking noisily through all its potential hiding places, until the only remaining space was a kitchen wall cupboard, my confidence returned. I opened the cupboard door and there, meeting my glassy gaze and filling every inch of space, was a puffed-out, muscle-bound, throbbing package of antagonistic vitality. Forget the starved-looking mud-caked dingy denizens of the garbage-strewn city; this was a rat in its virile prime. The colour of a lion, with its huge shiny teeth protruding beneath a sneering lip, its body was coiled to pounce. I slammed the cupboard door shut, and did the only thing possible: I went next door to get the neighbour. I then scuttled into the bedroom and was met head on by Michelle's French provincial swearing. When the invasion was reported to the local press it was decided not to alarm the locals. The next day the banner headline ran: MICE THE SIZE OF RABBITS FOUND IN EAST THOMAS STREET.

In the remaining time that I lived there with Michelle no further rats made an appearance, but they were obviously just lying low. Nine years later, when the tenements of East Thomas Street were demolished, witnesses saw platoons of them being led, Pied Piper style, up Easter Road toward the town centre.

Michelle never used her Gallic cuss words again. For a long time, I thought our mild but steady dope intake might have played its part in our happy and harmonious relationship. But maybe it was just her innately sweet nature and exceptional tolerance of my numerous faults that allowed tranquillity to reign. This was my first attempt at living with a girlfriend and there would be surprises ahead.

Though geographically barely a mile from the family home I might as well have vanished with Michelle to another country. I was beginning to appreciate the freedom of tenement life, away from parental strictures. The Edinburgh I was now inhabiting positively bristled with blackened tenements in various states of disrepair. My folk friends all lived in them, apart from a few stragglers who were still at home. I got to see a lot of their flats, navigating the shadows on the dimly lit, cat-pee-smelling stairs while climbing mostly to the top floors, where, with a shared toilet on the landing, minimal heating and no bathroom, the rent was cheap. Our two-room flat was on the ground floor, more cosy than cramped. We washed at the kitchen sink and once a week we walked along, soap in hand, round the corner to the public baths. There we immersed ourselves into the cast-iron Victorian bathtubs, which had been filled for us with luxuriously steaming hot water.

Life with my parents at Sydney Terrace had been very different: large, spartan rooms, dark lino and heavy brown furniture that had been inherited, passed down or saved for. This was their world, created carefully over time, before and after the war. The sound of the clock ticking on the mantelpiece provided comfort to them and induced claustrophobia in me. The smell of my mother's cooking seeped into every room. Lamb bones that had been cooked for hours to turn into broth mingled with grilled kippers, boiling tripe and onions. Once a week though, the sweet baking aroma of mixed spice, ginger, cinnamon and sugar took over the house, while the Home Service played soporifically in the background.

I would like to think that I wasn't ungrateful for the effort and sacrifices my parents made in their attempt to secure a profession for me. It was essentially a caring response to the uncertainties and hardships they'd experienced throughout their married life. They hoped I would come out of my training with a job for life, albeit in

MIKE HERON

a career that I had no aptitude for and no possibility of thriving in. Very early on it was apparent that I was totally unsuited for any type of office life. Neither did I have the intellectual or vocational drive that made my father such an inspirational teacher.

Even the songs I was writing didn't fit in, either with the rock bands I played with or the folk traditionalists. At that stage the songs I wrote came fully formed or not at all. But there was an audience emerging from the late-night bohemian coffee bar scene in Edinburgh that I was drawn to. Drink, drugs and late nights attracted a crowd who didn't have daytime responsibilities and were eager to hear live music. By now the folk circuit was opening up, and having an individual musical style suddenly seemed not such a bad thing. There was a glimmer of hope that I might be able do this for a living.

The charcoal-grey suit, carefully saved for and selected by my mother was carelessly discarded. It was replaced by the mismatched results of Saturdays spent rummaging through piles of second-hand clothes. Michelle and I favoured the basement at Madame Doubtfire's shop, where camouflaged cats slept undisturbed amongst the furs and trinkets. Chinese kimonos and silk scarves were flung over an appliquéd Victorian screen, which doubled as a changing room. Embroidered shawls and highland-dress jackets hung on the walls while below them sat a forlorn muddle of buttoned-up ankle boots, dusty ballet shoes and ice skates.

In my early attempts to look like a beatnik, my waistcoat and office shirt worn with denim jeans and moccasins still played a part. Later they joined the suit, and I moved on to a patchwork of handmade finery, cobbled together from Victorian nightwear and velvet curtains.

71

I'd gone straight from school to William Home Cook and Co. on a boy's wage and had been subsisting for years on parental pocket money. But by the time Michelle and I set up home together I was playing most nights and for the first time I had both freedom and some money of my own.

Just before lunchtime one Tuesday I answered a knock at the door. Standing in the doorway was a stranger. 'Sorry to call unannounced, but I couldn't get in touch. Joe Boyd gave me your address.' He went on to introduce himself: 'My name's Karl Dallas and I work for *Melody Maker*. I've been asked to do a piece on the Incredible String Band for my new folk column.' He had to stoop to get through the door and, looking round the chaotic room, it was hard for him to disguise his discomfort as he gingerly tried to find a chair hidden beneath the drapes and cushions. Michelle suggested he joined us for lunch. To his surprise, from the tiny kitchen cupboard she produced three sparkling wine glasses and a bottle of Burgundy. Finding the chaise longue under a discarded assortment of clothes, he relaxed as we ate, drank, smoked and talked into the night. In the next issue of *Melody Maker* was a nice article about the ISB.

The piece in *Melody Maker* felt like one foot on the map. The day after publication a little packet full of money turned up in the post. Joe's accompanying note explained that Jac Holzman wanted to sign the band, and the cash was to cover the cost of us flying (standby of course) down to London on Friday. Joe had already booked the studio for one day, which was all the time he thought it would take to make the album. We guessed by the economy transport and the allotted recording time that there wasn't a 'mega bucks' deal on the table in New York. But at least the second foot was hovering over the map.

News of the Elektra signing reached Clive via Mary's phone. He would have to come through to meet me in Edinburgh and we would fly together to London. After he complained that he had no suitable travelling clothes with him at Temple Cottage, Mary suggested that he select an outfit from the things on hooks by the front door, mostly abandoned or forgotten by the visiting singers and climbers. Mary had already left for work when Clive appeared the next day in his chosen attire. His gigantic shirt and trousers were pulled up and in by means of a partially concealed belt and braces, and his coat, made of thick waterproof black plastic, had been designed for veterinary use in the farmyard.

In 1966 Edinburgh's airport building at Turnhouse resembled a third-world military outpost. Complete with huts and scattered hangers it had been abandoned by the RAF. As Clive and I drew near we noticed a man in a watchtower with a brick-sized black walkie-talkie clamped to his ear. He was controlling the approaching traffic, which included the bus containing us.

On arrival Clive and I were sent to wait in the standby hut. There were no facilities, catering or otherwise, and when I asked where the toilet was I was directed to another hut. Looking back at me from the cracked mirror was a junior office clerk who'd ripped his tie off and rumpled his hair in the hope of looking hip.

When I returned, Clive was still the only occupant of the waiting room . . . Seeing him from a distance had allowed me to observe him properly for the first time, and as I took in his travelling appearance

I realised he was saved from ridicule by being at ease with who he was. At his feet was his banjo case, held together by electrical flex and brown parcel tape. Jumping out in bold white stencilling, his homage to Woody Guthrie: THIS MACHINE KILLS FASCISTS.

There weren't any obviously raised eyebrows as we were shown to our seats. Neither of us had flown before, but once the captain turned the 'No Smoking' sign off we relaxed and settled back into our thoughts: making the record, working with Joe, being in London. All of Clive's childhood years, and most of his adolescence, had been spent in various parts of London, and he felt nostalgic about his old haunts: sitting in with the Covent Garden Jazz Band, going to Hornsey College of Art and busking under the Arches in Villiers Street with his first banjo. I'd only experienced London fleetingly: once with Owen Hand, and once with my parents when, as a seven-year-old walking along the Thames towpath, I was suddenly transported elsewhere and not even the sound of my own splash disturbed me.

It was a noisy flight but a smooth landing. Reliving the highlights of his youth, his black coat flapping behind him, Clive strode across the tarmac with the easy confidence of a man returning to the scene of his triumphs.

Although it was mid-June, there was no chance of the farmyard coat being discarded – Clive had got used to the look. I was feeling hot in my white office shirt just trying to keep up. Clive was stepping out briskly, in spite of his limp, and by the time we had reached arrivals, was a thrashing plastic Dracula pursued by a perspiring tousled choirboy. Waiting to meet us at the barrier were the calm and cool Joe Boyd and Robin Williamson. Joe was wearing a white linen suit and Robin was in a light-blue cheesecloth smock. Joe, who was unable to stand the sight of even half a blank page in his diary, had scouted a location suitable for a photo shoot. We were heading for Moore's Early Music Store, where Joe would take pictures of us, one of which could hopefully provide the cover for our album. We selected three exotic-looking instruments from the shop display, and held them self-consciously.

Sound Techniques

After the photo shoot in Soho we piled back into Joe's beat-up estate car, and this time I couldn't help mentioning the spectacularly scraped, twisted and bent bumpers. As we sat in traffic on the way to his flat in West Hampstead, Joe passed the time by explaining at length the rudiments of his New York parking technique.

Arriving at his place, Joe waved us ahead into the front room, which would be our String Band base camp. All four skirting boards were obscured by LPs that had been arranged along the foot of each wall, lined up like books in a library. Joe then described the distinct categories they fell into, from Appalachian dulcimer music through Shape-note singing to Zydeco, each with its own alphabetic coding. It was clear that he took a little pride in the matching catalogue he'd compiled.

Three blue-striped mattresses occupied the centre of the room, along with piles of blankets and folded sheets. None of us was expecting five-star hotel accommodation, but it was becoming clear that this was a base not a home and we were beginning to wonder just how small this recording budget might be.

Although a six-footer, Joe was wiry and nimble. Being full of nervous energy he was always on the move and it wasn't long before he told us that we should get on with practising as he was going out to 'visit friends'. The instant the door closed behind him, Clive shot us a disbelieving look, implying that Joe's probable destination was more likely to be the wild side of city nightlife. Whatever the truth, we knew we wouldn't see him until the morning. We had the place to ourselves.

With no studio recording experience, and no idea which of our songs Joe liked, we needed to run through everything we wanted him to hear. We organised ourselves into a familiar semicircle of kitchen chairs and a muddle of instruments. Doping and playing with relaxed concentration, we began to run through our set. Bearing in mind the next day's recording, we counted the first song in . . .

> *Maybe someday she will come along*
> *Sitting here with my arms around my music*
> *Thinking of the girl that I might spend the whole of my days with*
> *Maybe some day she will come along.**

When Robin and Clive had asked me to join them, all three of us envisioned a guitar, banjo and fiddle set-up. An American old-timey

---

* The five-song demo that Joe had asked us to make for Jac Holzman had been recorded on a Grundig reel-to-reel at Atty's father's house in Edinburgh: we played 'October Song', 'When the Music Starts to Play', 'Everything's Fine Right Now', 'Maybe Someday', 'Empty Pocket Blues'.

roots trio, recalling Charlie Poole and the North Carolina Ramblers from the 1920s. We saw our set being built out of Carter Family material, jug band tunes, singalong chorus numbers and a few jigs and reels. A good-time, crowd-pleasing folk club act. Because each one of us loved what the other two were coming up with and wanted to encourage rather than restrict their creativity, the format had become twisted out of its original shape. There was a wider range of subject matter in our lyrics and influences from other cultures crept in. Nine months on, we were playing the kind of music we wanted to hear, sometimes abstruse and introspective, bathed in the sunshine of marijuana. We couldn't imagine what the album would sound like as a whole, or who it would appeal to, but decided that was up to Joe.

When midnight slouched by, we constructed a turntable from the mattresses, with our shoes where the spindle would have been, and, surrounded by three thousand records, lay down and hoped for a silent night.

Before he left, Joe had waved vaguely in the direction of the kitchen, saying magnanimously, 'Just use anything.' What we'd seen of his lifestyle so far hadn't implied much domesticity, so we weren't surprised when, in the morning, all we found in there was a pile of newspapers and three empty wine bottles. We could picture Joe weaving through traffic, munching ham-and-cheese on rye, late for a concert. We could see him striking a deal with a music business mogul over aperitifs at a chic Kensington restaurant, but we couldn't imagine him standing still long enough to flip us an egg over easy.

At 10 a.m., Clive and I, starving and laconically chatting at the bare kitchen table, and Robin, conducting a desultory search for an aesthetic teapot, were disrupted by the sound of Joe Boyd's size twelves on the tiles. 'Hi, guys. Are we all bright-eyed and bushy-tailed?' he said, to little response. 'Okay then,' he continued, 'let's make a move, I'll take you to my favourite breakfast joint on the way to the studio.' Joe himself was looking about as far from bright-eyed and bushy-tailed as you could possibly get. His hair and white linen suit were equally crumpled; his young face gaunt and cadaverous. But in spite of his appearance, he was pumped-up and exuding a youthful American get up and go.

The Hayloft at Queensway was an early example of stripped pine, dried grasses in carafes and blue-and-white checked gingham. Upstairs, Joe had to forgo his usual secluded table in the corner, where every morning he started the day with eggs benedict and the *New York Times*. Today's table accommodated all of us, leaving just enough space for Joe's briefcase on top and his long legs underneath. After his third black coffee it was time for business. Tilting his chair forward, Joe removed the contents of his briefcase. Out came our demo tape and sheets of liberally scribbled-on foolscap. He explained that these were notes he'd made about our songs and that with his production and Elektra's credibility this was our opportunity to reach an audience beyond the folk club scene. Leaving us suitably impressed, he finished off by saying we had a day and a half to make the album. An improvement on the single day we'd initially been promised.*

---

* The album project had been halted only the previous week when a bidding war had broken out. The £50 advance offered to each of us by Elektra had been trumped by Transatlantic records, who made an offer of £75. Elektra responded by upping the advance to £100 each. (Although they wouldn't increase our royalty rate from 1⅔ per cent. Where it remains to this day.)

Expecting a recording environment that resembled the photographs I'd seen of a BBC studio, it was a surprise to arrive at Sound Techniques, a redbrick building in Old Church Street off the King's Road. With a stone carving of a cow's head jutting out from a wall above the entrance it was immediately intriguing. By the time the visionary sound engineer John Wood thought of converting it into a recording studio, the building's life as a Victorian milking parlour had already long since come to an end, though a number of its unusual characteristics survived. Some were entertainingly out of place, like the cow's head or the downward-slanting corridors (designed so that water would escape when the cows were hosed down). But John also saw the advantages: walls lined with slate to muffle the noise of the cattle could work just as well as studio soundproofing, and the rooms of various sizes over three floors offered widely differing acoustic possibilities. John was a very experienced sound engineer, an expert at getting everything sounding as it should before the tape rolled, rather than having to fix it afterwards. Joe could then concentrate on encouraging the best performance he could from musicians without having to concern himself about the reliability of the recording. John had learned the ropes working mostly with classical music, and Joe knew he would be able to capture the characteristics of our acoustic folk instruments.

They sat together in the control room, looking down on us in the main studio, where we ran through the songs we'd played the night before that we thought might make it onto the record. We could hear Joe through an open mic but he didn't make any comment beyond asking us what each song was called. After playing for three hours we ran out of material and stopped for coffee. Joe kept leafing through piles of notes he'd been making as he decided which songs – some of which he'd only just heard for the first time – to record. He suggested that we begin by recording 'When the Music Starts to Play', and John started to set up mics for the band in the vaulted centre of the main room.

> *When sadness lays his cold fist on my shoulder*
> *And pushes me in icy waters drowning,*
> *The gentle hand of music lifts me smiling*
> *And through the sounds*
> *My heart takes bounds*
> *I happy am.*
>
> *And when the music starts to play*
> *Let me be around.*

After our third attempt at the song, Joe's 'That's a take, why don't you come up for a listen?' reverberated in our headphones. Never having heard a studio recording of ourselves we weren't prepared for the fullness and volume of the control room playback as it flowed around us. We felt like professional recording artists for the first time. But slowly it dawned on us that crystalline clarity was no friend to flat notes or fumbled strings.

Happy to get the first track down to everyone's satisfaction, Joe then showed us the list of songs and tunes he'd made. He chose twelve songs written either by me or Robin, and 'Empty Pocket Blues' by Clive, who also featured on the trio tracks and instrumentals. The ISB had moved away from our original format, and the

American roots music he loved, but he still threw all his musicianship and energy into the recordings.

In the eight weeks after 'October Song' had appeared Robin had written four more songs, all of them on Joe's list. Each was distinct in style and content – well-crafted, complete, meaningful. I had written many songs, but pitifully few matched that description. So far my songbook was sketchy and dog-eared, and would have had trouble standing upright on the shelf next to Robin's pristine volume.

I can't remember a single occasion when Robin or I asked the other what a new song was about. The first time we heard it we just absorbed it and after a while joined in with something we hoped might chime with the mood.

One of the songs that Robin wrote after 'October Song' was 'Dandelion Blues'. We were at Temple Cottage one afternoon just sitting around with guitars. I started playing along with him, not knowing that he was giving his new song its first airing. It had a catchy Everly Brothers-style chorus.

Much of what Robin came up with at that time was so beautifully crafted and fully formed ('Good as Gone', 'Smoke Shovelling Song', 'Womankind') that it was hard for me to find a way in. However, 'Dandelion Blues' was different, and I think Robin may have even imagined a two-guitar arrangement while writing it: my lines came easily, both sung and played, and the whole thing sat in an easy groove.

We must have played it live a hundred times, but it wasn't until I listened to the studio playback that I took in most of the words. The first verse was a relaxed, erotic romance, the second was beginning to lose me, and by the third any understanding that I had lay more in the ring of the words than their meaning.

By Sunday afternoon we'd recorded sixteen tracks that we thought could work as an album. The whole recording process was, for me, revelatory. Joe and John were intuitive about, and had an obsessive interest in, 'sound'; not just the ability to hear notes and record them with feeling, but also the gift to capture the best music live in the moment it moved the air. Sitting at the control room desk, John used his razor blade to splice the tracks together into Joe's preferred order. In those vinyl days, when it was usual to put an LP on and let it run through side one before turning over to side two, the sequence was important. Joe wanted the mood to build naturally over the course of each side. After hearing the playback he felt the order might be improved on and took the tracks home, where his own razor blade was waiting.

By the evening, Clive and I were back in the standby queue at Heathrow, hopeful for seats on the last plane home. It wasn't a long wait, which was a good thing as by now Clive's coat was somewhere between a hamster cage and a burning tyre. Airborne, and with the experience of our first flight under our belt, we waited for the 'No Smoking' sign to be switched off. We lit up and settled back in the dark to thoughts: making the record, working with Joe and leaving London. As we relaxed, Clive took the opportunity to tell me about the plans that he and Billy were making for a trek to Afghanistan. This didn't come as a great surprise, as Robin and I already thought that he might have some travel plans up his sleeve. I wasn't sure Clive would really leave though as he was often planning his escape and, as a natural dreamer with a drifter's nature, packing his bag didn't always mean travelling. By the time we started the descent to Turnhouse part of me was still clinging to the idea that the release of the album would provide enough glue to keep all three of us together. *We flew over the town at night; it spread like a firework of frozen light.* Leaning in towards me, Clive suddenly said, 'Are you going to be all right, Mike, when Robin's gone?' Stunned, I could hear him expand on this and as the echo of his voice grew clearer I heard him explain that Robin was leaving for Morocco in the morning and planned to live there with Likky. A song, which had been running in my head for days, now rolled through my mind like subtitles.

A strange thought just crossed my mind, paid the rains back in kind
'Twas the thought of sweet May coming on
The days are running so slow, my heart is aching to go
And my feet surely itch for the road.

Mmm the long hot summer
Oh now the summer long.

I have been tied to this land since the day I was planned
By the need to feed my body and mind
Look you can work till you're grey, waste your whole life away
What security then do you find?

Mmm the long hot summer
Oh now the summer long.

I don't have no one to cheat don't have no one to beat
You know I just need some room to uncurl
I don't have no aim in view just some dreams to pursue
As I wallow around in the world.

Things I must do, places to see
Things I must do, now I've nothing now to hold me here
And I'll take the southward road.

'Good as Gone' was one of my favourite Robin songs, but I'd always understood it to be a flight of fancy rather than a planned relocation. It seemed an abrupt way to end our partnership.

Clive and I emerged from the plane. We had nothing to say to each other on the airport bus into town, and at the terminal we parted with an ambiguous wave. Clive's putrefied coat, carrying a banjo, and bobbing from side to side, slowly dissolved into the dusty yellow streetlight. His head was full of travel and mine of home.

Unravelling

I trudged towards Michelle's place, my cheap cardboard guitar case shedding a trail behind me, my holdall getting heavier by the minute. The weekend spent with Joe had been exciting, and often inspiring, but lacking in comfort and sleep. Weariness had finally crept into me, and the dark tenements were looming – grimy and depressing. I was already missing Clive.

Drifting down East Thomas Street was a vaguely familiar song, but sung by a voice I didn't know. The sound was echoing and dreamlike, strong but lilting, and tinged with beautiful sadness – it chimed with my mood. As I reached the front door it slowly dawned on me that there were two voices, Michelle was duetting with an ancient recording of Edith Piaf, both at full volume.

I waited until the crackle and hiss of the track faded, before turning my key. When Michelle fell into my arms I noticed a glimmer of sympathy in her familiar smile.

She had already heard the news of Robin and Clive's departure through the folk scene grapevine. I felt a weight lifting from me as I realised I didn't need to explain my feelings of loss and disappointment.

Next day, pampered by the luxury of a night in my own bed, I was reluctant to appear fully awake, and kept my eyes seven-eighths closed as Michelle slipped out early on one of her regular visits across town to see her mother.

Michelle's mother's house on the south side was easy to find. In the street-level bay window, behind the watery glass, stood a large mannequin wearing only a corset. Michelle had pointed out many times how out of place it was in Edinburgh's demure Morningside, but there it remained; standing proud, dusty and unchanged. Her mother's window display had been admired when they lived in Paris, and how else could she so tangibly demonstrate her expertise as a corsetière?

When I did get out of bed I took my time just pottering in the kitchen and being at home. I'd only been away for three days, but a lot had happened. The flying, the new surroundings, the studio, all the playing and listening and the attention to detail from Joe and John, had made me feel that my writing and singing were both worthwhile.

With nothing to bring home from the sessions (Joe wanted everything to be complete before sending us a tape) I picked up my guitar and started to sing 'The Tree', one of the songs we'd recorded, just to remind me how it felt. Momentarily the cloud that was the trio's collapse came into focus.

I had a tree

In the dream hills where my childhood lay

And I'd go there in the wide long days

And my tree would listen to all that I'd say

And the sun was shining brightly and the sky was smiling

Then one day when the world had put me in its tomb

And my life was just an empty room

I went to my tree and I sat there in my gloom

And the light was fading dimly and the sky was crying

Then my tree bent its branches low down to the ground

And its green leaves shrouded up my mind

And I left the world somewhere behind

And I did not know what I would find

And the sun was shining brightly and the sky was smiling.

I twitched the curtain back, and the blue-sky morning swept in. Outside, everything looked sparkling and new, renovated by the June sunshine. I raked around in the bedroom for suitably carefree clothing, brewed up some coffee and dressed. I longed to be out breathing the brightness, but relaxed and slowly sipped instead. There was no hurry; the scented air would wait for me.

With all the time in the world, I sauntered through Queen's Park on autopilot, surrounded by all the shades of green there are, until I came to the cobbles and colours of the Old Town.

I'd been walking aimlessly, just enjoying summer in the city, but when I reached the intersection of the Royal Mile and North Bridge I realised I was less than a mile from the Crown Bar. A pale shadow of a cloud came into view once again, but it wasn't enough to break my stride.

When I shuffled through the pub door I was taken aback by how close to my expectations it was. Archie was off to the right at a small table, shoulders hunched, doing paperwork concerning the club, and Owen was perched at a bar stool leaning on the counter, writing notes. Hamish, pretending he hadn't been up all night, was addressing a pie and a pint. Wearing a gargantuan red cardigan, jeans, sandals and a twelve-string guitar, he was a sore thumb sticking out among the suited office clerks having lunch. Archie waved us all over to a table, and there was much hugging and back-slapping. I'd seen them only the week before, but I guess the label-signing, London recording and grapevine news had made me seem more missing than I actually was.

The time passed easily: Archie, as ever, was full of encouragement and Owen of understanding. Hamish, as he usually could, winkled out the humorous strand behind everything. They asked which songs we'd put down, what it was like recording with Joe, and when the record would be out. I knew we'd been helped massively by Joe and the roll of the dice, as the first Incredible String Band album was coming out on Elektra, the coolest folk label around. They simply couldn't believe that the group might break up completely before the album was even released. Owen said he was sure that Robin would take his time in a bohemian sort of way before returning, as if back from holiday, and that we would pick up where we'd left off.

The walk back home was easy. Two hours spent with Archie, Owen and Hamish had lightened my heart and put a bounce in my step. I could now begin to imagine Robin's return.

Archie had asked me to sing at his club night, so some future was sketching itself in. I wanted to hear the album, make sure everything was okay and find out the release date. I needed to call Joe.

I saw the sunlight glinting off a red phone box through the trees in Queen's Park, stepped in, called the operator and, reversing the charges, phoned Joe. He'd already finished the album and added that he'd spoken to Jac Holzman, who was now aiming for an early UK release date of 30 June. Joe said he had posted me a copy, which should arrive the next day.

Joe had learned, to his astonishment, that there wasn't a telephone at Michelle's, so had asked me to call him from a phone box at eleven o'clock every morning. 'Yes, it's fine to reverse the charges, Mike,' and, 'No, I haven't told Jac about Robin and Clive leaving yet.' Although I was obviously his third choice he then went on to ask me to do any press interviews required (keeping quiet about the absence of the other two) and write some of the sleeve notes. Joe added that he'd been playing the album to his music business contacts. Although it was hard to slot our music into one category, which would have made it easier to market, there was already a surprising amount of interest being shown. I was flattered to be involved in so much of the release process, even if my new role was largely due to Robin and Clive's unavailability.

The briskly efficient onslaught of crisp American syllables had threatened to go in one ear and out the other, but I soon adjusted and once again was suitably impressed by Joe's credentials. Looking out through the small panes on to a tranquil park – where ducks slowly circled on their lazy pond – I realised he had no idea where I was calling from. When I next called Joe, it would be from the grimy vandalised phone box round the corner from East Thomas Street, the view would be of a grey wall.

Since getting back from London I had dreaded the void of 'nothing to do', but the very moment that Joe's agenda landed, ways to while away a sunny afternoon formed a queue intent on seducing me. It was the seaside that prevailed. With tomorrow now mapped out I would bask in today.

Two straight downward-sloping miles led me to Portobello Beach. In addition to reaching the sea, the road reached into my teenage years. Branching off all the way down were side streets with strange names where my friends used to live. Ghosts of bikes, guitars, roller skates and girls haunted Vandeleur Avenue, Bryce and Kekewich. Bathed in memories, I came to the familiar promenade and sat down. It was a year since I last sat on that very same bench, having just walked out on both my career as an accountant and my parents. I couldn't have imagined then that so much would change over the next twelve months.

Then, with the sun high in the sky, and the sea the colour of dreams, I went home and wrote a song.

Michelle and I were in a fulfilling relationship, but that didn't stop me noticing the social changes all around me; it was the summer of '66 and I thought freedom and love might be good themes to explore in a song.

Michelle had a favourite regional French wine, Le Herisson, which had a scratchy black-and-white drawing of a hedgehog on the label. There was always a bottle or two in the kitchen at East Thomas Street, bought either by Michelle or her mother. It was very drinkable and evoked memories of long-gone family days that they'd spent together in France. I poured myself a glass. I'd had this ten-note motif in my head for some time. It was repetitive, jaunty and a little annoying, but was less strident and obtrusive when played with a slide. In keeping with Delta blues tradition the slide should have been a bottleneck or a dagger. I used a black plastic dice-shaker taken from a compendium of board games. Picking up my guitar I filled in a verse structure, and then a chorus emerged around the tune, and a song about an intrusive hedgehog pestering people with advice about their relationships began to appear.

Sitting on the bed the next morning I stopped playing my new song long enough for a slice of brioche and a sip of coffee. When I tried the chorus again Michelle shouted from the kitchen that she liked it. Just as I was wondering whether to sing it at the Crown that evening, the doorbell rang. I walked through with my coffee and saw Michelle taking delivery of a brown paper package that didn't look like the reel of tape we were expecting from Joe – it was the size and shape of an LP, but thick and heavy. On the front of the parcel there was a label addressed to me, and on the back was written: 'Sender: J. Boyd. Contents: one acetate.'

Before digital technology arrived, making accurate audio copies wasn't easy. Acetates were produced in the studio when the master recording of an album had been completed. It was a way of checking that all was as it should be before a run of vinyl was pressed. Acetates looked like records, but were in fact just metal plates coated with plastic (cellulose acetate) onto which an album was cut. They had a very short life, but enabled an artist to hear their record at home, away from a studio. This was useful for making sure that everything sounded as it should and that the running order worked.

In the parcel was a letter from Joe pointing out the limited number of plays possible before deterioration, and suggesting we read the pamphlet 'Getting the most from your acetate', which he had also enclosed. He went on to say that the cover design was at an advanced stage and my sleeve notes were needed urgently. Jac and he liked the album and could find no technical fault with it and so, as long as I approved the master, they would go ahead with a 30 June release. Since Robin and Clive were off the radar, I had been promoted by default. My apprenticeship was at an end; I was now a fully-fledged member, albeit of something that only now existed in the mind – a phantom band.

I ripped the disc out of its remaining packaging and slipped it onto the turntable. Michelle budged up on the sofa, where we sat agog as Robin's fiddle rasped out from the Dansette. Michelle, who'd heard the opening song, the Bulgarian-flavoured 'Maybe Someday', enough times to be blasé about it, wasn't. We then listened entranced to 'October Song', astounded by how much studio sound was flooding the room, but by the third track realised we ought to lift off the pick-up arm. Feeling a need to share this experience and unsure of the number of plays that were possible on an acetate, we wanted friends to be listening with us.

My eyes were drawn to a plain white postcard that had arrived the day before:

> *Mike, I'm in your patch on Tuesday around teatime, going to a beer and skittles night with Allan Coventry and Mike Smith. Worry not, I don't expect you to come, but the three of us could call round to yours on the way if that's ok? Atty*

Slick American ten-pin bowling had yet to reach Edinburgh, but primitive alleys had sprung up in the backrooms of pubs. The Abercorn, a huge, sprawling inn half a mile from East Thomas Street was the only one I'd been to . . . never again. Using both hands you sent a very big, very heavy wooden ball scudding towards nine rustic skittles, collapsing on your knees once the ball had been dispatched. Beer was guzzled, and halfway through the evening a huge tray of lukewarm meat pies was ushered in. To add to the futility, at game's end it was usually discovered that the designated scorer had gone home, and anyway all interest in winning had long since dissipated.

I rushed out to call Atty from the grey wall telephone box. 'Yes,' he assured me, 'we'll be with you at half past six. Actually, I don't know why I keep going on these office skittle nights, you just bruise your knees, drink gallons of beer and never seem to get pissed.' I mentioned the acetate and he said the boys would like that.

With the afternoon stretching ahead I wrote another verse for my hedgehog, and when I sang Michelle the whole thing she thought it sounded ready for the Crown. Archie Fisher had done me a big favour by suggesting I do a spot there every week. I really wanted to keep on writing, and he had dangled a big carrot in front of me by providing a regular audience for my new songs. If Robin didn't return I would have my own material, and if he did we could combine our sets. I knew him well enough to know he wouldn't be idle in Fez.

Atty, with the precision you would expect from an apprentice quantity surveyor, rang the bell at exactly 6.30 p.m. Mike and Allan were in the outside toilet, puffing a joint and sipping a quarter bottle respectively. When we convened in the front room of number 12, our chairs formed a vague circle round the record player. Talk was all about the making of the album, music being our shared obsession. Then the acetate was weighed, fondled and passed around, before being placed gingerly on the turntable. Michelle lowered the pick-up arm, and Robin's familiar fiddle screech soared into the room. We looked around at each other with anticipation before we realised it had abruptly stopped, to be replaced by a bass scratching sound like the zip of a big boot being repeatedly dragged up and down. All eyes were on the turntable, where the acetate was unravelling like a black pullover. Mixed in with the constant low whirring came the sound of little squibs exploding as plastic showers intermittently shot upwards. Back at the turntable pin a molten pool was piling into a mini volcano, set in a sea of silvery spinning metal. In the half-light things slowly settled and ground to a halt. The eerie silence was broken by Mike's awestruck voice: 'Wow, man, monochrome fireworks.' Behind the thick lenses of his glasses, Allan's eyes were huge. He was thrust forward in his seat as if anxious not to miss the lighting of the next sparkler. In the disorderly black-peppered room it was Atty who picked up the page covered in bold red lettering – GETTING THE MOST FROM YOUR ACETATE – his gaze was drawn to the last paragraph.

> *Before playing your acetate ensure your stylus is not chipped or otherwise damaged. If you habitually play old records, for safety you should replace your stylus. A damaged stylus can completely destroy your acetate.*

Michelle and I looked at each other.
Silently her lips formed the word . . . 'Edith.'

Apart from the expected disapproval from the traditionalists 'The Hedgehog' went down well that night at the Crown, and a day of mixed fortune tottered to an end.

The following day, as I made my way to the call box, I wasn't too worried. I was sure that Joe would make despairing noises when I told him the story of the damaged stylus, and be disappointed at my inability to comment on his clever track order, but would grudgingly send another acetate. He'd feel that at least one band member's approval was needed before the record was pressed.

Although I had a new, unblemished needle waiting when the acetate arrived, Michelle and I agreed that this time we would listen alone. There were more than a few anxious moments as the new acetate began rotating. The previous incident was fresh in our minds and the black plastic aftermath was still being discovered in and behind things. We soon forgot to worry though as we were carried away by the music. Because we were so familiar with the songs, the thing that surprised us most was how present and clear the instruments sounded. The tracks followed each other in such a natural way that the songs might have been written in the order Joe had chosen. As the realisation hit me that the album would actually be released by the end of the month, a track that I'd tended to ignore crept out of the speakers.

> And I've nothing to do
> And I've nowhere to go
> I'm not in the slightest way upset
> I'm not chasing a hope
> Or a dream or a plan
> And I'm not even chasing the sunset.

I had never played 'Footsteps of the Heron' at the Glasgow club, and thought of it as coming from the same mould as 'Can't Keep Me Here'. They were both about the shock that accompanies freedom from hidebound work and study schedules, but each had a different take. Their common thread was an acknowledgement of the hitching thumb that had dumped the nine-to-five work ethic by the wayside, but 'Footsteps' had a thought that felt relevant to me as I listened. I needed to realise that not every lull was the prelude to a storm of creativity.

Instead of treading water until Robin's hoped-for return, I tried to fill the days usefully. I continued writing and, armed with my new songs, looked forward to my weekly spot at the Crown, but most of my friends who shared an enthusiasm for smoking and folk music seemed to be on the road. Feeling nostalgic for the ballroom days, I re-enlisted Atty and we ambled past our old haunts up to the Palais, but twisting had now been replaced by loon dancing. We moved on to the Gamp, where Rock Bottom and the Deadbeats were swinging like crazy under Andy Hampton's jazzy spell. Their repertoire was now mostly Liverpool beat group songs but made looser and more danceable by a lurch away from solid 4/4. It was impossible not to foot tap, or at the very least sway along.

Terra Firma

It had been raining for three days straight when one Saturday in early October I set off for Milngavie, heading to Mary's. Without warning, after passing a small, grey-stone primary school, the B road became a dirt track and snaked up sharply alongside Balmore Golf Course. The sky was dark and still full of rain, and the mud was now thick and sludgy as I peered like a mole through the swishing wipers of the borrowed Mini. Three hours earlier the car had been pillar-box red. Now, under its opaque coating, the colour was anybody's guess. Skidding around trying to hold the horizon steady, I was steering to avoid three previous victims of the hill: two cars and a van and, on its side, the rusty green tractor that had failed to rescue them. Whistling to myself in defiance of the mud, I saw, through the spattered windscreen, a thread of white smoke. That's when I knew Temple Cottage was within reach but, stuck with the wheels spinning furiously, I was contemplating failure, and dreading the descent. Suddenly, for no reason at all, there was a gripping, grinding noise, and with a surge the little car reached terra firma and the cottage garden.

I slumped back in my seat. It wasn't just relief that swept over me, I was engulfed by a sort of spiritual anxiety, and thought I might be having an acid flashback. Tiny circular rainbows were dancing in front of my eyes as I tried to see the four monkeys more clearly through the murk. They were jumping around waving sticks in the top branches of the three very tall pines behind the house. It seemed they might be trying to communicate, but the wind was carrying their rasping chattering cries off as they hopped up and down with increased vigour. Silently I cursed Billy's sugar cube.

My first LSD trip had taken place earlier that year when Billy returned from London with a batch of impregnated sugar cubes. Nobody in Edinburgh really knew anything about acid then, but Billy's alternative pals were eager to wander in the psychedelic terrain they'd heard all about. Between gulps of hookah, Billy explained that we couldn't just sample a little to see what we thought; it was essential to take enough to transport us on a mental journey. He assured us that the world we returned to would be different, touched with magic. Reminded of Alice in Wonderland, I expressed an interest, as did Mike Smith and Eddie. Billy promised he would guide us along the route, lest we get lost and confused.

The following Saturday morning we all met up as arranged and were welcomed by Billy, who was wearing a long brown monk's robe, a large silver cross at his neck. With his hands in prayer position he greeted each of us with a subtle nod, and ushered us into the front room. Incense and the sparse sound of angular Japanese *koto* music filled the air. A sort of manual had come along with the LSD and, as we sat around on scratchy mirror-work cushions, Billy prepared us for the trip. His preamble was delivered in a hushed, sanctimonious voice, peppered with words like 'sacrament' and 'awakening', and oiled with phrases like 'cosmic consciousness' and 'inner space'.

We were eventually allotted a sugar cube each, but our instruction hadn't quite ended, and we were treated to a chapter on contact highs and acid flashbacks, even as the sugar dissolved on our tongues. After an hour, and though I was not at all convinced that anything had happened, Billy decided it had and led us down to the street. We were a patchwork crocodile crawling towards the nearest open green space – the Meadows – the pavement dancing under its feet. *The purple sail above me catching all the strength of summer.*

As we made our way through the guns and tanks there was rising panic, with Billy (the only non-tripper) trying to restore calm: 'It's all right,' he said, 'they're only recruiting.' Having slipped into a time warp, Eddie took this to mean he was going to be press-ganged and was all for fleeing in his kilt. Clipboard-holding soldiers didn't even bother to ask if any of us would like a career in the army.

We wandered down to the Old Town, where shimmering buildings unveiled themselves, revealing their past so vividly that I felt I could see it all for the first time. I peeled off to the park past the ferns and down among *shadows crawling through the green bush trees.* Breathing in the quiet sounds of evening I watched the sun setting over the ancient city. I wasn't ready to go home, so headed for the Traverse in James Court, where the poets of '66 were gathering.

Alone in the dark, holding on to significant words spoken with new crystal phrasing, I ended the day having returned to my familiar but changed self.

'Mike, Mike!' Mary was knocking on the windscreen, stooping to look into the driver's window: 'You look shaken, come on in.' I slithered to the front door. 'What's happening in your trees?' I asked, once we were safely inside. 'Oh,' she smiled, 'that's only Chris and his climbing buddies, a drop of rain doesn't stop them, they're just checking their equipment before going north. I'm sure you've met them a few times, didn't they say hi?'

The little round rainbows had now joined up to form a big hoop at the edge of my vision, but the rest of my sight seemed to be returning to normal. Although large, the rooms at Mary's had a cosy feel, with chunky couches, armchairs and thick velvet curtains that were not usually fully open. I was sitting on my own in the corner, Mary having gone to fill the kettle, when in the half-light, with my improving eyesight, I began to see people far off at the other end of the room. A man dressed like Lawrence of Arabia was sitting on a sofa, stroking a cat with his right hand while waving at me with his left. Next to him was an Edwardian lady botanist wearing a fitted floor-length white cotton dress and holding a butterfly net. Not entirely confident that I wasn't hallucinating, I walked as firmly as I could across the room, my hand outstretched in greeting. At the third step there was a flash and a clunk, and my memory and senses returned together. The cat became a lute, the net an umbrella, and I knew why I was there.

It hadn't been a heavy Friday night, but Michelle and I usually didn't surface till late morning, which meant the arrival of Joe's telegram at 9 a.m. had been a prolonged and noisy affair.

> *MIKE HERON ESQ*
> *ROBIN BACK STOP AT TEMPLE COTTAGE STOP*
> *YOU GO SOONEST STOP CONCERT STOP*
> *JOE BOYD ESQ*

I should have known that they wouldn't look exactly the same after three months in North Africa, but these were different people. They were beyond recognition. Robin was clean-shaven, with flowing, long, sun-bleached hair; any exposed skin was as far away from his previous Scottish pallor as was possible. With his bronze toes thrusting out of sandals he looked totally at home in a cream djellaba with a thin, pale-blue vertical stripe. Silver bracelets circled his wrists. There no longer remained any sign of their beatnik Edinburgh past, as he and Likky sat there glorious and shining. I looked at my olive-green cable-knit jumper sagging over my ill-fitting damp jeans and then down to my mud-encrusted Hush Puppies. Not for the first or last time, I felt I knew my place.

I dug into my sodden pocket and fished out the telegram, presenting it to Robin, who glanced at it without obvious excitement. 'Later, Mike,' he said, putting a full stop on my overenthusiastic babbling. 'Let's just eat.' Of course Robin had already been in touch with Joe and was more informed than I realised. When I tried again to blurt out the news about a proposed concert he raised his hand: 'Please, Mike, try this first, it's called couscous and we brought it all the way back from northern Africa.' I looked down at the slop in the brown pottery bowl on the table and fell silent.

During the meal Robin was able to quietly fill me in on the finer details of the offer that was being made by Joe. The album was doing well and gathering good reviews, which had given Jac Holzman the confidence to agree that Robin and I should open for the touring Americans Tom Paxton and Judy Collins at the Royal Albert Hall on 4 November. As a duo. Over coffee in the dimming light, with the fire crackling and the rain continuing to fall, we eventually unfolded, remembered each other, and talked.

Before I arrived, Likky and Robin had settled into a room on the upper floor so I was allotted the unconverted rafter space, which was only accessible via a climber's rope. So, luckily, or sensibly as it turned out, we agreed to rehearse the next day in Robin's room.

Having managed the ascent, I slid sleepily downward the next morning and headed for the kitchen to collect coffee and my guitar. The smell of last night's woodsmoke lingered in the house and on my clothes, along with a backdrop of incense. Drawn by an exotic, plucked, woody sound I'd never heard before, I headed to Robin's room. He was sitting on the bed playing a Moroccan oud. Beside him, a canvas knapsack was overspilling with flutes, whistles, bows, finger cymbals and a pair of small clay drums. The rain had stopped and a shaft of light caught the careful arrangement of a small bronze Buddha, cowrie shells and a jar of dried honesty that had been placed on the low bedside table. Inspired by the unfamiliar sound, I drew up the only chair and started to play along. I slipped into a new song that I'd been living with for some time, curious to hear if the oud might colour it. As *the bent twig of darkness grew the petals of the morning*

Robin put aside the oud and took a small, more primitive-looking instrument from a nail on the wall. Sitting on the side of the bed he picked up a bow and placing the Gimbri upright on his lap he drew the bow over its three strings producing an otherwordly primal wailing that was somehow weirdly right. It transformed my song and changed everything.

I looked up and standing at the doorway was a small boy with red hair and a sweet, puzzled face. The door opened a bit further and he edged his way in.

> Listen to the song of life
> Its rainbow's end won't hold you
> Its crimson shapes and purple sounds
> Softly will enfold you.
> It gurgles through the timeless glade
> In quartertones of lightning
> No policy is up for sale
> In case the truth be frightening.
> You know what you could be
> Tell me my friend
> Why you worry all the time
> What you should be.

Part II

In the Footsteps of the Heron

ANDREW GREIG

Tidings that I have been untrue to my word will not go back to the land to which I myself cannot return.

Cuchulain

Outer Groove: A Prince of Boredom

It's back again, late autumn '67 in our wee town on the east coast of Scotland. I have turned sixteen, the house is empty, the parents out somewhere. It has been dim and wet all day – *gey dreich* in my father's tongue – and the roof guttering can't cope. I am standing at the sitting-room window while *Revolver* clicks on its inner grooves.

They say it has been a Summer of Love, but not noticeably so in these parts.

I am fixated on the overflow, at once rushing and stuck, which is how I feel. In the street below, water bubbles up from the stank to run down past Auld Jeannie's house, then on by Duncan's the draper (it's Sunday, the yellowed blinds are down). The swelling flood swerves onto Rodger Street, down past the garage where they sell air guns to anyone, then gushes by the locked doors of the Royal Hotel, where men who prefer to drink standing dry their behinds at the coal fire.

Opposite Eddie Clark's café (closed, of course), by the eroded Market Cross on Shore Street, girls in damp frocks and coats stand shivering, waiting for the bus to Leven – which won't come for ages, because it's Sunday. Behind them the rain-river swirls through the gap in the sea wall, digs a channel through sand, meets turbid sea and vanishes.

Fifers half-jokingly still call it *the Kingdom*. Despite the Forth and Tay road bridges in the early sixties, Fife remains a place apart, defined by estuaries and a reputation for thrift and canniness. *It takes a lang spoon tae sup wi' a Fifer.*

I can never quite be a Fifer, because we moved there when I was thirteen and my father retired from medicine. He might as well have been my grandfather, for he fought in the Great War, about which he said only *You had tae look after your feet*.

If this is the Kingdom, I am its prince of boredom. Elsewhere, momentous changes are afoot. I sense in my fizzing body that it's all happening in Liverpool, London, San Francisco. Meanwhile I could finish my French homework, put the Byrds 'Tambourine Man' on the gramophone one more time, or practise Tom Paxton for the school Folk Club.

Raindrops squirt down the glass, pause, then jerk on towards the sill, like the falling lines in Apollinaire's calligram:

```
I        w        a        w        i        i        t        e        m
t'       o        s        e        n        t'       o        n        y
s        m                 r                 s        o        c        l
         e'       t        e        m        r        o        o        i
r        n        h        d        e        a        m        u        f
a        s        o        e        m        i        a        n        e.
i                 u        a        o        n        r        t
n        v        g        d        r        i        v        e
i        o        h                 y        n        e        r
n        i                          a        g        l        s
g        c        t        e        n                 l
         e        h        v        d        y        o
         s        e        e                 o        u
                  y        n                 u        s
                                                      o
                                                      f
```

Give me a name like Guillaume Apollinaire and let me live in Paris, and I might accomplish something! As it is, I am a supersaturated potassium permanganate solution in double chemistry, awaiting the seed crystal that will turn me solid blue.

Ah, sod this. I lift the needle then hurry downstairs. In the back garden, my brother is playing solitary keepie-uppie with a tennis ball in the rain. I unhook the olive-green shorty raincoat, pull on my beloved Cuban-heeled square-toed Chelsea boots.

I hesitate in the dim porch. Peaked caps like Ringo's in *A Hard Day's Night* or Bob Dylan's on his first LP – you can't get those round here. But it's really wet outside. I'll be *drookit* – my father's word again, coming from a different part of him.

I reach up for his deerstalker. It smells of pipe and is tight on my head – his skull must be narrow, though his hands seemed huge when they last clouted me a year back. I step out into the rain. Older folk may look twice ('*Yon's the doctor's laddie*') and laugh in that Fife way, a mere twitch of the lips. I am bothered and not bothered by that. The lassies in the bus shelter are another matter, I would not enjoy their scorn.

My feet take me along the back ways, past the town hall into Cellardyke, which is a world of its own, with smaller houses, tighter streets and a different accent. My boot heels clack past closed wee net-curtained shops run by fishermen's widows.

Damp, dreamy, on fire, I am walking, inevitably, towards a grey pebble-dashed council house. I have been hopelessly – and I use the word advisedly – in love with a classmate, the girl I think of as Cherry. Cherry red, cherry ripe. To sit next to her through double French, our shoulders inches apart in our thick uniform jackets, is to suffer exquisitely.

I asked her out at a few weeks ago, and she looked at me with her lovably crooked full-lipped smile then said quietly *I'm going out with somebody else*. That somebody else is a year older, very possessive, quick with his fists.

My walks, like my thoughts, all trend in her direction. I might see her washing up at the lit kitchen window, or drawing curtains in the living room. She might see me, come out and change our lives for ever.

A voice keeps me company. It doesn't tell me I am Napoleon in exile, or that our phone is tapped by aliens. Instead it murmurs *Fall, flow and ache*. It adds *Our town overflows like an old ash can*. It tells me things just beyond my understanding, like French poetry. Recently I have started writing down and playing with these voices. It's fun. It helps.

Wet is seeping through the shorty raincoat as in the failing light I stop at the corner of the street that will always be *her street*. (At this age so much happens in italics.)

Cherry's house has a pulley beam sticking out above a wee door high in the attic gable, marking it as a fisherman's home. Lights are on, curtains drawn. In the kitchen, the diffused shape of her mother at the sink. A shadow passes across the front room's curtains – is it her, or her sister? – then gone.

I squelch off homeward for my tea, certain that Real Life happens elsewhere and nothing will ever change.

I am so wrong. On the coming Friday at the school Folk Club, I will encounter something that redirects the flood of my life. As I pass under the fuzzy haloes of streetlamps, the dripping wires that zing like the voices in my head, just outwith the range of sense, I cannot know this will be the last Sunday of Before.

Track 1: Chinese White

The overflowing guttering, the restless yearning boredom of Sunday afternoons, the glow pulsing behind the grey of our dreich, cherished village – I am reinvented in these memories. None are faked but all are shaped by the craft I have been, for better and worse, pursuing most of my life.

The teachers and kirk elders, the sweetie-shop wifies and drapers of my youth, are all gone. Our parents are all dead, dying or demented. The younger brother who played keepie-uppie in the rain has retired to concentrate on croquet. Phantom fishing boats with names like *Spes Melior*, *Bright Star* and *Wilhelmina II* bob in Anster's pontoon-crammed harbour. That council house in Fowler Street has been bought and sold, and with it went that post-war world and its welfare state, which surrounded us then, unremarked on and ordinary as air.

Now I sit in a writing shed in our garden in Edinburgh, at sixty-four, listening to the blackbird pour song from our neighbour's solitary pine. Pale liver spots shift like freckles of rain on the back of my hand. How did it come to this?

Of course we misrepresent birds when we say they sing. They emit signals of territory, warning and mating, and they do it in response to light and hormonal stirrings. We are not so different, except we do it consciously, alone in the shower or to paying audiences. Whether receiving or transmitting, song remains one of the great joys.

The blackbird clutches the topmost of the swaying pine. I watch its beak open then, a moment later, the song arrives from the world outside. At the same time, from within, so clear and immediate, a song arises from near-on fifty years ago, written one sunny morning in upstate New York in 1968 by a man who has improbably become my friend and sometime stage partner.

Even the birds when they sing
It's not everything to them.

Our school Folk Club had been started three years earlier by senior pupils inspired by the rising Protest Movement. They took over the Music Room one evening a month, rearranged the chairs and dragged in straw bales to signify Folk Music.

The early offerings were earnest renditions of 'Where Have All the Flowers Gone?', 'Kumbaya', 'This Land Is Your Land', 'All My Trials', shoulder to shoulder with 'The Wild Rover', 'Mhairi's Wedding' and 'Loch Lomond'. Though a couple of the teachers would do their party pieces – genial Mr Leslie on the mouthie playing bothy ballads, Eddie McGeachy belting out 'The Muckin' o' Geordie's Byre' – for that evening the school was ours.

No matter how rough and unskilled, everyone got a clap, even the recorder group. Perhaps we sensed we would need all the support we could get. Most joined in the singing, as unselfconsciously as was possible for young Scots, and there were times when our voices stacked together and the harmonies felt stirring, right and strong.

Like a tree standing by the water side
We shall not be moved.

We knew little about the American Civil Rights struggle. We just liked the song, and sang it with feeling, while sensing deep down it was not true – whatever was coming our way, we would most certainly be moved.

The Folk Club was only partly about music. Other than the annual school dance, it was the one time you could mingle with the girls in numbers, out of school uniform. Who knows what transformed being might sit nearby in her vivid frock, hair up; reshaped by lipstick, mascara and eyeshadow hastily applied once out of the house; and what might accompany her passionate interest in Joan Baez?

It would have been the black polo-neck sweater with mod waistcoat and Chelsea boots. Round the time I bought *Sgt Pepper* back from St Andrews earlier that summer, I stopped using my dad's Brylcreem for my Elvis look. Now I combed it forward in a fringe, keeked in a mirror then roughed it up at bit. Took off my glasses, peered at the result, felt myself a work in progress.

I stuffed the Spanish guitar into its plastic cover, checked I had the right harmonica, then out into the salt-stiff night.

In my memory, which is as unreliable and myth-making as my *Collins Golf Illustrated Diary* entries for the time are near-indecipherable, that evening I sat on the straw bales and rushed through Donovan's version of 'Candyman', then Dylan's 'Love Minus Zero/No Limit'. It was the first time I had sung solo, and I struggled to pick chords while playing the harmonica. How could anyone possibly do that?

I dropped beats like grain through my fingers, the harmonica clogged up with nervous saliva. I did not feel easy on stage, and I had little faith in my voice or guitar-playing.

Why do it, then? Ego? An anxious but fierce need for approval?

In the light of everything that came after, all those years of risking rejection and looking ridiculous (both things I deeply feared), the self-exposure in putting what you have made in front of people – there has to have been more to it than ambition and ego.

In the end it was, I think, like this: I loved some songs so much I wanted to play them for myself. And it wasn't enough to play them alone. I wanted to play them in the presence of other people so they would feel what I felt.

A hunger for connection – to the song, to myself, to others – drove me to practise till my fingertips stung, then go onstage lacking much by way of talent, confidence, or experience. I believed in the songs like the Summer Seaside Mission people believed in Jesus.

When done right, it's not about you. It just looks that way.

My classmates George Boyter, Rick Cebula and Phillip Gay, came on as the Travellers. They stood in front of the bales. I saw that was a smart move.

Phillip was the good-looking one that girls fancied, and he had the voice. Rick and George had been playing guitar for months longer than I had, and were both natural musicians. They could both sing well enough to fit harmonies around Phillip.

They sang something conventional. 'Loch Lomond', perhaps, plus 'Jamaica Farewell' and 'Abilene'. It was enjoyable and familiar. I sat at the back, cooling down, and slipped my glasses back on in the dimness.

Then George announced they were going to do 'something different.' Richard produced a small guitar that was . . . pink, with some swirly green bits. A muffled giggle from somewhere. Phillip shifted from foot to foot, stared out over the audience.

This curious guitar had only one string. Rick tuned it down, listened carefully, adjusted the tuning knob. *Boing Boing!*

'It's called "Chinese White",' George announced. Another giggle. What kind of title is that?

He began to play four notes based on a D chord, and kept repeating. Then Rick came in on the single string with a droning buzzing whine. He began to play up and down the fretboard. Something odd was coming.

Then Phillip Gay opened his mouth and rather self-consciously sang

The bent twig of darkness grows the petals of the morning
And shows to them the birds singing just behind the dawning

Then like Yuri Gagarin I was weightless and gone.

> *Oh, will your magic Christmas tree be shining,*
> *Gently all around?*

The pink guitar buzzed and faded. A long pause, then hesitant applause. I sat astounded.

The Travellers looked relieved. Richard put away the pink guitar. 'Thank you,' George said. 'There's another one.' Another one? How can there be more of *that*? 'It's called "Painting Box".'

In some ways this song was an antidote to the strangeness of 'Chinese White'. It was sweetly melodic, harmonised between Phillip and George. Some sort of love song, but one that involved purple sails and talking fish and Friday evening footsteps plodding dully through this dark town (summoning up my lovesick ramblings through Cellardyke). The singer liked the sea he was on and didn't mind if he drowned. And there was a catchy refrain some of us began hesitantly to sing along with:

> *For somewhere in my mind there is a painting box*
> *I have every colour there, it's true*
> *Just lately when I look inside my painting box*
> *I seem to pick the colours of you.*

The only thing it had in common with the previous song was that neither were pop or folk, protest or beat music. It wasn't even Bob Dylan, the other person who sang unexpected words. These two songs were something utterly new and unmoored from tradition, as we believed ourselves to be.

> Richard Cebula: *My brother Karol had taken an old Spanish guitar that had a slightly warped neck and painted it pink, with a few colourful swirls of paint on top. The guitar wasn't really playable so ended up with one string and the idea was to use it to provide a drone effect. George did most of the hard work working out the chords. I don't recall Phillip being too avid about the ISB.*

'They're called the Incredible String Band,' George said.
'?'
'Because they're incredible,' Richard laughed.
'They're from Edinburgh,' George added.
'They're *Scottish*?'
'Oh, aye.'

I boggled. Scottish was Robin Hall and Jimmy Macgregor, Moira Anderson and *The White Heather Club*; Matt McGinn at best. It was rumoured that Donovan was Scottish, but he didn't sound it. All the music we cared about – Beatles, Stones, the Who, Kinks, Paul Simon, Dylan, Mamas & the Papas – came from far away.

'Could I have a listen to the record?'

Richard hesitated. 'It's a loan from my brother Karol.'

'And we're still working out the songs,' George said. George and Rick had been pals since primary school. I was still an outsider in Anster, and Pittenweem, a mile along the coast, was another world. We'd been getting to know each other only in these last months, in the smaller classes of fifth year.*

'Ach, come on over at the weekend,' Richard said, grinned his

---

* In the Scottish system, fifth year was equivalent to year eleven. One more year and we'd be free, or chucked out, depending how you looked at it.

toothy smile. 'I'll play it to you then. The rest of it is incredible too!'

Once in a while you feel the need to double-back on your life, sensing there is something left behind there that you could really do with now.

Track 2: Unpeeling the Onion

I spent much of yesterday with George's diary entries, laid down so many years ago: raw data like raw spirit, unfiltered and non-matured, catching in the throat.

> George: *Friday 15 December 1967. After school helped Kirk decorate Folk Club Room. Netting, fairy lights, candles, posters and Merry Xmas. Folk Club great. Extremely high standard of play. Philip Bolt OK. Johnny's Crowd great. We played 'Chinese White' & got great applause then did 'Painting Box'. After one of the best FC's ever at the end, Kirk, us and Johnny's Crowd did Wild and Gypsy Rover for rammy. Afterwards we went to play at Scout Dance at Craw's Nest Hotel. Home at 2a.m.!*

It is the diary of a sixteen-year-old – unconsidered, unguarded, all enthusiasm. And, without pushing the point into a postmodern bog where this book would slowly founder, George's diary also points up the limits, partiality and inaccuracy that any account of the past is doomed to.

So, remove the straw bales from the Folk Club scene that night! George and Richard agree that they were brought in sometimes, just not this time. In their place, drape ethnic fishing net and seasonal fairy lights. I nearly wrote candles into my original account, but then thought that couldn't be – too messy and too dangerous, what with the straw bales. Now we have candles restored.

And it is not October but shortly before Christmas. No wonder my moody Sunday walk through Anstruther a week earlier had been so dark. And I smile to think of that Folk Club evening concluding in a thrash of crowd-pleasing, communal-singing 'Wild Rover' and 'Gypsy Rover'. Of course it did.

Reading George's diaries has crowded with dear ghosts this shed in a garden of the Edinburgh flat I live in with my wife. How did this happen, how did we come to own things, to be married? Does our magic Christmas tree shine, gently, all around?

Will it? Does it? Can it still?

The day after that revelatory Folk Club, I biked over the hill to Rick's, went up the stairs into the garret hung with posters. George sat cross-legged on a cushion strumming a guitar, as with a knowing grin Richard handed me a record sleeve.

'It's *psychedelic*,' George said helpfully.

I still wasn't sure what that meant, nor how to spell it, but what I was holding was surely it.*

---

* I had seen the word used about *Sergeant Pepper*, and sensed it was something to do with drugs, but had no knowledge of these drugs, what they were or what they did or meant. Cf. 'vagina'. How limited our information was.

The colours were so . . . *weird*. Twisted, squiggly, yellow-and-red lettering unfurled right across the cover, below one open rainbow eye. *The Incredible String Band*. Above that rose a two-headed human, one male and one female face, and a blue-green globe where the dual being's heart would be. And below the lettering was, well, an outsized mauve onion.

I turned the sleeve over.

The band turned out to be not a band at all, but only two people who seemed to be crouching inside a bush (they were): they had the air of fugitives. One was dark-haired, strong-featured, serious. The other was blond, fierce-eyed and long-jawed, with scruffy beard and moustache. Below them, distorted yellow lettering set against red fringed with yellow flames proclaimed *ROBiN WiLLiAMSON AND MiKE HERON*.*

Above the picture of the 'band', orange-pink distorted hand lettering said *THE 5000 Spirits Or THE*, and below that, lime-green lettering bulged forth LAYERS OF THE OniON.†

'Mad, eh?' Richard said.

And below that, at last, something recognisable, a track listing, albeit one printed over prismatic light spraying from the word *AND*.

I looked up at George and Richard. Glee, hilarity, awe, expectation, multiplied between us. The cover alone was *radioactive*. It made *Pepper*

---

* Misled by the layout, for months we assumed the dark one was Robin, and Mike the fair beardie. We knew no one who could put us right.

† Only now, transcribing this from the cover, do I register the extreme oddness of the mix of upper- and lower-case lettering, previously obscured by the extreme oddity of everything else.

seem normal. Nothing like it had ever existed in the East Neuk of Fife.

'I can loan you it for a week,' Rick said. 'A swap for your *Rubber Soul*?'

I biked back over the hill to Anster with the LP in its carrier bag flapping from the handlebar. The tide was high, the day brimming. A lad in the year ahead of us had recently been killed on this road, his motorbike crushed between two cars as he overtook. *His head split open like a melon*, someone had whispered. I cycled carefully, off the road where possible. I must not die before hearing this record.

My mother was in the kitchen making lunch, with the Home Service on our valve radio.

'It'll be an hour or so,' she said. 'Your father's out playing golf.'

'Fine,' I said, and scooted up the stair, into the sitting room, and lifted the lid of the gramophone. I tipped the black circle from the pulsating sleeve, got it on the turntable. I lowered the needle, heard the crackle-hiss of *presence*, then stood by the window where I'd been maddened with boredom just a week earlier.

I spent the afternoon playing that record over and over, incredulous. I stared out at the rain, the bare branches thrashing in the garden of the Clydesdale Bank, the occasional Morris Minor passing in a sizzle of tyres, my English teacher frowning a poet's frown as he stalked nervily around the corner and out of sight.

Meanwhile, from my parents' gramophone's Bakelite grille streamed a universe of Mad Hatters, reproachful clouds and chiding hedgehogs, red hair falling as I kissed you (if only), the smouldering book unreadable, Orpheus charming the sunrise. From this disc unfurled flute and buzzing sitar, mandolin and bongo drums, harmonica, glad cries and kazoos.

Folk music seemed mostly about long-lost battles, failed weavers' strikes, drownings and lovers with poor facial recognition. Then 'Please Please Me' blew in like a warm and joyful gale. 'Satisfaction' strutted the horn we boys had no choice but to live with. Dylan's 'The Times They Are a-Changin' made sung words matter. But *5000 Spirits* was something else again, transforming both me and the Anstruther I looked out on. It conjured a world made wondrous, playful, poignant. Made . . . incredible.

The String Band made music that had just been born, without limits. It was the sound of what we could be. Impossible to love it and be unchanged.

I got out of bed after midnight, pulled on a sweater and went back into the sitting room, carefully closed the door. I turned the volume down low, lowered the needle then lay on the carpet with my ear next to the speaker slats.

'Chinese White' sung by the Travellers was arresting enough. On the turntable, I recognised the opening guitar figure George had played, but then rose a sobbing sound, at once animal and soul, visceral, ecstatic.* Something between a falsetto muezzin and a tomcat in heat.

---

* Like the opening chord of 'A Hard Day's Night', the sound was a declaration of intent, a threshold into the new.

This yearning cry was the North African gimbri, apparently bowed by Robin Williamson. It was like nothing heard before. It was, though we did not know it out in the sticks, the sound of LSD.

It was also – though I am queasy over the word, disliking its other-worldy postcode – a profoundly spiritual invitation. It announced a space where we had known none before.

Mike Heron's 'Chinese White' was followed by Robin's 'No Sleep Blues', which wasn't a blues at all. It was funny and celebratory, daft. Mice played football. Washed feet got clean and the water got dirty. A line about what happens when you let the pigs decide things might read as cutting and scornful, like one of Dylan's put-downs, but sung it had a lightness, a liberating on-the-wing quality. If our consciousness is a game not a given, it's possible to choose how to play in the world.

At a time when every month brought something new, this music was not like anything I'd heard before. It was like being an astronaut in the Space Race: unnerving acceleration, then abrupt release into wonder and weightlessness.

Yet for all its overdubs, the whole album sounded natural and unforced. With its oud and gimbri, mandolin, harmonica, sitar, bongos, guitars, kazoo, flute and double bass, this music came from all over the place. And it also came from Edinburgh, just forty-five miles away.

The sleeve credits suggested Heron and Williamson did not write songs together. They were unhyphenated. Mike Heron songs sounded earthy, humorous, with a sort of calypso delivery. Robin Williamson was spacey, swooping and warbling, harsh then sweet. But who was Licorice? What of Soma and his twangling sitar?

Lying on the carpet after midnight as that music poured from the radiogram, or sitting in this shed nearly fifty years later listening to it streamed from the Cloud, my response is the same: wonder that such a thing can be. Lyrics are too expensive to quote at any length, but in any case don't do the sung words justice. How can they possibly? A song exists in its singing.

None of us had heard anything like this before. 'Good Vibrations' was still recognisably a pop song, with a recurring chorus and refrain. Even Dylan's tumultuous 'Like a Rolling Stone' had a conventional structure of rhymed verses plus refrain. But Williamson's 'The Mad Hatter's Song' contained seven or more songs in four minutes. It flowed like consciousness itself, continuously developing, never repeating or returning to its origin.*

The track started with busy acoustic guitar, wordless vocalising and sitar whining. Then abruptly the vocal, chilly-harsh, prophetic and ecstatic, *Oooohh*—

The sitting-room door opened. My father, looking ancient, wild-haired, in dressing gown.

'What the hell are you doing?'

I scrambled up from the floor.

'Listening to a record. I've only got it till the weekend.'

We looked at each other, uncomprehending. Behind me, Robin Williamson was conjuring the land of the blind. I braced myself.

'Back to bed, laddie,' my dad said, almost gently. 'You have school the morn.'

---

* Lennon, with his short attention span, was particularly affected. 'Happiness is a Warm Gun' would be unthinkable without 'Mad Hatter'.

He turned and padded off to the loo, this man who had fought in the Great War, survived the Blitz in the Second, and now in his old age was having to deal with secret sitar sessions in the small hours.

At the time, I was relieved. Now I sit here watching the wind shake the laurels outside my writing shed, and feel gratitude, obscure shame and absence rise like acid reflux in my throat. He was only five years older then than I am now, but he seemed the ancient of days. I thought he didn't know anything that mattered.

I switched off the gramophone and went back to bed, leaving the record on the turntable for the morning.

To Pittenweem with my guitar, up to the garret where George and Richard confirm they have discovered an earlier String Band album, simply called *The Incredible String Band*.

We sit cross-legged on the floor (painful but essential) and pass round the cover. The band's hair is much shorter and there are three of them. The third is called Clive Palmer and he looks unwell, in a strange plastic coat. They stand looking out at us confrontation-ally, clutching very odd stringed instruments (none of which, we gradually realise, are played on the album). The colours are muted, the typeface stark. No hand-lettering, no winged figures, rainbows or purple onions. The effect is ascetic, challenging, offhand.

Though made just a year earlier than *5000 Spirits*, this album already comes from a different age: the era of mono, of TV only in black and white. So much has changed recently, and we are part of it. We examine the sleeve, looking for clues.

'Clive Palmer plays the banjo and wrote one really good song,' Richard says. 'We've nearly got the chords worked out!'

'I read in the *Melody Maker* that Clive disappeared to Afghanistan after they recorded this,' George says, as he lifts the record arm. 'That's why there's only two of them now.'

And then we listen.

It is a bare room of an album, immediate and raw.* Shrill whistle, metallic banjo, Robin's keening voice and scraping fiddle, Mike's syncopated, jerky, laughing vocals and picking. Without double bass, it is full of empty space and sounds like a demo. It isn't mellow. I see from the credits that only three of the sixteen tracks have the whole band playing at the same time. About half the songs are solos. There are two instrumentals.

It is altogether very odd, recognisably folk, but not as we've known it. There's something off in its quasi-Bulgarian rhythms, the hint of wailing Arab harshness in Robin Williamson's vocals, and Mike Heron's curious, laughing delivery. If this is Scottish, it is a very different Scotland from that of Jimmy Shand or Matt McGinn.

'We're working out the easy ones!' Richard announces.

This music is doable. It is odd but credible. With much laughter, tea, retuning, we get down to play.

——

* Perhaps analogous to Dylan's first album recorded in a day some two years earlier – at once a feint and a calling card.

I walked home over the hill with guitar in hand, copies of the scrawled lyrics and chords in my coat. We'd focused on the Mike Heron songs, 'Everything's Fine Right Now', 'How Happy I Am', 'The Footsteps of the Heron', plus Clive Palmer's 'Empty Pocket Blues'.* These were immediately likeable, quirky and earthly songs evoking drink, girlfriends present or absent; perfect for folk clubs, parties. They were good for cheery harmony singing, without being the 'Wild Rover'.

These we could do ourselves.

There were songs in my head that we hadn't attempted, like Mike's 'The Tree', a stark solo, passionately delivered from where the ribs divide. It made me ache for my Bannockburn childhood, when the river ran more clearly.

Recently Mike told me it was about an apple tree in his parents' back garden. I'd imagined some towering beech or oak. 'No, it was quite small – though it seemed big then!' And those green hills were the Pentlands? 'No, just Arthur's Seat – you could see it from our house in Portobello.'

'Footsteps of the Heron' took a simple tune and lyric:

One day as I sat in a big noisy crowd
There was me and the whole of my conscience
And I thought that I wouldn't be missed if I went
And my going would be of no importance.

---

* To be played again in May 2010, with Billy Connolly on banjo, Aly Bain on fiddle, me on white guitar, in a tent below Norman MacCaig's *Loch of the Green Corrie*, snowing outside and whisky within. 'I *loved* those guys!' Billy exclaimed.

So far, so teenage angsty. But the twist that followed was pure Mike Heron.

And I've nothing to do and I've nowhere to go
And I'm not in the slightest way upset
I'm not chasing a hope or a dream or a plan
And I'm not even chasing the sunset.

That lightness of spirit marked a parting of the ways with the earnest folk music that had come before. Instead of alienation, angst and anger, it proffered the just-being of childhood, the joyful liberation of dawdling and daundering. To a Time-haunted boy prone to pessimism and the elegiac mode, who would always be chasing the sunset, this throwaway song came as a counter, a reminder, a much-needed lichtsome companion.

The other song, the standout of the album, was 'October Song' by Robin, which left us breathless. It was a complete life statement that put paid to the temptations of politics, religion, insurrection and conformity alike, and it was so damn beautiful we hadn't the gall to massacre it ourselves.

Track 3: The Hangman's Beautiful Daughter

Preoccupied with the guitar and songs, I told my maths teacher I was dropping out of the golf squad, and his baffled turning away left me guilty and liberated. I still played rugby, semi-detached at the edge of the scrum, but was increasingly concerned with self-preservation rather than glory. I needed my hands undamaged.

Now the Prelims loomed, and I was both competitive and interested in all the subjects I was doing, including maths and sciences. Playing guitar and singing might have remained something I dabbled in, then grew out of on the way to being a chemist.

Then, in the Easter holidays of 1968, came the hangman's beautiful daughter.*

---

* *The hangman is death and the beautiful daughter is what comes after. Or you might say that the hangman is the past twenty years of our life and the beautiful daughter is now, what we are able to do after all these years* – Mike Heron

ANDREW GREIG

For many, *The Hangman's Beautiful Daughter* is the ISB's creative peak. It took the breakthroughs of *5000 Spirits* and pushed them way beyond 'folk music' to merge with the growing audience for psychedelia and generally *out there* exploration.

Pantheistic in outlook, celebratory in mood, sensual, wildly various, *turned on*, supported by haunting melodies and even wider instrumentation, it remains definitive of its era. Paul McCartney hailed it as the most important album in a year of extraordinary music. Robert Plant and Jimmy Page later said they founded Led Zeppelin on its inspiration. It was world music twenty years before its time.

For George and me – Richard was increasingly away – riveted with the sleeve in our hands and the record birling on the gramophone, it seemed we were being given the keys to the kingdom.

Here were the cues, hints, markers on which we would build our version of their world: pan pipes, invocations, masks and plays. Childhood as inexhaustible source of delight and nightmare. Above all, it gave us the living, breathing back country.

If the music hadn't been miraculous, the covers would not have mattered so. But it was, and they did. I now know the back cover photograph (which quickly became the front, so talismanic was it) is not quite what we and many others assumed.

A raggle-taggle player-family halt in wintry woods, leaves thick at their feet. All four young men are in odd apparel; Mike holds a crude cardboard mask, Robin offers up a mysterious red object that might be the key to the riddle. Five haphazardly dressed children stand or crouch in the group, one biting her fingernails, her big sister Tink grinning confidently. Likky in a striped cloak is front

133

right, clasping Robin's dog Leaf, smiling inscrutably at the camera. The other woman – essential to the balance of the whole – is at the centre, clasping a branch, her face half-hidden by long dark hair. She appears strong yet also as if she does not quite belong there.

She doesn't, but she soon will. She is Rose Simpson and her presence is pure happenstance.

Rose was a spirited but fairly straight student at York University. President of the Mountaineering Club, she had come north with a friend hoping to do the winter traverse of the Aonach Eagach ridge in Glencoe in her Christmas holidays. It was the climbing connection, not music, which brought her to Temple Cottage, in deep country beyond Milngavie, north of Glasgow.

Mary 'Spud' Stewart worked at the vet school in Glasgow. An active climber who loved singing, her Temple Cottage had become a kind of rural Alice's Restaurant for passing climbers, folk musicians, refugee monks, free spirits and lost souls. People stayed for days, weeks, in sleeping bags, chilly rooms, tents and outhouses. With Mary's five children, it was crowded, chaotic, but it somehow worked.

At this point Robin and Likky had been living for months in the attic, and Mike came to work with Robin on the songs of *5000 Spirits* and *Hangman*. Clive Palmer had stayed there. As did Hamish Imlach, Billy Connolly, Wizz Jones, Bert Jansch, Chris Bonington, Tom Patey and Dougal Haston, and two young Tibetan refugee monks who would soon found the Samye Ling Monastery. Spud was the intersection, the place-giver, without which revolutionary lives and times cannot flower.

Rose and her companion, plus Spud and 'Glasgow Jim', set off for Glencoe, but the weather turns bad, Jim freaks out, and they abseil off. Back at Temple Cottage, Rose's friend goes home but she stays. She turns on. She loves the company she is keeping.

Then Iain Skinner comes to take photos for the new album. It's a cold, bright winter day, just before or after Hogmanay. Because it's lovely and the times are what they are, it becomes a mass outing. Spud's kids, plus current residents Roger and Nicky, come for the laugh. Likky drifts along. And Rose is around, so she goes too.

They raid the dressing-up box. Forty years later, Spud identifies Roger Marshall's necklace as one of her belts. The oldest boy, Allan, pulls on a waistcoat made from suede cleaning cloths. Likky sticks a little green-and-purple triangular felt hat she has made on nervous Edie's head. Robin picks up a red item from the sideboard,* then with painted masks, assorted hats, cloaks and striped coats, they all go down to the wintry woods.

We assumed Rose was already Mike's partner and part of the band like Likky. But she was a near-stranger to the people round her – thus perhaps her half-hiding quality.

Iain Skinner gets his shots, and may have had in mind the cover of Dylan's *John Wesley Harding*, released a few weeks before. That is another group in a wood, but the Dylan one is sepia, old-timey, inhabited by weathered outsider males, whereas the String Band are colourful, young, fertile with children and two women.

Children and friends wander off home. Mike and Robin and Iain Skinner follow a drystane dyke up the field behind, and that's

---

* I recently mentioned to Mary that I'd long wondered what it was. She smiled, reached into a drawer and put in my hand a home-made, red-painted, jointed wooden snake. 'We called it the Red Dragon.' The gap between Then and Now closed, leaving me faintly faint.

where the original front cover photo is taken. Perched on the snow-rimmed wall against a winter sky of deep dazzling blue, shot from below, Mike and Robin are two heraldic figures in cloak and cape, travellers on a mythic quest, briefly poised mid-flight.

On a recent visit to Temple Cottage, Spud and her son Robbie – formerly the infant on the cover wearing a blue dressing gown and vast, floppy straw hat – directed me to that coppice. I located the trees, the crumbling wall. Impossible to say exactly where that group photo was taken – in forty-seven years trees grow, fall down, are replanted. But that corner of the woods was still haunted for me by a motley gathering: the children shouting, the excited dog, the laughter and glances between the young adults.

I looked up and saw, across the next field, a drystane dyke rising against the skyline, and knew it was *that wall*. Their brief day was so bright.

A few days later, Rose went back to York University. That could have been an end to it. But, sometime before Easter, Robin Williamson in full Wizard of the North regalia floated into the student refectory and took her off to London. She remembers wearing a paisley-patterned dressing gown on the train, the only remotely hip thing she had. And something happened in London, probably at Joe Boyd's flat, where Rose relates she realised she was 'in the wrong sleeping bag', and went to find Mike.

Robin was a bit put out, but, as Mike points out, he was supposed to be with Likky, so he didn't really have a leg to stand on. Soon Mike and Rose moved to nearby Roman Camp, and all was cool.

Ah yes, the sixties. No screaming rows, no severed ears, no clothes thrown onto the street or punch-ups among the band. Bloomsbury revisited, without the posh folk.

What did George and I take from *Hangman*? Not, in the end, many songs. Most of them were technically beyond us. We had no sitar, could not do Robin's vocal range, nor pull off the delivery that made Mike's 'Mercy I Cry City' and 'Swift as the Wind' so arresting.

Robin's pastiche 'Minotaur's Song' – the equivalent of 'With a Little Help from My Friends' on *Pepper* – we sometimes did with friends at the Folk Club and parties. Above all we finished on Mike's astonishing 'A Very Cellular Song', and that became our finale to many communal nights of raised and raucous happy voices.

What *Hangman* did was validate our provincial rurality. Alone and together, George and I began following the Dreel Burn upstream, by the ruined mill, the old lade, the farm lanes. Carrying guitars, mandolin and whistles, we found the lost, magical places, the last patches of wildness amid the fertile, practical farmland of east Fife. We chose ragged hawthorn hedges, little dells and lonely copses where we could hunker down out of the wind.

We bore witness to sunsets, winter storms, autumn moonrise over stubble fields. We began to haunt Crawhill Woods, found foxes' dens, thrilled to the creaking woods, the pigeons and pheasants calling at roosting, gulls rising like shredded paper from the tattie dreels, desiccated weasels and stoats strung on barbed wire.

Perched high in swaying trees with mandolin and whistle, we imagined into existence gods and spirits, nymphs and dryads, sensed the back country as a living thing that whispered, groaned, squeaked and moaned the song of itself. With eyes closed, it sounded very like the sea.

Inspired by *Hangman*, the back country became our playground, rehearsal space and theatre. We found Kittlenaked Wood, and lit small fires at its fringe to cook sausages, drink cider, sit cross-legged and try out our first songs. We perched high in the trees, silent as we watched the setting sun, red and wobbly as a water-filled balloon, settle down on the stubble fields. Dogs barked from distant farms, tractors coughed and died and left the world to us and the rising moon.

In fifth year at Waid,* all roads led to Highers, and beyond them the fearsome question: *So what are you going to be?* In addition to English, French and Latin, I was sitting chemistry and physics and maths. After the exams, I'd have to drop some and go on with others, and that would determine my life.

But I found them all interesting. Algebra was ingenious and good at establishing the number of cows in a field. Trigonometry was useful for calculating the heights of ships and spires. Then, with

---

* Like cream or like scum, we were rising towards the top. The hard cases had already left, to work in their fathers' trades or at the fishing, occasionally glimpsed on motorbikes or even cars, with the faster girls we fancied.

advanced calculus, I hit my ceiling. Abruptly, I had no idea what it was on about. End of maths.

Physics was interesting because of the patterns that underlay the movements of planets and tides, cannonballs and feathers dropped from towers, collapsing bridges and the Van De Graaff generator. Unfortunately it would take a lot of high-level maths and calculus to graze on *quantum fields*. So, further physics was out.

In fifth-year chemistry we had gone round the futuristic ICI plant near Grangemouth, and the oil refinery. The Periodic Table was elegant and complete as any sonnet. To know what things are made of, how they are made, what holds them together!

Our chemistry teacher gave handouts of his lessons then went methodically through them. This left a lot of time for daydreaming. It was said he had been a research chemist before he had a nervous breakdown. He became animated one afternoon, talking about Linus Pauling, the Nobel Prize and the hybridisation of atomic orbitals. This was inspiring and hard to fathom as Rimbaud's poetry.

I sat in his class, wondering what a nervous breakdown would feel like, thinking about Linus Pauling and ICI. Several things abruptly became clear: I was not a genius chemist. I would not win a Nobel Prize. The reality would be working for ICI, developing some new substitute for something else, making them money.

Why do chemistry unless you are a genius? End of chemistry.

Meanwhile, despite the government banning pirate radio, and the Home Service and Light Programme of our childhood becoming Radios 1, 2, 3 and 4, brain-changing music was pouring from our transistors. Records and their covers were becoming ever weirder and more ambitious, with all the hybridisation and resonance a mind could hunger for. And, unlike organic chemistry, you could hum it, dance to it, play a crude approximation on the guitar.

You didn't have to be a genius to enjoy making music. You didn't have to be a great poet to get a kick from making a poem or a song. You just had to be yourself, whatever that might be.

I approached Highers in the manner of a date with someone when you both know this is no longer where it's at.

I had lately had just such a session at Anstruther's Regal Cinema. Afterwards we waited for her bus, neither of us knowing what to say. The bus came. A muffled embrace of coats, *Cheerio*, then her bus shuddered off into the night. That was it over, whatever it had been.

I walked the family beagle to the end of the pier and stood watching the swell curve and break into the harbour mouth, rush out again. The regret. The relief. I remembered the lurch of inadvertent truth when we had sung together at the folk club: *It ain't me, babe*.

Soon we sat in uniformed rows, turned over our exam papers and did our best to answer the question. We wrote with one hand while the other was flexing chord changes; and, while setting down the causes of the First World War, I was humming 'Swift as the Wind'.

Something had to give.

Over kippers one July morning in 1968 I announced to my parents I was going to drop all my science subjects, and instead do another year of English and French, and learn typing so I could type up my future poems, lyrics, articles and plays. (I had the sense to keep my music ambitions to myself.)

My mum looked to my dad. He lowered the *Scotsman*.

'Are you sure, laddie?'

'Yes.'

'Will they let you?'

'I hope so.'

He sat back and began to rub tobacco whorls between his palms. I knew my mother had once wanted to be a writer or a journalist. Instead the Second World War came, then she'd had us. My father lit up, glanced at her.

'Better go up there this morning and sort it out,' he said; then went back to the newspaper to frowningly read about inflation and a distant war.

He had made his life what he wanted it to be, and he trusted his children to do the same. Across forty-four years and from this side of the grave, I salute him.

Then, abruptly, Richard Cebula was gone, moved to Buckie with his family. We would no longer meet in Karol's garret, amid the bare floorboards, posters and the background whiff of incense and the ghost of parties innocently snogging to 'Anyone Who Had a Heart' on repeat.

I sat with George in the spare bedroom up the stair in 'Francisville', Pittenweem. He had cleared out the bed, leaving only a couple of chairs, a small couch, table, tape-recorder on the floor. His mum brought up the first of many laden trays: teapot, cups, biscuits, pancakes, jam. I thanked her as I'd been taught to. She smiled then left, closed the door behind.

'Is he coming back?'

'Nobody comes back from Buckie.'

We contemplated Richard's absence. Phillip Gay was off the map – a divergence of musical tastes, an argument over a girl.

George picked up his guitar. I lifted mine and we looked at each other.

'I've cracked "The Minotaur Song",' he said.

Track 4: The Birth of Fate & ferret

Buoyed up with our inchoate musical mission, in mid-August 1968, as the Beatles released 'Hey Jude', with 'Revolution' on the flip side, we returned to Waid Academy for our final year, to a half-empty timetable and a warm wind at our backs.

At the time you feel yourself and your friends unique. From a distance it is evident you were an *instance*, one grain in an ear of barley swaying in a generational field, moved by the same wind.

I'm looking at the black-and-white photograph of sixth year, Waid Academy, 1968. We are a skinny, lumpy, half-formed bunch, but for that year we will be each others' mentors, peers, audience; each large as life and fully grown. No one else is entirely real, or matters as much.

We know without saying it – unlike some of our predecessors, we are not very political – that the schools, the water, electricity, gas, Post Office, buses and trains are ours. The coal mines of west Fife are ours, like the steel and the National Health Service and half the houses. From school milk to our grandparents' old age pensions, the state looks after us. We will be paid to go to university, and then offered jobs for life. All this is natural and unremarkable as the salty air we breathe.*

There are twenty-four of us, and half are girls. That alone marks a huge shift.

We are all white. We are all Scottish-born, with maybe one exception. All but four are Fifers born and bred. Anyone from outside Fife is regarded as a bit, well, foreign.

The Waid is a small local comprehensive. Everyone goes to it. In the photo I identify Cherry the fisherman's daughter, and her best pal, also from the fishing. Here is the joiner's son, the gamekeeper's lassie, the farm boys. The skipper's plump and busty daughter. The baker's, the bus driver, the electrician. The other joiner's lass, the minister's son, the shopkeeper's diffident boy.

In those days grown-ups had jobs that needed no further explanation.

All of us in that photo are bound for university or colleges of further education. Most are going to be the first person in their family to go – another social revolution. It will cost our parents nothing, or next to nothing. We will pay no fees. We will get support grants which, if we are canny – and we will be canny, being Fifers – will just get us through each term without debts or having to work evenings or weekends.

---

* We might have been less sanguine had we known Scotland's nuclear bunker, the country's post-Apocalyptic command centre, was hidden below a farmhouse a few miles up the road. Though it had two cinemas, it is unlikely *The Layers of the Onion* would have featured in its substantial record collection.

ANDREW GREIG

In any case debt is impossible – there is no question of students having an overdraft. Credit cards don't yet exist. We have what we have. Such austerity! Such wealth!

It is worth repeating: *we will be paid to go to university*. This has been going on since the Second World War, in ever-increasing numbers, though the lads and lassies standing awkwardly in the photo still make up about only 7 per cent of school leavers. Going to university or college seems an extraordinary privilege. It is.

In the cottages, council houses, farms and solid merchants' homes of east Fife, on the sideboard or mantelpiece, alongside the great-uncle who died in the Great War, the yellowing wedding group, babies sprawled in christening gowns, in pride of place is the son or daughter in graduation gown, clutching the scroll that gets them out.

It goes with the Space Race images on our televisions. The parents and grandparents are putting their children into orbit, to where they themselves have never been and will never go. Their labour and their taxes built the launch vehicles, and we fortunate few sit – apprehensive and glowing, in our black school uniforms with red piping and the badge of the ship passing through between pier heads, underscored by the motto *Multi Pertransibunt Et Augebitur Scientia* * – at the tip of the rocket, heading for the unknown.

---

* 'Many will pass through and knowledge will be increased'. Waid was the first school in Scotland to be created under the 1882 Education Act, and pretty much did what it said on the blazer. There was no secondary modern, nor grammar school. The Waid was simply 'the school'.

Now teachers called us by our first names. There were so few of us in sixth year, most were made prefects simply because they were there. I was not a prefect, due to an incident involving lager cans being found under my youth hostel bunk on a school trip. I was happy not to be prefect material, having no desire to be an example.

The Rector *(the Headie)* was new, fairly young, progressive. Mr Fraser was unlike the daunting, black-gowned, chalk-ridden, strap-wielding Headies who came before him. He made our biggest troublemaker, the one who had quick fists, smoked and drank and was said to have *gone all the way*, into Head Boy.

Scobie, our school legend. He would have a quick cigarette on the rugby touchline, then charge, knees pumping, elbows flying, small fry clinging to him as he cleaved like Achilles through the Trojan ranks. Smart move, making the Headie's problem into an asset. As Alpha Male, Scobie ruled.

He was not a classic bully, for he wasn't interested in tormenting weaker boys. I showed him due respect, and he was surprisingly decent to me, even when I captained him at cricket. He was looking to pick a fight, but not with the likes of us.

That final year was the high-water mark of Scobie's life – Head Boy and rebel, sporting talisman when he could be bothered, fancied by girls, admired and feared by boys. In the photo he stands taller than any, proud, glowering and wary, directly behind the Headmaster.

I saw him again in the late eighties, glimpsed stooping at a bus stop on the St Andrews road in the rain, now bald, a plastic carrier bag in his fist. He coughed into a cigarette, and seemed an old man. I nearly stopped, but did not.

Next time I asked, I was told *Oh, he died.*

I look at Scobie again in the prefects' photo, and I see him stern, frowning slightly, at once belligerent and wary, ready to take on the world in a fight he could not possibly win.

In the Scottish tradition, students went to university from their fifth year, often at sixteen. That had begun to change. A sixth year was added on, along with a post-Higher grade to give us something to do. Most of the hard exam lifting had already been done, and many of us had provisional acceptances into university. All we had to do was grow up a bit. Sixth year was not so much a pressure cooker as a pan of simmering soft fruit.

For that one year, school became what it always should be – an open resource, a place I wanted to go, not because I had to, but because much of what I wanted was there.

Absurdist plays in sixth-year French (Genet, Artaud, Beckett, my favourite, Ionesco) led to me reading N. F. Simpson, Pinter, Ann Jellicoe. A school trip to Edinburgh gave us *The Resistible Rise of Arturo Ui* with Leonard Rossiter. Still reeling from that, George and I caught the bus over the hill to St Andrews to be confronted by *The Sport of My Mad Mother* and *Who's Afraid of Virginia Woolf?*

Suddenly plays were where it was at. We went to the new Edinburgh Fringe hit *Rosencrantz and Guildenstern Are Dead* – loved it so much we bought the script. George and I learned and performed the opening act to the senior classes.

I wrote and directed a short sub-Pinter play, my pal Jim in the central role as a put-upon, potentially murderous son in an oppressive family. On stage, Jim's shyness and diffidence dropped away. He thrived on being someone else. I knew acting wasn't my talent. I was only any good at being myself, whatever that might turn out to be.

Like that childhood game of Finding, we were all directed by inner promptings murmuring *Cold, warm, warmer Hot! Colder, cold. Warmer, warm, Got it!* Some of those voices might be deluded, but they were all we had to go on.

Like hundreds, thousands of others, George and I were, very tentatively, starting to write songs. Anyone who was anyone – Beatles, Dylan, Buddy Holly and Chuck Berry, Cohen, Stones, Who, Kinks, Donovan, Paul Simon, Joni Mitchell – wrote their own songs. It couldn't be that hard.

I began with other people's poems, starting with an English translation of Mallarmé's 'Le Lac', and sang it over finger-picked chords. Then I tried that with the scraps of poems and monologues I was writing – the usual things: sunsets, ungainable girls, rain-drenched woods, the solitary coast, mist at night out along the pier, the god Pan.

Perhaps songwriting was not my talent, but it was fun.

George was naturally mimetic. He listened to songs, instinctively understood what made them work, then started to make his own. Proper songs, with verses that rhymed, a middle section, a chorus or refrain. It was amazing to me that he could do this, and delightful that I could pick up the guitar or harmonica, and see what I could do that went with it.

I still hear his nasal voice, the light thumb-strum of his red guitar, the faint whirr of the tape recorder on the bedroom floor in Pittenweem. The day was fading in the skylight window and out over the back country the song evoked: that lone bare thorn bush, last light on the Dreel burn, the distant sea and the stir in the back-country willows as my friend's song re-enchanted our corner of the world.

> *It's getting late, night time's round here again*
> *The sky is still, quiet blue over darkening hills*
> *And black trees where four men were hanged*
> *Have found no sleep . . .*
> ('Balance & Turnover')

More than any other musicians, the Incredible String Band released us to have a go. Their songs seemed to have no rules, no pattern or traditions you had to master before starting. You didn't have to sing close harmonies like the Everlys, or three-part like the Beatles. You didn't need a drummer, bass player and amps.

The String Band made a virtue of looseness. Robin and Mike didn't so much sing harmony as voice two different renditions of the same song. We could do that!

We entirely overlooked the years of playing solo and with others, in different traditions and taking on multiple influences, which made it possible for Mike and Robin to play as they did.

We lacked technique, experience and ability, which is normal at seventeen. We were vaguely aware of this, but reckoned we'd pick it up along the way. For now, we'd make our bid through imagination and enthusiasm, and our provincial ignorance granted us freedom of a kind. It left us – forced us – to make it up ourselves.

I have a notion that originality arises from failed imitation, limitation and misunderstanding, as much as from eventual mastery. For instance: Joni Mitchell's childhood polio driving her fingers towards open tunings; left-handed Hendrix using a right-handed guitar; a provincial harmony group stuck in Liverpool; a Jewish hardware shopkeeper's son in wintry Minnesota with his ear riveted to the failing radio. It can help to be far from the supposed centre, and have to approximate and make things up.

George and I inherited the school Folk Club. The 'Wild Rover' and the 'Irish Rover' would rove no more on our watch. We agreed on a set of ISB songs plus one by David Campbell, a Guyanian singer we'd heard at the St Andrews Folk Club, and my rendition of 'Love Minus Zero/No Limit'.

After a rehearsal in Pittenweem, George walked with me over the hill to Anster (in reality a slight rise, but locality's lens magnifies everything). We had a couple of cans of lager under our coats, my guitar. We crouched by a hedge above the golf course and thoughtfully drank the beers as dusk came in with a whiff of rotting seaweed.

We needed a name for our Folk Club gig. All bands had a name, many including the word *Band*. We agreed we wouldn't do that. We played with words like *fantastical*. Too close to *Incredible*. We sipped and burped lager. *Fatalistic? The Eyes of Fate!* we choroused.

Nah. Too pretentious, even for us. Fate sounded good, but needed to be undermined or at least balanced. *Fate and fiddlesticks?* That got us thinking along the lines of English pub names. The Pig and Whistle, the Cat and Fiddle . . .

'*Fate and ferret!*'

'With an ampersand, like e e cummings poems!'

'*Fate & ferret.*'

We looked at each other. It was deep, it was silly; it had an ampersand.

We were no longer two starry-eyed provincial youths of limited musical pedigree. We were a band.*

I slipped into the Royal Hotel and asked for a quarter bottle of Smirnoff vodka. The barman looked at me, I shiftily looked back. He must have known, yet he reached up for a bottle and I handed over the money George and I had pooled, then hurried home, glass cool against my palm in the raincoat pocket.

'Got it?'

'Yes!'

In my bedroom, George produced his stage gear, which included an embroidered waistcoat and a tan beret with a pheasant-feather plume. I put on the sealskin slippers my elder brother had brought back from Greenland, then the blue smock with a huge strawberry heart shape on the back that my mother had quickly run up the night before. I tried on my dad's deerstalker but George firmly shook his head. I went down to the kitchen and came back with a selection of tea cosies.

---

* George remembers this scene as being by the old thorn bush above the Dreel burn. We drank cider, not lager. He remembers walking home, imagining how he might letter *F & f* on posters. Wouldn't have mythed it for the world.

The big quilted satiny one fitted just fine. We checked each other out. George looked the part of the vagabond minstrel. He was a visual person, intended for art college, and he understood appearance. I recognised that, though physically slight, shy and uncertain, George had an inner toughness. Maybe it was Pittenweem saltiness hardening the system over the generations.

I felt excited, but not ready. The rehearsals had been so much fun that I'd never really considered doing the songs in front of people, dressed in daft clothes. They might not get it. Someone might laugh.

'Lets start the vodka,' I said. No time to get glasses, so we had it swig-about, straight from the bottle. It was truly vile.

Then we stuffed harmonica, rack, kazoo, mandolin in our duffel bags, picked up the guitars and headed up the road. Somewhere near the school gates, the alcohol hit and we started laughing – at ourselves, at the night, at the wondrous daftness of our lives. Our friend John Myles emerged, wearing a satin snooker waistcoat and a tweedy bunnet, guitar slung down his back. We were not alone.

'Got the voddy?'

'Aye.'

We passed it round. It still was foul, but the effect was liberating.

That first time we dressed to go to the Waid Folk Club, not as 'George and Andrew' but *Fate & ferret*, I did wonder if we'd gone too far. It was hard enough singing in public without being dressed like a chump.

I could not have done it by myself. Maybe George would not have either. Maybe we were a classic *folie à deux*. Come to that, maybe so were Robin and Mike. Perhaps all creative partnerships, from the calamitous to the sublime, are mutually reinforcing follies.

I looked at my pal George, and he looked the part. That made it possible to greet our friends when we came into the Music Room, and later pick up the guitar and walk onto the stage (devoid of hay bales: *uncool*, we'd decided) and launch frenetically into 'You Know What You Could Be'.

The plectrum flew from my sweat-slicked fingers so I kept thrashing with the back of my hand. People laughed at the flying plectrum, and I laughed too because the song was a gas, and the kazoo prompted the laughter it invited, and that was right too.

Accelerated by nerves, we played way too fast. Our vocals made the String Band sound barbershop-tight as our first-ever set went by in the vivid blur of all our future ones.

But for us it was a wonderful evening. Some of our pals got it, and the String Band songs would bind us for the rest of that year and the remainder of our lives. We walked out of school feeling anything was possible.

Track 5: Shrine

In a corner of my bedroom, an area evolved that wasn't for sleeping, practising putting, or school work. My granny's tartan travelling rug defined the space. A chunky salt-bleached branch carried up from the beach became an altarpiece-cum-candle-holder. The Laughing Buddha my father had brought back from Penang in the twenties now bore incense sticks in his red jug, and developed a scorch mark across his pale porcelain face. A few fancy cushions purloined from the sitting room made for exotic lounging.

A small stack of devotional books grew – Mallarmé and Baudelaire, *Four Greek Poets*, Alastair Mackie's *Clytach* and *Les Yeux d'Elsa* by Louis Aragon. Also a book on yoga, Robert Graves' *The White Goddess* and *Greek Myths*, *The Importance of Living* by Lin Yutang (what male hand had dedicated it to my mother on Christmas 1941? I never dared ask, and now cannot) and Allan Watts' *This Is It*, all intuitively recognised as part of the world of the Incredible String Band.

I sat up late in my little corner shrine, straining to read by candle-light. On mild nights I'd open the window to hear and smell the sea slurping outside. The spectral cry of gulls entered Baudelaire's 'L'Invitation au voyage'; the intermittent flash from the Isle of May lighthouse lit the curtains while I read of Apollo's return to Delos riding on the back of dolphins. My cramped, dark, old-fashioned village became magical and charged.

By daylight, the corner was dead. The school jotters, timetables and golf clubs took over the bedroom. But at night, when the house had gone quiet, I lit the candles and a sandalwood joss stick, settled cross-legged on the travelling rug, and, as Radio Caroline murmured, opened a book.

Sometimes words would condense out of the watches of the night. Sometimes I'd reach for the guitar and stroke it quietly, murmuring words to see where they'd go: part-song, part-poem.

Sometimes I padded down the stairs, to slip out the back gate across the sand to the water's glimmering fringe, or go out along the pier. I watched the dark swirl of sea, cold moonlight hosing down the pantile roofs of Cellardyke, picking apart the ribs of the trawler taking shape on its cradle. I felt the rising tide, sensed my own life becoming buoyant.

Elevated by solitude and yearning for connection, I stood on the pier-end of my teens till the shivers sent me homewards. In the morning, scribbles on paper, sand on the travelling rug.

It happens mostly when we are young and malleable, when someone, perhaps inadvertently, gives us a glimpse of where we might go and what we might be.

In an empty classroom at day's end my English teacher Alastair Mackie handed back the poems I'd shown him. He recommended I read more. He said reading other people's poetry was not cheating – it was essential.

'Bones, Andrew,' he insisted. 'You have to get to the bones of a poem. Write less!'

He suggested I try George Mackay Brown. I didn't read Scottish poets, apart from Norman MacCaig and Iain Crichton Smith and Mr Mackie. I liked American Beats and early T. S. Eliot, and European poets in translation. I instinctively avoided anything I was meant to read.

Mr Mackie hesitated, picking out grains of chalk from the grooves of his greenish corduroy jacket. 'George lives in Orkney,' he said. 'I used to teach there.' He stared at me through his black horn-rims. 'George doesn't teach or have a job. Of course he is poor as a church mouse. He just writes . . .'

His voice trailed off, as if distracted by some miraculous prospect. He was a scrawny, abrupt man, given to twitchy head movements as though trying to dislodge something inside. He picked up his leather homework briefcase and strode to the door.

'Keep writing,' he announced. 'Find the bones!'

It was rare for a grown-up, let alone a teacher, to give you a glimpse of what they were about. The longing in his voice when he said *George doesn't teach, or have a job*. As I walked home, my inner voice murmured *Warmer, warmer.*

How much instruction we have taken from so many! I used to emphasise our difference and distance from each other, but now

I see our communality. Even the words we think with have come from others. We are so filled by each other the individual self scarcely exists, except as a leaking bucket.

We came to call her *the Boss*. Her kingdom was Commercial, tucked away off the main corridors. It was the girls' equivalent of the boys' technical drawing and navigation.

George and I knocked and went in. We were stared at by girls sitting at typewriters, operating copying machines, bent over books with columns and numbers instead of words. This was still a time when we went into school through separate entrances. These lassies were too young to be intimidating, but we felt ourselves in a strange land.

'We would like to learn typing,' George announced.

'Not shorthand or bookkeeping,' I added. 'We just need to learn to touch type.'

The teacher was a slightly taller and younger version of my mum – comfortably built, neat perm, amusement sparking in her eyes and mouth.

'Why would I be doing that?'

We told her we were writing songs and poems and plays, and it would be good to learn to type them ourselves. We needed access to typewriters, paper and correcting fluid. We were interested in the duplicating machines, for making programmes for folk clubs and distributing poems, plays, songs and stuff.

She told the giggling girls to get on with their work. Were we serious about this? We would have to apply ourselves. If we were happy to work alone and did not disrupt the classes, we could come anytime.

It was a small, peripheral kingdom, but the Boss ruled over it with wit, wisdom and firm kindness. We learned to nearly touch type, stencil and operate the inky bander machine. Because she was not our parent, we found we could talk with her at length – at great length, I'm afraid – and we would listen to her. Because she was not formally our teacher, we could learn from her.

Commercial became Fate & ferret headquarters, and our pals started to drop by in their free periods. It developed into a would-be literary factory, a setting for therapy and guidance, and a dating agency of sorts, as the Boss tried to help us grow up.

When it became evident that this was too big a job to accomplish at school, she asked us to come for our tea at her wee house in Lundin Links, with a few of her favoured pupils, and much would come of that.

Track 6: A Half-Remarkable Concert

The first concert I ever went to was Jimmy Shand and his Band, in Stirling, probably 1960. The kilted, elderly Mr Shand stood stage centre, stern and unblinking as he worked his massive button accordion like a chest expander. The music was a disciplined gale, and its energy contrasted with Shand's grim poise, just one polished shoe tapping.

He did not seek approval. He did not smile. He made my father seem flighty.

Jimmy Shand just named the tunes, then played them: head-spinning reels, the more lyrical strathspeys, the offbeat bouncy polkas. His fingers flickered over the buttons while he remained as immobile as an institution. This was a man who had a locomotive named after him.

Jimmy Shand junior sat in the tartan ranks behind his father, and every so often would rise, play a chorus, then sit again. This was music-making, Scottish style, a serious business. Jimmy senior's bald pate and black horn-rimmed glasses gleamed in the spotlight when he nodded briefly in acknowledgement of the applause at the opening bars of 'The Bluebell Polka'.*

Jimmy Shand senior had been a miner as a boy until, after playing benefit concerts on his moothie and fiddle for striking workmates, he was banned from the collieries. He had an improbable passion for motorbikes. He was very dry. At one B & B he requested honey for his toast, and was brought a tiny jar. He said, 'I see you keep a bee.'

He was incredibly hardworking, constantly touring Britain on one-nighters through the post-war years. He recorded more tracks than the Beatles and Elvis combined. He played Carnegie Hall in Dunfermline and Carnegie Hall in New York, and I doubt if he smiled at either.

I loved it, especially the jerky polkas.

My second concert hall experience was the Incredible String Band at the ABC on Lothian Road in Edinburgh, 30 August 1968, and that was a very different occasion.

We caught the bus to Leven with our dressing-up gear in duffel bags. The connecting Edinburgh bus left five minutes before our bus got in, so we stood in the drizzle defiantly singing snatches of 'How Happy I Am' in that depressed town.

---

* His biggest success and signature tune. It was produced by George Martin, who had already overseen our *Children's Choice* favourites 'Nellie the Elephant', 'Goodness Gracious Me', Spike Milligan, *The Archers'* theme tune and 'Right Said Fred', before taking on a provincial harmony rhythm group. Despite his accent, Martin was as working-class in origin as Shand.

Scarcity creates value, as though Puritans secretly wrote the script for hedonism. We had seen the Corries in Elie folk club, Archie Fisher and Jeannie Robertson at the Waid. We had goggled at the Beatles on *Juke Box Jury*, the Stones and Donovan on *Ready, Steady, Go*, but this was a trip to Edinburgh to witness our gods made manifest.

The Edinburgh bus came and we got on it. Some project was growing in our hearts and minds, and seeing – perhaps even meeting! – Mike and Robin was part of it.

It wasn't that we were lazy and couldn't be bothered serving our apprenticeship. Rather, we were in a hurry. This was our last year at school, soon we'd be passed on into the world, where we'd be expected to go to university then get jobs – *aargh!*

There wasn't time to become great guitar pickers or master the sitar, flute, mandolin or harpsichord. With more work, we could learn to play covers for wedding dance music, or thrash out traditional folk at Scout huts, but three ISB albums had made that seem not the point of existence at all.

We wanted to get to *where it was at*, and the local bus couldn't get us there soon enough. Like all provincial youth, we were painfully aware that by the time we'd got the records, learned the songs and grasped what was happening, we'd be behind again. Perhaps we would always be behind. Or maybe we could *make it up*, and be what was happening.

Or maybe we were two damp schoolboys on a perversely time-tabled bus, chuntering through the dreich afternoon towards a chimera.

We caught a town bus to Leith, then walked to Christine's flat at the edge of Leith Links. I'd heard George's sister sing at the folk clubs. She was thin, jumpy, curly-haired, smiling. She gave us our tea and our tickets. The concert was billed as a festival night, and didn't start till 11.15. We went upstairs and changed into *Fate & ferret*, covered our finery with coats and set off into the night.

As we passed the Lyceum and Usher Hall, among the well-dressed and, to our eyes, elderly folks coming out of Edinburgh Festival events, we began noticing *weird people*, flashes of colour among the black and grey. Berets, floppy hats, bright scarves and striped waist-coats, peacock feathers jammed under a broad belt. Girls had bright gypsy skirts, long loose hair, many gold and silvery clacking bangles. And they were all going our way.

The strangeness and the colour concentrated round the entrance of the ABC. Vivid eyes, black-outlined but not at all like Dusty Springfield or the girls on lager cans. Exotic smells, not my Old Spice. A preponderance of stripes, fringes and swirls. Inside the hall was a buzz and blur of ruby satin, velvet and fur.

There were some *Pepper* military uniforms, but mostly it was do-it-yourself, raided from grannie's wardrobes, theatrical costumes and charity shops. Old necklaces worn as belts, and belts worn as necklaces. The air was furry with sandalwood, jasmine, tobacco and something earthy-sweet. Someone wore a tricorned jester's hat. A girl had bells tied to her waist that tinkled as she walked barefoot. A very tall man had a black top hat and a full-length green cape.

'God, I hope he's not sitting in front of us!' George said.

Joyfully we peeled off our coats and revealed our finery, my electric-blue tabard with the big strawberry heart, George flashing his tan French beret, green velvet breeks and striped satin river-boat-gambler waistcoat. We were not alone. We were legion. We had not known there were so many joyous, colourful, strange people in Scotland. It was a convention of weirdness.*

At that time, a yellow-fringed silk scarf with green satin trousers could get you beaten up anywhere from Stornoway to Hawick (probably still can). Young men of all classes still wore a suit and tie when going out – look at the photos of football crowds, or dance hall nights in the sixties – and the gypsy mediaeval-magician look was as offensive to many of one's peers as to our parents' generation.

It was nothing as organised as Fashion, and owed more to the dressing-up box than the boutique. A step on from scruffy down-beat beatnik, this was dress as Play, incorporating elements of the *commedia dell'arte*, the raggle-taggle gypsies meeting the *Lord of the Rings* in a harem. I had seen Summer of Love photos in newspapers and *Melody Maker*, but that had been London or San Francisco. Seeing it in dour, smoke-blackened, fiscally-minded Presbyterian Edinburgh was a revelation.

Still happily boggling at our fellow audience, clutching a large bottle of cider under my tabard, we went in. George and I agree we were in the stalls, left of centre, near the front. Because the ABC was essentially a cinema, the stage was untheatrical. But there were two chairs, an Eastern carpet, cushions, some microphones and

---

* Experienced again in 1977 at the Edinburgh Playhouse, the first punk concert in Scotland. Very different times and outfits (mostly black) and different drugs (alcohol, amphetamines, glue), rows of tense police outside and in – but the adrenalinised mood had the same sense of joyous recognition, of coming out, of being many.

an intricate ragbag clutter of instruments – guitars, mandolin, various flutes and whistles, bongos, harmonicas, an electric keyboard, assorted stringed things, bells, a thrilling sitar. The lights went down for a moment, then up again.

And here without announcement was the Mage, the Wizard of Changes: Robin Williamson floated onto the stage, followed by his partner/accomplice/foil, Mike Heron. They nodded in our direction, looking happy and slightly stunned at the numbers and the roar of approval.

It was a triumphant homecoming, their first Edinburgh concert since *The Hangman's Beautiful Daughter* had put them at the cutting edge of what was happening. Their music had demanded a new genre title: *psychedelic folk*, and across the country, thousands were rolling joints on their album covers. Our lads had filled the Fillmore in San Francisco, the Carnegie Hall in New York, the Albert Hall in London.

As they settled down, Mike Heron had a sizzling grin the size of a new moon, and that seemed to be his default expression throughout. Robin was more distant, as though viewing the whole occasion benignly from somewhere beyond the asteroid belt. He seemed to be, if not the leader, the spokesperson.

We looked, absorbing every detail. Robin had long, curling, blond hair. He looked beautiful, with a long jaw, strong nose, cheekbones like arrowheads. The surly beatnik of the first album had bloomed. You might have said he looked like a girl, but his features were as much those of a young knight or a magician.

Mike just sat with huge white melon of a smile, looking out over the audience. He was as short, black-haired and solidly handsome as Robin was fair, elongated and nebulous. They were Sancho Panza and Don Quixote, Watson and Holmes, Pan and Apollo, Earth and Air.

Finally, in a strangely derived Edinburgh accent, with a breathy, light intonation, Robin looked up from his guitar, leaned towards the microphone: *Hi, I'm Robin Williamson and this is Mike Heron.*

A roar of approval, laughter and applause, though this was scarcely news. Mike's lighthouse-bright grin stretched even wider. Retrospectively, one might say it was a stoned beam and very possibly he was, but it was active, sizzling, outward-going. Robin adjusted his tuning yet again, glanced at Mike, then launched off.

A gasp, spatter of applause for 'Koeeoaddi There', the opening song on *The Hangman's Beautiful Daughter*. Then the Usher Hall was attendant to the ecstatic unspooling of young Williamson's Edinburgh childhood: winter skating, ministers and soldiers, cherry-tree blossom, head-high snow, the baker's stubbly chin eliding into standing on sands by an ocean that stretched out for ever, then the riddle of a basket bound with skin. It was all our childhoods flashing by – then abruptly left behind, driving across the moors on a misty morning with one's lover towards adulthood, still bearing that riddle of being a human, perishable life.

Mike added Jew's-harp, sitar, vocals. Without its studio over-dubs, it was the same song we knew in every detail, yet came out differently and fresh. I suddenly got it: this is an Edinburgh 'Penny Lane'. And forty years on I add: combined with the LSD interiority of 'Strawberry Fields'.

A roar of applause at its end. George was on his feet, clapping; he turned to me with shining eyes, 'Fantastic! Truly incredible!'

I shook my head, thrilled beyond speech. The concert had only begun and already it was more than we could ever have hoped.

As the clapping subsided, a dog wandered onto the stage, and behind it drifted two barefoot girls in gypsy dresses – Likky and Rose.

Another roar of applause, shouts of greeting. They smiled, waved, sat cross-legged on the carpet. The dog sat down beside Likky, looked at the audience, decided we were harmless, put head on paws and seemed to go to sleep.

We were near the front, close enough to see Rose and Likky were bonnie but not in the way of models. When they smiled, they had uneven teeth with gaps. Their hair was long, had not seen rollers or had a perm in many a moon. Their eyes were ringed with kohl, but they wore no lipstick. They were exotic yet real, even homely.

Surrounded by cushions, incense, instruments, the four of them were an illustration in my mother's *The Rubáiyát of Omar Khayyám*.

There was a lot of tuning-up. This was not a tight act, knocking out the hits, backed up by roadies and instrument technicians. Nor was it like folk clubs, with their solemn historical introductions and terrible jokes.

ISB concerts were as singular as their music. They did not have an act. Perhaps that was their act. Rose and Likky sang a little, most notably on 'Painting Box', where Likky also tinged finger cymbals. To our excitement, Rose played bass guitar on a couple of songs. Unlike the mysterious 'Mimi & Mouse' in the ISB 'Mystical Pantomime' we had read about in *Melody Maker*, they did not dance. For the most part, they just sat and smiled, swayed and nodded. They were part of the band and they were part of the audience, who happened to be sitting onstage.

It was a sharing rather than a show. Robin's dog, Leaf – who else brought a dog on stage? – snoozed on his cushion. It was the *Hangman* cover-group extended, and we were part of it. It had something of the folk club ethos, with its rejection of the Star-and-Audience set-up, but without the political and aesthetic earnestness. It was informal, yet sacramental.

The word *shaman* hovers, ready to descend like a mantle on Robin Williamson's shoulders: one who alters reality in the group by altering it in himself. Mike less so – there was always an element of earthiness and monkey-mischief and human emotion in him. He was having too much of a good time to be an out-and-out shaman.

It was a given that the point of being there – for the four people on stage and the thousand or so around them – was to *get higher*. To alter our reality. To be transformed.

It is a very big ambition, way beyond mere entertainment, but it was fulfilled that night. It crystallised my sense of the point of performing arts – music, theatre, dance, even poetry readings. And, to a degree, even the point of a book: though they only address one reader at a time, I hope still for words to uncoil off the page like incense, to pass along the neural pathways of the brain, to alter and alert it.

Give me back the world! Return me to myself! Turn me on! Set me loose!

It's a high hope, that flood of *presence*. Perhaps it marks me as one of my time, yet who does not yearn to be untethered, made buoyant, borne out into that gong-tormented sea?

In the upper gallery, Atty Watson, Mike's school friend and co-strummer in Heriot's cloakrooms, then bassist with Rock Bottom and the Deadbeats, was having a very different experience. He sat appalled in suit and tie next to Mike's mother and father, who had never been out so late for years. They had come to see their son's first big concert in their home town and were formally dressed.

'Mike and especially Robin looked weird, but I half-expected that. But I was amazed so many of the audience did too!' Forty-seven years on, in his orderly and recently extended house in Goldenacre, Atty shook his head. 'And I couldn't believe how much time they spent tuning. How unprofessional it all was. The sound was not good, and sometimes they strayed off-mic. And allowing a dog on stage!'

In the dance bands Atty still played in, the aim was to be tight, nail the harmonies, get the changes, start and finish together. Keep the songs coming. What he saw in the ABC was, to him, a shambles, as if they were just making it up. And Mike's songs weren't like the Buddy Holly ones he first wrote. *Amoebas are very small* – what was that about?

'And the other thing that struck me,' Atty said, as we chomped his wife Sandra's lemon drizzle cake, 'was how many people applauded and cheered when they heard the opening bars of songs they clearly knew! I realised that though it wasn't my kind of thing, these people loved it. I was still embarrassed by the presentation, but I had to recognise that my old friend and Robin had become a real success, and I was really pleased for him.'

That concert was a high-water mark in my young life, leaving a multi-coloured stain high in my heart, but I scarcely remember what songs they played. There were some we knew from *5000 Spirits* and *Hangman*. They did 'Minotaur's Song'. Shock and pleasure coursed down my spine when Robin began 'Waltz of the New Moon', and there was deep recognition-glow when Mike sang 'Painting Box', with Robin, Likky and now Rose singing harmony.

I am sure they did Mike's 'Swift as the Wind'. I was stunned by its passion and volume, the emotion when Mike opened his chest to the night terrors and deliriums of childhood. Those throaty *Aaaahs* were not ethereal but fearsome.

But a large proportion of the evening was songs we did not know. (Mike says Robin always wanted to do new material, 'which was fun, but made it difficult for the audience.' Later, perhaps under the influence of Scientology, they focused more on giving the audience what they wanted – and so maybe gave them less.)

Some of the new stuff was revelatory. Mike possessed the sitar passionately, the music poured unimpeded from his mind out through his hands, and the whole hall, like some stone flying saucer, up and left Edinburgh while Robin sang about finding a meteorite on Cramond Island, which somehow morphed into dragons and glittering jewelled caves ('The Iron Stone'). Another piercingly beautiful Robin song, 'The Half-Remarkable Question', posed a question that had been waiting for me all my life and lives in me still.

At this distance it is tempting to envisage the band as floppy and stoned. But there was nothing wilting, tremulous or passive about the Incredible String Band. They were vivid young men, glowing with energy, throwing open the doors of possibility, and their music banished sin and dross and drowsiness.

When Robin called for audience volunteers, we were out of our seats and clambering onto the stage like ferrets up a drainpipe.

Robin passed me a bell. Twenty of us stood in a line, facing the rest of the audience. Like much of the String Band ethos, it was generous, openhearted, undisciplined. It was probably indulgent. It was also extraordinarily democratic, trusting and inclusive.

It was not what people had paid for, to wait for ever before Robin conducted us through a 'piece' of ringing lasting maybe a minute. At the same time, it was exactly what we had paid for.*

We climbed down off the stage. Soon Robin announced they were about to play their last song. We sat expectantly as Mike moved to the electric piano, with his wide unfaltering gleeful grin, while Robin adjusted his whistles, checked the mandolin, retuned guitar, took up the gimbri and its bow. Up in the gallery, Atty Watson would have been sighing while Mr and Mrs Heron checked their watches. So late! Would there still be taxis?

---

* Rose and Likky likewise added fairly minimal additions, mostly vocals or finger cymbals, little drums and rattles, hand-claps. Yet they were a part of what we had come for, that spreading out of talent, charisma, participation. Few, if any, bands have ever instinctively looked to spread the limelight so generously.

A couple of false starts. Laughter on and offstage. Likky adjusted the bongos between her knees. Rose plonked the bass, glanced over to Mike. The octopus-armed musical prodigy Robin was ready. Strange sustained high chords on organ setting, and then the bowed gimbri, that visceral yearning essence of wonder. I felt it in my gut and what I had come to hesitantly name my soul. Then Mike leaned to the mic and sang huskily:

Winter was cold and the clothing was thin
But the gentle shepherd called the tune.

We were into Mike's masterwork, 'A Very Cellular Song'. Its thirteen minutes can seem a lifetime or two blinks of an eye, depending on how lost in it you get. We had snuck a bottle of cider each into the concert, but had been too enthralled to drink much. Then again, the air was very fragrant, and we probably had a contact high.

Looking round, I noticed people were mouthing every word. I suspect there are many still alive who have lines about riding backwards on a giraffe inscribed along their neural pathways. In our core we still hear a rasping kazoo turn the spiritual inside out like a duvet cover, refreshing it as cosmic joke – that liberating manoeuvre at the heart of the ISB's vision.

The benign acid trip of that song flowed tumultuously on finally to emerge into the shining delta of its coda, sung over and over by us all (apart from an appalled Atty and Mike's parents in the upper gallery) until Leaf the dog got up, stretched, then followed Likky and Rose offstage as the last chorus faded into cheers and applause. Mike and Robin stood up, the short and the tall of it, waved and drifted away, Mike's grin lingering in the air like the Cheshire Cat's.

George and I looked at each other.

'Backstage?'

'Absolutely!'

> Atty: *Sandra and I did not go backstage as, if truth be told, I think we just wanted to get away from all the weirdness of the evening and the proximity of the great unwashed who had emerged that night.*
>
> *Mike's old man sat next to me and, although he was an English teacher, he was a pretty down-to-earth character and I do remember his 'My God!' as he surveyed the state of the audience.*
>
> *I was always amazed that ISB songs could arouse such devotion in the fan base, although I was impressed, especially as their recording period got underway, by the excellence of the playing of their multifarious instruments and the beauty of the lyrics. My main reaction to the whole thing was pleasure in seeing a close friend making good on the musical scene, albeit not exactly in the genre to which I subscribed.*

There was no muscular security barring the way. A longhair asked if we knew the band, so we said 'Yes!' and went in. A dozen or so exotics were greeting the band like old friends, which they probably were. Mike perched on his own on a stool, still with the smile bright as a lighthouse banishing shipwreck.

His glee was almost intimidating, so we swerved past him and greeted Robin Williamson. I said the first thing that came into my head.

'Would you like some cider, Robin?'

He looked at us, at the proffered bottle.

'Ah, sweet apple-ghosts,' he murmured. 'Thank you.'

The celestial being who wrote 'Three Is a Green Crown' and 'Waltz of the New Moon' was drinking my cider! His Adam's apple convulsed, he handed back the bottle.

We gibbered how much we had enjoyed the evening. He said he had too, though, 'We were a bit nervous at first – it is always harder playing your home town.'

We filed this away. He got nervous! George started telling him about how we were playing ISB songs at our folk club, and were starting to write our own. I said we were also writing Absurdist plays and poems, Baudelaire, Rimbaud, Walt Whitman . . . Robin said he had long been into poetry, was interested in mixing songs, poems and theatrical masques.

We offered to send the band some poems, stories and drawings, by way of thanks. Robin said that would be cool, and suggested we ask their tour manager for the address.

Then an old friend cut in to greet Robin, and we drifted away. We found the nerve to talk to gap-toothed Likky, then a beaming, friendly Rose – I fixated on her strong, bare feet – who pointed out their tour manager.

We introduced ourselves to a strikingly tall woman, long black hair down to her hips, white skull-like face, a deep, posh voice: Morticia in *The Addams Family*.

'So what kind of songs do you boys write?'

George and I looked at each other. Our few efforts to date were patched-together mood pieces, incantations of night, Pan and the back country, instructions for making fudge, with a generous dollop of free modal wailing.

'Our own kind,' George said firmly.

'That *is* good news,' she said, and scribbled down an address we could send our relief parcels of F & f goodies to. Our notion, invented only minutes earlier, had been to put together a 'thank-you' package for the String Band, but then she added, 'If you send your tapes to Joe, I'll make sure he'll have a listen.' That casual remark would reconfigure everything.

Unable to take any more, we reeled out into the Edinburgh night. I see us crossing Leith Links in our bedraggled finery, exhausted, brimming, as first light swells into day, two small-town country boys clutching that scrap of paper, our ticket to the life that was truly ours.

Track 7: A Glencoe Pan

In 1968 they were still known as *the tattie holidays*. Because agricultural children didn't turn up at school while the potatoes were being lifted, the authorities eventually made it an official October break.

I picture us gathering on the farm road by the school in freezing half-light in jerkins, wellies and woolly hats, getting a hand up onto the trailer, clutching a bag with Thermos flask, corned beef sandwiches and chocolate.

The tattie-howking was brutal work but decently paid. It was, in its way, romantic, this collective, seasonal labour. I liked the clean, hard dawn, the short-flaring sunsets, and even the scouring wind across the chocolate-brown fields of Fife. It was great when we stopped for our break, and a greater sweetness when the tractor broke down and we would wander to the edge of the field, groan and lie out flat. Some sat in their shallow wire gathering-baskets, like coracles rocking on a sea of mud.

(A brief romance with one of the farm girls. Kissing behind the bare trees, caressing with our muddy hands and broken nails, sharing flasks, hurrying through our dreels so we could have an extra minute together before the tractor lurched back to open up the next row and we all descended behind it like the gulls in the wake of the homecoming boats out in the Firth.)

At the day's end we clambered painfully down off the trailer and queued for coins and notes, then hobbled homeward visioning food and hot bath. The tattie-howking was money in the hand, without paperwork or deductions – the sweetest pay there is, a tangible reward for physical effort.

Doing it lifelong would be a different matter. I've seen enough labourers with broken-down backs and knees, or the bent, retired fishermen with their knotted, arthritic hands rolling cigarettes at the pier-end, not to be romantic about manual labour.

The tatties were hard, but five days could get a couple of LPs, with money left for the Elie disco and a share in a quarter bottle of vodka behind the bus shelter. But, in October '68, Fate & ferret forsook the tattie-howking. We decided to go on the road, hitch into the Highlands with our guitars and sleeping bags, and let it happen.

The ancient Army rucksack was metal-framed, with heavy, smelly canvas and perished leather straps. Spare jeans, socks, shirt, notebook and *Greek Myths*. Performing gear. Flask, torch and Swiss Army knife. Rubbish Spanish guitar in plastic case, kazoo, harmonica and stand. Emergency money from my seventeenth birthday a few weeks earlier.

In our minds we were travelling players, part Roger Miller's 'King of the Road', part Provençal troubadours. Also wandering Taoist poets, and the fiddler stepping to the road in 'Visions of Johanna'. We got most of our notions from songs and books – at that age, where else were we to get them from?

George's dad dropped us off near St Andrews bus station. We walked with our guitars to the edge of town, stood in cold wind watching the golfers. Soon enough, a car stopped. Then a lorry took us across the Tay, and its driver told us a local competition to find a slogan for the new bridge had been abandoned after the one with the most votes – *It's all downhill to Dundee* – was felt to be unsuitable.

We laughed, but George recalls staring down into the turgid waters, feeling a distant echo of his childhood fears of the ferry crossing, the terror of going down, the chill waters closing over his head.

No longer in Fife, F & f descended into the abrasive city of Dundee. In the Gallowgate we unfurled our guitars, spread the plastic cases on the pavement, donned our feathered bunnets in the light rain. My dad had told me that through this public space Yeats had walked to the students' lecture hall, Buffalo Bill Cody had ridden stiffly on his great white horse, Ulysses S. Grant had commented, *What a mighty long bridge to such a mighty little old town*, and William McGonagall flogged his dreadful penny broadsheets. And now us.

We opened with 'Oh, Lord How Happy I Am'. A few pennies, tanners, the odd, chunky threepenny bit spattered on the guitar case like discoloured rain. Mostly we got sceptical glances. Dundee had spent much of its history in recession. At that point it had the highest per capita murder rate in the country. It was like Glasgow without the leavening influence of Highlanders and Irish.

So, not the happiness capital of Scotland. We bashed on with 'Empty Pocket Blues'. A few short people stopped, a child was given a coin, tossed the sixpence then ran away. The rain petered out, but the chill wind got up. It was hard to say whether we were playing an impromptu concert or begging for money. We glanced at each other for courage, then launched into 'You Know What You Could Be', with kazoo solo.

'Eh, do ye play "Bonnie Dundee", pal?'

'No.'

Three lads, our age but infinitely harder, stared at us. One cupped his burning cigarette inside his palm, gangster style.

'How aboot "The Wild Rover"?'

Pause. George and I looked at each other.

'Na, we don't play that.'

'You're no much fuckin' use, are ye?'

One of the lads reached down and scooped up our few coins.

'But we do play "The Gypsy Rover"!'

'And Buddy Holly,' George added.

The lads stared at us. One or two folk hung near, just watching. The biggest lad nodded to the one with our money, and he dribbled the coins from his fingers back onto the pavement.

'So play it, pal.'

We launched into 'That'll Be the Day'. The trio listened to the first verse then stalked off with their high-shouldered, stiff-legged strut.

We finished the song, picked up our few coins. We asked a wee man if he knew a pub where we could play music.

'This is no bluidy Ireland,' he said. 'Are ye Fenians or whit?'

We went to a non-musical pub, had a pint and considered our options. This town was not for us, any more than it had been for our fellow Scot and aspirational, delusional dreamer, William Topaz McGonagall.

> *Well, my dear friends, the next event in my life that I am going to relate is regarding me and my Mistress McGonagall leaving Dundee in the year 1894, resolving to return no more owing to the harsh treatment I had received in the city as is well known for a truth without me recording it. Well, I went to the Fair City of Perth, one of the finest upon the earth, intending to remain there altogether. So I secured a small garret in the South Street, and me and my mistress lived there for eight months, and the inhabitants were very kind to us in many respects.** *

We left the pub and caught the next bus to Perth, a city altogether more bonnie: genteel in parts, rough in others.

By the time we got there, it was getting dark and too chilly and damp to play on the street, so we went into a promising pub for a pie. Someone noticed the guitars and called for a song. Someone else bought us a pint. Soon we were in a warm corner, eating pies

---

* If McGonagall were shown a glimpse of a future where he would be famous as the world's worst poet, and another where he would remain unpublished and unmocked, which he would have chosen? Would he have opted for immortality on those terms? Would I? Would you?

then playing with greasy fingers on the strings. We found the Buddy Holly songs went down well, as did the Scottish standards, though we still drew the line at 'The Wild Rover'.

Encouraged, we glanced at each other and launched into 'Everything's Fine Right Now'. Some bafflement, but the mood of it seemed to work, and people laughed at my rasping kazoo. 'You Know What You Could Be' was perhaps a bit philosophical, though one fella with a partial moustache nodded thoughtfully as he sang the refrain back under his breath.

More drinks. 'Nowhere Man' was taken up by our group to the point where we were sternly told to *Keep it doun, lads.* This is a Scottish pub, you're here to drink not enjoy yourselves.

Still, it was great, playing and singing in a pub for pies and pints, among older men. We felt we were spreading some message about the new times we were in. We talked about these Edinburgh lads, the Incredible String Band, then played 'The Hedgehog's Song'. It worked. We were bought whiskies on the strength of it. An elderly man – meaning about fifty – kept on shouting *Gies that sang aboot the pair wee hedgehog!* till we played it again. And again.

Then it was chucking-out time (still ten o'clock) and, as a chill smirr of rain ghosted down, we were on the street, unsober, with guitars and packs, and sleeping bags that would be useless without a tent. If there was a youth hostel in Perth, we didn't know where it was. Our money didn't stretch to a B & B. Our frontal cortices not fully developed, we hadn't planned at all.

George said he'd heard the police have to put you up in the cells if you've nowhere to stay. So we went looking for a policeman. It's true – you just can't find one when you want one. Someone directed us to a police station. We hesitated outside. We were cold, damp and exhausted.

We presented ourselves and made our request for a cell for the night.

'Hae ye committed an offence?'

'We've been busking in the street,' I offered.

'Without a licence!' George added.

The mouth of the man behind the counter twitched in what might in Fife have passed for a smile.

'We didna see you.' He leaned forward, it was a quiet night. 'Look, lads, we're no a hotel. You'd best try Skinnergate House if it hasna shut fur the night.'

Skinnergate House, place of last resort for the dossers, tramps and winos. It's the smell that I remember, long-fermented sweat, pish, fags and booze, the rancid guff of humanity on its uppers.

There were grilles on the windows, distant arguments, shouting. Someone bawled 'The Wild Rover'. Another moaned, possibly in protest against the song or the state of his guts or just life in general. The lighting was dim and yellow, the walls a scarred green. The man at the counter asked for 2/6 each and wrote us out a receipt.*

We were shown to a cell-like room. Two wooden platforms and one chair. I may be inventing the tin bucket, the single, low-wattage,

---

* I found it in a package George sent recently. I picked it up gingerly, sniffed. It still smells of decay, cigarettes, and our youth.

naked bulb. I believe we were locked in, and that we felt grateful for that.

The worn blankets looked dodgy and did not smell good.

'I bet they've got lice.'

I examined the stained, flattened mattress. Our mothers would kill us if we brought lice or bugs home. We gingerly pulled the blankets off the platforms, unrolled our sleeping bags on the bare wood. The lights went out. We lay in the dark, listening to the cries and moans and curses. I fumbled for my torch and played it on the flaking ceiling.

'Far out,' George said quietly. 'Skinnergate House.'

We laughed. It was beyond grotty, but this was what we had come for. In time there might be a song or a poem in it. In another cell a ruined voice ventured *And it's no, nay never, no nay never no more!* A shout, a cry, then silence.

I lay with my torch on for comfort, thinking about William McGonagall. The man had many of the traits of artistic genius – the embrace of poverty, the ambition, self-belief, discipline and sheer hard work. He heard the calling 'William, be a poet!' and walked away from his clattering loom. He wrote over 200 published poems. He put himself out there, risking (and finding) ridicule. He had all the essential qualities of a significant artist, apart from talent.

Fervent teetotaller and passionate Presbyterian, he seems a totem of the Victorian age, tragic, ridiculous and profoundly Scottish.

If he had not existed, he would be an inspired creation and cautionary tale. What would-be writer does not once in a while hear that dread whisper and wonder if they are in fact absurd, ridiculous, a joke? *Am I in fact William McGonagall?*

I switched off the torch and, appalled and thrilled, surrendered to the stinking dark.

Next day, Perth was kind to us, as it had been to McGonagall. Images of the broad river, sunny streets, a noisy corner near the AK Bell Library that drove us back to some green space near the river, where we sang our hearts out, largely to the ducks.

Restricted by our rucksacks and guitar, we couldn't take a decent walk or head for the hills. We dawdled away the day, propped on our packs, strumming guitars. George had the makings of a song, rejoicing in the title 'Ablative Absolute', taken from our Latin grammar book. The chords are long lost to us both, but the opening lines remain grooved in my brain:

Carry on living for the rest of your life
There's plenty of time on the side
And plenty of room on my running board
If you're coming along for the ride.

Then it was evening, and pie and beans in a cheap café, and then a pub for warmth. We were told to shut up or get out – this is a Scottish pub and we'll not have music here! We finished our gassy pints of McEwan's Special and left.

We found another pub, ordered Export, which was darker and sweeter, fit for sticking up wallpaper. There was a snug where the barman said we could play if we kept it down. So we did the now-familiar set of ISB songs mixed with Scottish traditionals, Buddy

Holly, 'Abilene' and 'I Saw Her Standing There'. We deflected requests for 'The Wild Rover' and 'Flower of Scotland', still just able to afford some integrity.

A group of drinkers gathered around. We politely declined the cigarettes but accepted pints and coughed in the blue-grey air. We took a break, supped our drinks, hinted at a record deal. We had some original songs but our manager wouldn't let us play them till he'd secured copyright.

A last blast of 'The Hedgehog's Song' and we were on the streets again, pissed and without a plan.

One of the men who had been sitting with us offered his place. So we walked for ages through the streets into a poorer part of Perth, and there was his home, a warm council house, and mugs of tea. A woman made an appearance in a dressing gown – she had long fair hair, seemed kind and amused or perhaps merely sleepy and tolerant. We could sleep on the fold-out couch if we didn't mind sleeping together.

George and I looked at each other. Shrugged. It was better than Skinnergate House. Her husband opened the fold-down and left us to it.

My head swirled like water draining down the plughole as I slid anti-clockwise, down into sleep.

Morning was bright sun in a kitchen with a blue formica-topped table. There were two small children excited to see strangers. Our host was not much older than us, and the children seemed

RIGHT: Clive's Incredible Folk Club
Membership Card

Owen Hand, Robin Williamson, Lesley Hale
and Clive Palmer at the Traverse Theatre

CLIVE'S INCREDIBLE FOLK
CLUB
La Cucaraccia Buildings,
134 Sauchiehall Street, Glasgow, C.2
The best in Late Night Folk and
Country Style Entertainment.

Rules:

This Membership Card is NOT trans-
ferable, and must be shown on request
to club officials.

All members' guests MUST BE SIGNED IN,
AND PAID FOR by the member.

Consumption of alcoholic beverages in
clubs is illegal therefore cannot be allowed on club premises, any individual found
in the possession, or under the influence
of alcohol will have his/her membership
confiscated, the management regret that
under these circumstances membership
fees cannot be refunded.

The management reserve the right to
refuse admission.

EVERY SATURDAY from 11p.m.
till SUNDAY at dawn.

Mike Heron, Robin
Williamson and Clive Palmer
backstage at Clive's Incredible
Folk Club, 1966

RIGHT: Atty Watson, Edinburgh,
1960

RIGHT: Mike Heron, Clive Palmer and Robin Williamson on stage at Clive's Incredible Folk Club 1966

ABOVE: First American album cover photo shoot, 1966

LEFT: Clive Palmer, Robin Williamson, Mike Heron, with instruments from the music shop wall, 1966.

LEFT: Publicity shot for the Incredible String Band

BELOW: Mike Heron, Robin Williamson and Clive Palmer at Temple Cottage, 1966

RIGHT: Mike Heron plays mouth organ to Robbie Stewart outside Temple Cottage, 1966

LEFT: Mike playing Robin's guitar

Mike Heron, and Trembling Bells at Glasgow Necropolis, 2012. From left: Alex Neilson, Georgia Seddon, Mike Heron, Simon Shaw, Mike Hastings; seated in front: Lavinia Blackwall

RIGHT: Mike Heron and Ashraf Sharif Khan rehearsing in Berlin for Wasser Music Concert at House of Culture, 2015

ABOVE LEFT: F&f + Fiddler Tom
ABOVE RIGHT: Andrew Greig, Netted,
1969

LEFT: Andrew Greig, Kilconquhar
Inn, Dec 1970.

RIGHT: F&f
tune in to
Bearsden, Jan
1970

ABOVE LEFT: Back Country Brouhaha

ABOVE RIGHT: Cherry, F&f and pals, Kilconquhar 1970

RIGHT: Bedroom Dream Corner

BELOW: How to find Robin

Robin, 4th Floor
25 Gordon Mansions
Huntley Street
London

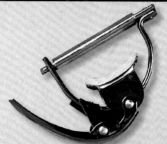

London To-Do List

Meet Malcolm & Roddy at 10.0.
Phone Joe 11.30.
Zel Records
Joe — what to do w tape
          Gigs for summer?
          Krysia?
          Programs/Songbook
Anthea - chicks for concert

Andrew - Cockneys 2.30 - 3.0.
          ,,   6.0

ABOVE: *Electric Ferret*: Eric Plectrum, Andrew Greig and John Myles

Back country roof

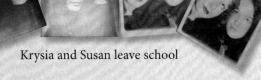

Krysia and Susan leave school

Frogpocket, Andrew Greig, Mike Heron, Mike Hastings and Georgia Seddon, House Concert, 2011

Strangely Young, Green Note Café, 2011. From left: Tim Booth, Andrew Greig, George Boyter, Ivan Pawle.

Mike Heron and Andrew Greig return to Hangman Woods, 2015

improbable but lovely. Boiled eggs, sunlit kitchen, tea and toast and giggling children. I wonder where they all are now, those kindly people.

We had coffee and biscuits and played songs for the kids by way of thanks. I have a sense we went Scottish because it felt right, what with children and being on the edge of the Highlands. We would have played 'Mhairi's Wedding', the 'Mingulay Boat Song', and, most probably, 'Wild Mountain Thyme' before shouldering our rucksacks and out the door and onto the road again.

There was, maybe still is, a notable transport caff at the edge of Perth, where lorry drivers meet to fortify themselves with mugs of tea, white sliced bread stacked high beside egg and chips. We went in and started going round the tables, asking for anyone heading west or north.

Crianlarich, son? Crianlarich was part of Gaeldom, not our culture, but all the better for that. The Lowlands had formed us, no doubt, yet the pragmatic landscapes of Fife, its coastal villages of sceptical fishermen, dour farmers and canny shopkeepers, left little room for the Golden Bough.

Soon young Fate & ferret were sitting high in the warm cab of a brewery lorry trundling into the Highlands, telling their story of a night in the cells of Perth.

As a hitch-hiker you have a duty to entertain and to listen, to soak up stories then pass them off, suitably amplified, as your own. I learned from myself never to trust travellers' tales, though with their process of borrowing, incorporating, altering and embellishing, they share much of the procedures of Art. Portrait of the artist as a young hitch-hiker.

When we clambered down in Crianlarich, we bought and wrote a postcard to the Boss, to say we were in her native place, thinking of her. But nothing much seemed to be happening, so we stuck out our thumbs again. There was little traffic, and none stopped. We drifted back down to the bus stop. The Glasgow to Fort William bus was due soon. It went via Glencoe.

'What you reckon?'

'Glencoe? Out of sight!'

The country bus grinds up Black Mount onto Rannoch Moor. We traverse our country's desolate heartland, flare-lit by a low orange sun. Then Buachaille Etive Mòr, the *Big Shepherd of Etive*, soars on our left, the broken saw of the Aonach Eagach ridge threatening on our right. The bus twists and plunges down into the pass, by the Meeting of the Three Waters, then sharply kinking down towards the valley floor. Splinters of sunlight on the upper peaks, dark backdrops and low-level cloud up ahead, the rain just holding off but threatening, it is a fitting place for a massacre.

We get off the bus where the wee road branches to the Clachaig Inn and the youth hostel where we intend to spend the night. The wind is strong and penetrating. We climb over a wall to change into our Fate & ferret gear.

We look at each other. George seems confident. He might think the same about me. We shoulder our packs, pick up the guitars and hurry down the single-track road towards the Clachaig Inn through the dismal light.

By the door of the Clachaig Inn we check the sign:

No Hawkers
No Campbells

It's a joke, of sorts. There are still people who spat at the mention of the name Campbell, three hundred years after the event. *Murder under trust* it was called under Scots law. Many of the troops were in fact Lowland Scots, and the slaughter part of the wider political struggle to keep the Protestants William and Mary on the throne, in place of the Catholic Stuarts.

But to us this is all *vieux jeu*, a preoccupation with the past that we are impatient to leave behind. I pocket my glasses, then, being neither Campbells nor exactly hawkers, we push on the door and go inside.

The bar is packed, steaming, hot and loud. The men are bigger and older than us, with hairy sweaters (the age of the fleece has not yet descended), some of them straight off the hill, for this is the epicentre of Scottish mountaineering.

Some stare as we push through the crowd, drop our packs and join the press at the bar. We must look weird, young and puny in our purple tunics, tabards, tasselled scarves and feather-sprouting bunnets.

But the hair is getting longer, and I will learn climbers are more unconventional individualists than macho squaddies. In common with young Fate & ferret, they have a passion that most people consider pointless, that earns them nothing other than intense experience and the respect of their peers. Like us they are here to do what they love, because it makes them feel more alive.

Perhaps that was why instead of being mocked, beaten up and thrown out, we get served our viscous pints and a small space clears for us, and we launch into the song of Mike's that had become our banker, our signature tune, our starter for ten: 'Everything's Fine Right Now'.

The beers go down like bittersweet glue. We drink, sing, take a break. Three girls, perhaps a year or two older than us, come over and ask about the songs. They are trainee nurses from Glasgow. The taller one with wavy brown hair has heard of the Incredible String Band, and we get talking, shouting into each other's ears above the hubbub. She may be called Susan, or Suzanne. There is a spark of mischief in her eyes.

We sing again, drink, sing and shout ourselves hoarse, finishing with a throat-ripping 'I Saw Her Standing There', then 'Mhairi's Wedding'. More drinks come. Then it is closing time. We knock back the pints, zip our guitars into their plastic cases.

The three nurses go to the Ladies. George and I stand by the door, grinning at each other, open to whatever comes next. Only two trainee nurses come out of the loo and even I realise something has been settled. Susan or Suzanne puts her arm through mine, says they are staying in the youth hostel down the road. I say we probably are staying there too, and we head out into the night.

The night outside is breathing hard, moon and stars and clouds are wobbling above the darker dark of the hills. Susan staggers into me as we set off down the road, and I register she's half-pissed too. The third nurse comes up from behind, grabs my guitar, mimes strumming it, before overtaking George and his girl and vanishing into the darkness ahead.

We walk on, drifting from one verge to the other of the dark road, stepping aside for erratically driven cars. We talk about our lives and hopes. She says she's Catholic. I have only recently been informed I am technically a Protestant, but I gather for Glaswegians religious background is relevant information. This may mean she is even less likely to have sex.

She has three sisters and a brother, and wants to emigrate to Australia. I pass over school, claim to have no plans for the future other than writing and singing. I imply trouble with drugs. Her moonlit face looks more concerned than impressed, so I add this is largely behind me now.

Every so often we stop, and kiss swaying on the verge. Her lips are cold but her mouth is warm and wet. Struck by the contrast of outside and inside, I mention this, along with the moon riding high, several times. I am intoxicated by the Glencoe night as much as beer.

George and his girl have disappeared. We stumble on a side ditch, and end up in it together. It is surprisingly comfortable, nearly dry, out of the wind. We lie looking up at the moon straining on its invisible leash. We kiss and fumble, stare at each other to check how this is going, and fumble some more.

Then excitement morphs into distaste for what we are about. Or not quite distaste – for this is much better than the tattie-howking – but some unexpected reluctance. The Gypsy Rover is all very well, but the prospect of having my first advanced sex – even if that is on offer, which I doubt – half-cut in a Glencoe ditch with someone I scarcely know does not meet my aspirations.

She seems to have come to the same conclusion. I clamber out of the ditch and reach down to give her a hand out. We agree we'll have to hurry to get to the hostel before closing time. I'm more relieved than disappointed. I suspect she is too.

She pulls on woollen gloves, I dig out mine and we hold gloved hands as we make best time down the road, more children in a fairy tale than horny teenagers.

The hostel is closed. Lights out, silent, door locked. Shit shit shit.

Susan/Suzanne and I stand whispering in the hostel porch. No sign of George and his girl. I try the front windows but they are snibbed. I encountered the warden of this hostel on a school trip the Easter before, over the matter of the lager cans under my bunk. He was not a friendly man. I have a sleeping bag in my pack but Susan is not petite.

'Where's your dorm?'

'At the back, round the side,' she whispers.

'Let's try the window there.'

I must get her inside, then take off with my rucksack and sleeping bag. I must find George.

We go round the side. I grope, reach up, find a window. It feels slightly open. I ease my hand in, finger the bar, lift it off the catch. Open the window wide.

'I'll help you up,' I whisper. 'I'll need my guitar in the morning.'

'Sure,' she says. 'Goodnight.'

A formal, friendly kiss. I link my hands and she steps onto them, and I start to lift her. I hear her breathing heavily, faint grunts as she gets her elbows on the sill.

The lights come on bright. *Hey you! Oot o there, ya wee bastard!* But it isn't directed at me, or at Susan, who slithers away into the room with a thump. Off to my right, George stands like a pheasant in headlights, caught in the act of helping his nurse out, reaching up towards her protruding head and shoulders.

We sprint round the front, I snatch up my rucksack, then we're on the road and pelting into the night. A door bangs and the warden comes running our way, torch in hand. We swerve off the road into trees and shrubs.

We plough on, twigs whipping our faces and hands. Down a bank and lie still. We ease off our packs and wait. Look at each other, trying not to giggle. The torch beam prowls the road, sweeps our way. We duck down. Surely he'll give up.

The branches above us light up. We hear him crunching our way through the undergrowth.

'Come on oot, ya bastards!'

We can't outrun him with our packs. He has the torch. We're done for.

'I'll draw him off,' George mutters. 'You take the packs and my guitar – meet you up the road.'

He gets to his feet, poised leaning forward like a sprinter on the blocks, then he's off. George is fast and light, plays inside centre at rugby.* He jouks away to my right, through the trees. The warden bellows and is after him. I grab two packs and one guitar and set off

---

* Captain of the 2nd XV through our tumultuous final year at school, phenomenally unsuccessful. Played fifteen, lost fourteen, drew one. But they stuck at it, turned out every Saturday morning, thin and shivering, to be tramped into the mud again. Mr McGeachy our pugnacious gym teacher praised their gallantry.

by moonlight in the opposite direction, working up towards the road but staying off it. I stop, hearing shouts and curses on the breeze, crackle and thrashing from among the trees.

So the warden hasn't caught him yet. I am very impressed at George's decisiveness and possible self-sacrifice. In the pagan night of Glencoe we are combining John Buchan and Robert Graves, 'The Wild Rover' and *Kidnapped*. This is just right.

I hunker down in a thicket where I can keep an eye on the road. The moon comes and goes. The night is thick with the hulking hills, the shades of murdered MacDonalds.

I shiver as the sweat cools and the breeze rises. More woman and children died that night from exposure than men were killed by the sword. I pull on my fisherman's sweater and consider. I haven't heard anything for a while. I have no idea where the warden is, or George, or where we might meet up. The night is mercifully dry and I have my sleeping bag, but my friend's is in his pack beside me.

Then comes deliverance. Down the brae, somewhere near the river, I see a torchlight stab and slash. Faint shouting, glimpse of something running towards the village. That decides it.

I scramble onto the road and hurry along it, quick as two packs and a guitar allow, away from the hostel. I need a vantage point so I might spot George if he escapes the enraged warden and gains the road. There is a break in the trees to my right. I go through there and cautiously start to climb the open brae, feeling exposed. Cloud tears away from the moon.

Someone is standing on top of the hill, against the skyline. Facing my way. His arms spread wide then he steps down into the shadow.

I hesitate. Who the hell? It can't be George or the warden, I'd seen them a couple of minutes earlier down in the valley. A second warden? A wild rover? A still-fugitive MacDonald?

I cannot outrun him, not with the packs and the guitar. Hesitantly I carry on up the hill. The figure reappears in moonlight, closer now. He stops. I stop.

'George?'

'Andrew?'

Reunited, we hurry to the top of the knoll, then over the back, off the skyline. We lie so we can see anyone coming, and try to settle the mystery of the torchlight pursuit in the valley.

'I thought it was the warden chasing you.'

'Wasn't me,' George replies. 'I gave him the slip early on, but I didn't know where he was or where you had gone. So, when I saw the torch, I knew it must be you he was chasing, so I scarpered up here.'

'It wasn't me. Who was he after?'

We grow wide-eyed, feel the wonder swell in us. Only one possible explanation.

'Pan!'

The mighty Pan is not dead. He has merely moved to Glencoe, and come to the aid of his followers in their hour of need.

We had first been alerted to Pan by Robin Williamson's pantheistic invocation 'Waltz of the New Moon'. This had grown into the Fife back country becoming peopled with minor deities. We wrote songs about them, lit fires, drank votive cider, nearly glimpsed them capering in the moonlit stubble fields.

Then in Graves' *Greek Myths* we found that passage from Plutarch, and looked at each other, dismayed. *Pan ho megas tethneke. The great god Pan is dead.*

We were unwilling to believe it, yet it rang true. Of course Pan was dead. The Christian world had overrun the classical, and then the medieval world was replaced by the scientific outlook to which I subscribed. There was no magic, no other order of beings that existed alongside us, moved through the trees, gurgled in the burns.

The Periodic Table was astounding yet verifiable in a way that Pan and owl messengers and spinning castles were ... not. The Incredible String Band were Scottish, but so was the Enlightenment.

George and I did sciences at Waid. We cannot drop that world view. But we also know what turns us on. Lying on that hill top below scudding moonlit clouds, thinking of the torchlight pursuit that has saved us from the warden, we do and do not believe that Pan has intervened. But, by Apollo, it feels like he has.

We wriggle into sleeping bags. Dig into our packs for pork pies, Kit Kats, raisins, cheese. We crack open the Don Cortez, a rusty razor of a red wine.

We toast Pan. The String Band. The Glasgow nurses. The Boss. George's girl had got into the hostel just before it closed, having arranged to climb out once the lights were out. Mine had been the opposite, due to our time in the ditch and change of heart on both sides.

With the wine quickly inside us, swigged straight from the bottle, it is all perfect. Our virginity will persist a while yet – but so what? Nothing beats watching mist come pouring up the valley with great force, feeling the chill damp air on our faces. To be seventeen and on the loose in old Glencoe, while down in the valley Pan and the long-dead MacDonalds lead the warden astray – it is wonderful and more lasting than sex.

We get cool, then very cold. At one point the fog rolls up and smothers where we lie discussing future albums. Then the mist sinks, and the near-full moon is riding high again, and we begin to shiver continuously in our dew-damp bags as we talk of ancient Greece, doze, talk, lie wide-eyed through the Glencoe night.

A grouchy start to the day, numb, sleep-starved and hungry. I needed my guitar back. We crouched in the undergrowth near the hostel. An hour passed, then three young women left the hostel and headed towards Glencoe village. One, thank Pan, was carrying a guitar.

We caught them up near the Massacre memorial. I got my guitar back, and we said the bare good-manners minimum to each other, all parties embarrassed. There was no talk of exchanging addresses. Their bus came and to mutual relief they got on and, with a tentative wave, were gone.

The night's magic had departed, leaving us hung-over and hungry at the roadside. We had our last biscuit and a short tetchy argument about something. We had no mechanism for sorting disagreement, any more than Robin and Mike had, beyond disengagement.

Not speaking, we wandered down the road to keep warm. Into the silent morning a murmuration faintly swelled, not exactly music or wind or burn. We walked on. The sound seemed to come out of the air and the ground, in an irregular pulse.

It was unmistakably human, oozing from a plain, grim little kirk.

Of course, it was Sunday. But it was not singing as such that passed through its small windows and unadorned stone. We stood outside, transfixed. These were not upstanding Victorian hymn tunes, nor even Church of Scotland psalms. For one thing, there was no accompaniment. Nor was there quite a tune.

We put down our gear and stood attentive as pilgrims or anthropologists. The faint, fervent voices were foreign to us. It was a cappella, in some kind of ragged unison. There was nothing as evident as a melody, and yet it was an extraordinary music, at once individualistic and collective. It nailed us as we stood, heads bowed in concentration, outside that Free Presbyterian church as the Presenter laid out the line and the responding congregation unfurled Gaelic psalms in praise of God into the morning.

What we listened to that grey hung-over morning in Glencoe was as strange as anything Robin Williamson ever picked up in Morocco, or that Mike Heron had heard in Bulgarian or Bahamian music. It struck George and me to the heart, though we were not Gaels and our songs praised Pan, not the Calvinist God. It made my eyes prickle and opened an ache where the ribs arch away from each other. It still does.

The Gaelic psalms defy musical logic. The Presenter leads with the opening line of the verse from the Psalm, and he – of course it is a he, what do you think this is, the Church of Scotland? – chooses the melody and phrasing that comes to him as most appropriate. Then the sitting congregation (ever contrary, Wee Frees stand to pray, sit to sing) responds, working off what the Presenter has proposed, each completing the line in their own time.

It shouldn't work. It should be the equivalent of what happens when you mix all colours together and end up with sludgy brown. There is no drilled choir to follow, no organ or piano to sustain it (the regulative principle dictates that nothing is brought into worship except what scripture requires). But in its modesty and fervour, Gaelic psalm-singing is one of the world's most remarkable musics. It cannot be taken on just aesthetically, filtering out the God part and enjoying what's left over.

All you can do is stand as George and I did outside the kirk, heads instinctively bowed, riveted, eyes and hearts prickling, getting the extraordinary drift of it.

Two days later we are back in double English, in school uniform, warm and clean. Our pals have been earning money at the tatties. Alastair Mackie is introducing a haunting Iain Crichton Smith poem 'Culloden and After'.

I glance over at George, who turns his head and looks at me. Glencoe. Pan. The Glasgow nurses, children, boiled eggs, Don Cortez, moonlight in Glencoe. Kind strangers, lorry cabs and fibs. Many beers, Skinnergate House. Cold fingers stinging on the strings, coarsened throats, unexpected harmonies. Brown-haired girl in a ditch. That unearthly earthly singing.

George winks, I grin back, feel immeasurably enriched as I turn my head to the front and enter the world of the poem.

Track 8: The Joyful Long Player

It was the time of thrilling, pocket-money devouring double albums: *The White Album*, *Blonde on Blonde*, *Wheels of Fire*, *Electric Ladyland* – and the String Band's *Wee Tam and the Big Huge*. Double albums may indicate talent in its pomp, or an erosion of quality control. Perhaps both.

Wee Tam was the Incredible String Band and their times in fullest bloom, with just a hint of the petals over-extending. We loved the smell, look and feel of the albums, the cursive lyrics all over the cover, the lads long-haired, beautiful, radiantly assured with beads, neck-pieces, floppy hats and clinging, swirly shirts.

And the songs that awaited us post-Glencoe! Robin's monumental 'Maya' was a celebration of all human existence, juggling multiple mythologies, committed to none. Wonderfully melodic, beautifully structured, stunningly sung, it seemed his masterpiece. And when Mike finally came in on the 'Maya' refrain, the song lifted from cerebral lyricism into pure heartfulness.

A quick rummage through the school library informed us that Maya is Illusion, that which conceals the underlying Void. In other hands this would signify meaninglessness, something to do with Samuel Beckett and that cool but depressed fifties thing. But in the ISB universe it announced the Joyful Player – one who recognises life is but a game, and responds not with bitterness but with joyous, all-embracing assent. It doesn't matter that it doesn't matter.*

'Job's Tears' was lengthy, hymn-like and strikingly Christian in imagery. Were they having a laugh or did they mean it? Or both? In the same way, Likky's thin, quavering, cracked choirboy descant was both funny and touching.

Robin's 'Ducks on a Pond' was fine, though perhaps one long song too many. But 'The Half-Remarkable Question', ornamented by Mike's sitar, was a wonder – focused, fluid, almost succinct, with another gorgeous melody. It struck me to the soul, and through all the years has kept murmuring in the background. Walking down the street or lifting a glass of wine, it remains a fair question, perhaps *the* question: what are we? What are we part of?

But it was the Mike songs we zeroed in on – scribbled lyrics, identified chords, lifted the needle and tried again, looking for songs we loved and could do at folk clubs and parties. We found them in two gorgeous and very different love songs: 'Air' – humming, intimate, sensuous, an audio incense stick – and the sprightly, delighted 'You Get Brighter'. Good wooing songs, we reckoned.

---

* Years later I found it again, in Rilke's death-interrogating *Duino Elegies*: '*Just to be here is a delight! Don't you know that yet?*'

'Log Cabin Home in the Sky' was a tongue-in-cheek fiddle hoe-down with a catchy refrain. It became our next banker, ideal for Fiddler Tom, and the tune was simple enough to double on my harmonica. 'Greatest Friend' sounded like a hymn, yet its imagery of mountains, wells and sacred trees was right in our pantheistic groove. With its few chords and emotional tune, it would become an anthem at family weddings, sung with my busker brother-in-law Lawrence in woods and gardens, and finally, improbably, shared onstage with its maker.

The jug band sources had almost entirely disappeared, yet the songs were driven by melody and conviction. Rose and Likky had more integrated roles on fiddle, vocals, keyboards, bass and percussion. Mike's sitar playing was all over the twin albums. He was not trying to sound earnestly Indian. In a fearless, unselfconscious way, sitar poured out through his fingertips, announcing we have unmoored from the known.*

We took what we could reasonably reproduce, and those songs spread to our friends, to be sung en masse at Waid folk clubs and parties. We kept the finest songs – Robin's lovely fragment 'The Yellow Snake', and 'The Circle Is Unbroken', which would so astound us at the Usher Hall concert, Mike's gimbri-enhanced 'Puppies' and the profound testament of 'Douglas Traherne Harding' – for solitary nights leaning on the windowsill, looking at the stars as our youth unwound like smoke from an incense stick.

---

* Probably Mike's best instrument, he sold it when Robin left the band, knowing he'd not have use for it again – he only took it up to accompany Robin's songs, choosing an instrument that that multitalented musician couldn't already play.

The String Band did much more than form my musical taste, which moved on. Despite utterly changed times, stiffening body, diminished senses, my prevalent anxiety colluding with the piling up of deaths of those we care for, my gloomy culture and the monetisation of our world – despite all this in my heart of hearts, like many others from that time, I still fly, like a battle-torn standard, the Joyful Player.

That winter of 1968–69, we had great hopes of mead. Brewed by monks, it seemed the sustenance of mediaeval wandering scholars and singers, with a hint of debauchery. Mead was the drink of poets and of Pan, the discoverer of honey. One cup, ideally a goblet, of mead would bestow fuzzy wisdom and harmony. Shared with a girl, it might lead to happy fondling. Among friends, to joyous anarchy.

George bought a bottle of mead in St Andrews. The lettering was ultra-Gothic as the drink itself. We tried it out after a rehearsal, along with the cinnamon sticks we'd taken to smoking.

'This is . . . interesting.'

We toasted Pan, and had another sip. It managed to be at once overly sweet, thin and bitter.

'Man, those monks must have been desperate.'

The mead bottle sat for months on a shelf in our studio room. George would offer it to friends who had come to record. No one liked it. Eric Plectrum necked it straight from the bottle. Raised his bushy eyebrows, scowled and took another slug.

'Yon is shite.'

That bottle was never finished, only abandoned – as a poem is, according to Paul Valéry, though I notice he prefixed this with the less-known proviso: 'To one who pursues perfection'.

And what if one does not pursue perfection? What then?

Deep in the online infinite wood of forking paths, checking up on Valéry, this jumps out like a startled hart: *Despite what people say about handing it over, a book is like the flying knife of the magician – released without ever leaving the hand.**

I sit in my shed, transfixed, as though pinned to my chair by a volley of those flying knives.

Say the knife, the song, the poem, the book – are only *apparently* thrown. The version that materialises at the other side of the room, thudding home beside the reader's head, or in her heart, appears to be the same one weighed in the hand of the writer/magician, held up by its gleaming tip, then flicked away – but it is not. The original has been palmed, and remains with its maker. The other was planted while the eye was distracted by flourishes.

In which case the cry that leapt from Mike Heron's lips during 'Swift as the Wind' at the ABC in Edinburgh in 1968 remained with him, in his heart, and the cry that rose in mine was my own.

The magic trick is in the song, the poem, the memoir, the play. Each is the flying knife that never flew.

---

* From *Fortress Besieged*, by Qian Zhongshu. Quite wonderful and very funny.

I sit in the shed, staring vacantly at the bamboo rattling on the window. My wife Lesley is away. My old friend George, with whom I sat up late last night, struggling to breathe through laughter about our daft days, is on his way back to London. I am alone, as is my daily practice.

In my body, in this shed, my fingers flex over the keyboard, and the flying knife gleams for a moment as it apparently crosses from one solitude to another.

From one apparent solitude to another.

Track 9: A Misty Night
by the Crusoe Hotel

Saturday evenings at the Boss's became essential. Once or twice a month, by invitation, we would go there by bus. The core was George and me, her star pupil Helen and Teri, the golden girl George fancied in the year below. Sometimes Johnny Myles, Fiddler Tom and a couple of the Boss's fifth year girls were there. Our future guitarist Eric Plectrum was later adopted.

The Boss would cook, and we were always hungry. Helen and Teri, some parlay over, would be laying the table as we came in off the bus and set down our instruments and records. The Boss provided wine, Martini, sweet sticky liqueurs. We would bring chocolates, cake, some cans.

It would seem odd now, even ill-advised, to have senior pupils along for such freewheeling evenings. Shades of Miss Jean Brodie, without the fascism. One night the Boss let slip there had been a fiancé who died in the war. Her normally cheery face stopped moving for a few seconds; then she went on to a yarn about a haunted glen and never spoke of him again.

We needed and valued her, and she gave us so much. She listened to us talk for hours about ourselves, our hopes, problems, confusions, latest enthusiasms. She acted as interpreter between boys and girls, trying to explain each to the other. She was a teacher of emotional etiquette.

She could take the huff, as suddenly and bafflingly as any teenage girl, if one of us had overlooked her birthday, or thoughtlessly treated another of her brood. Her face would harden, she would be too busy to give us time at school, invitations to her evenings were withdrawn. Eventually a message would come through one of her girls, saying what needed to be done – an apology, an explanation, a card, a poem – before we were favoured again.

But for the most part she dispensed warmth, laughter and stories, along with drinks then food. She was very much of the Gaeltacht, and our evenings were ceilidh-flavoured.

On arrival there would be a drink and general talk. Feet up, music on – Leonard Cohen, Moody Blues, Beatles and the String Band, alternating with Scottish dance music and *South Pacific*. Then food was ready and we were directed into action. Build up the fire. Heat the plates. Open that bottle. Put down that guitar. Let's hear the record you've brought.

Most of us came from stable, affectionate, if uncommunicative families – Teri and Eric Plectrum were more troubled souls – but the Boss's evenings gave us room to open up, to be heard, advised and guided.

After the meal came the crux of the evening. The kitchen was down a short corridor and a step. She would nominate the dishwashers, and I can see now they were not randomly selected. The two in the kitchen had twenty minutes to sort out whatever needed to be resolved, and another Boss-led discussion would be going on in the sitting room. It might be an intense therapy session or a stream of stories, or songs and poems, or a telling-off.

When the two people came back from the kitchen, friendship sorted, or newly holding hands, or silent and chastened, it was time to 'take a walk'. The Boss would stay behind, sipping Drambuie or having a one-to-one, while we, full of food and pleasantly fuzzy with drink, would go off into the charged night.

Did we decide who was walking together, or did the Boss orchestrate it? How much was prearranged in discussion with her favoured girls? One night that November I found myself walking with the Boss's protégée Helen through misty streets down towards the sea. I liked Helen, appreciated her help in typing poems and with the temperamental copying machine. She was bonnie, self-contained, with calm, wide-set eyes. We were friendly if not friends.

Middle-class Lundin Links became the more louche Lower Largo, birthplace of Alexander Selkirk, the real-life model for Defoe's *Robinson Crusoe*. By the fuzzed light of the sodium streetlamp, we gazed up at the statue of the goatskin-clad castaway gazing out to sea for release from his solitude. Something made it possible to take her gloved hand.

We followed the sound of water down to the harbour. Behind us soared a railway viaduct, in front the sea slopped against the pier. The mist, the angles and the streetlamps made it seem the set for a play. Unsure what to do next, we went into the Crusoe Hotel.

No one challenged our age. I put my glasses on to order our drinks, then slipped them off again (most of the time I was with a girl I was half-blind, which now seems apt). We sat at a corner table with a pint of lager and a Sweetheart Stout. We glanced at each other, then away. As she spoke about her plans for the future – she was bright, and clearly had ambitions – I found myself watching her moving lips. I haivered about writing poems and songs, maybe becoming a lighthouse keeper.

We exited, buttoning our coats against the haar. This time she had no gloves on and her hand was chill, smooth and damp. We stopped under a street lamp and faced each other. She didn't seem to be indicating Yes or No, so I took a chance and kissed her.

How different each mouth is! Her lips were mist-damp, cool, faintly salty. Tongues did not come into it.

We separated, tried again, then looked at each other and sort of smiled. It wasn't revelatory like in films. No bells or soaring music, just the soft smack of waves on stone and a passing gull maligning the dark. We took hands and walked back to the Boss's house. George and Teri the golden girl were already back, looking harmonious. Everyone looked at us and drew their conclusions.

The Boss smiled. Drambuie or Cointreau? We were into the last part of the evening. Sweet, lip-sticking liqueurs, head fuzzy and warm, damp jeans roasting from the fire. I took off my shoes, put my feet up on the mantelpiece, accepted the laughter at my unmatched socks and felt utterly at home. As we talked and laughed, sang 'Mhairi's Wedding' and 'Mingulay Boat Song', our lives seemed blessed.

Then the rush for the last bus. We hugged the Boss as we never did our parents. Wave and *Hurry up! Hurry up!* Then the yellow lights of the bus shoogling through the night with two whispering, giggling couples. Teri got off at one stop, then Helen.

George came and sat beside me.

'What a great night!' he enthused. 'So, are you and Helen . . . ?'

'I think so,' I said. 'Maybe.'

Track 10: *Scottish Love and Death in A Minor*

'You might recite a poem at the Burns Supper,' Mr Leslie said.

I hesitated at the classroom door, pleased to be asked but ambivalent about Burns Suppers. It was all a bit hearty, too many kilts.

'I thought perhaps the opening of "Tam O'Shanter", Andrew.'

Burns seemed awfully . . . Scottish. Backward-looking, the tartan world of jolly heather-tramping songs, brilliantined hair and fixed smiles to camera.

'What if I did a song with George Boyter instead?'

Mr Leslie hesitated. A stalwart at the Folk Club, with his good humour, mouthie and bothy ballads, he had already been exposed to Fate & ferret.

'A traditional one?'

'"The Twa Corbies"?'

'That would be grand.'

His hawk is to the hunting gane
His hound tae fetch the wild fowl hame
His lady's ta'en anither mate
So we can mak oor dinner sweet.

As ISB fans we were fervent apostles of joy, positivity and a generally benevolent outlook, but the ruthlessness realism of "The Twa Corbies", its relish in the details of death, betrayal and abandonment, the body taken back into nature to the bitter wind's threnody – in our bones we knew that to be the truth of it.

George had the Corries' version of 'The Twa Corbies'. We associated them with Aran sweaters, but every so often they did something different, and when they did it tended to be good. They had recorded 'October Song' and gave the ISB an early leg-up, so they were okay with us.

'It's only two chords, A minor and D minor,' he enthused. 'Shall we give it a go?'

Our – my – lack of musical ability had showed up when we tried to copy the Corries' version. The song sounded dutiful and plodding. We decided to take it into the back country where it belonged.

We stopped in Crawhill Woods, tuned guitar and mandolin and gave 'The Twa Corbies' a go. The wind pierced our performing gear, the bare trees groaned, the Dreel burn gurgled malevolently, inland gulls squalled overhead as we played. The thin pinging of the mandolin was bleakly out of tune.

We pictured the stalwart Burns Supper audience, and knew we weren't there yet. It needed to be *more weird*.

We followed the Dreel burn on round the bend where big trees fell away to shrub and broken willow. A couple of miles off, Kellie Law rose, bare and yellowed. We cut off across the stubble fields, sliding on the thin mud on top of frozen ground. A couple of hoodie crows tugged at something in a ditch, glared as we went by. Some days our world was charged with portents.

We crossed the farm road, louped the dyke, then up onto the rough pasture of the slopes of the Law. It was much colder up there. We passed colourless dead thistles, a rabbit skull, dried-up bits of gulls. Higher up, the jawbone of a sheep, the teeth yellowed and worn. The snell wind moaned through battered gorse.

'Here?'

'Definitely.'

Hot tea from flasks, scones courtesy of George's mum. Then I placed the sheep jawbone and rabbit skull before us, wrapped my cloak tighter and looked back towards Anster and Pittenweem, the East Neuk tilting off towards Crail and Fifeness. Flat, hard light shifted over the gunmetal Firth of Forth.

It looked like home, the place we'd soon be leaving. We were running out of time. George had applied to Dundee Art College. I was expected to go to Stirling. We reflected that when our bones were dust, the wind would still be blowing up here.

We were ready.

We abandoned notions of audience, structure and rehearsal, and just played. We gave ourselves over to 'The Twa Corbies' for however long it took. When the last notes blew away, we looked at each other.

'That was . . .'

'Amazingly far out!'

It was the first time we'd truly gone out there. Everything else had been copying.

'Lets do it again! Further out!'

We began with a long, harsh, *A-a-a-h!* that began feathery, turned to leather, then to stone. A shrill mandolin announced the melody, then pinches of whistle played one-handed, thudding drumbeats on the body of the guitar with my other fist. The opening verse rose, fell, randomly stuttered, picked up again.

> *As I was walkin all alane*
> *I met twa corbies makin a mane.*

Another verse, sung unison and solo and harmony. Alternating lines, repeating and extending lines. Peewits, curlews and gulls rose and fell above our heads, a few Blackface sheep lay immobile as depressed boulders. A lengthy extemporisation in the middle disintegrated in the wind. Towards the end I chant-spoke, George thrashed the mandolin to a crescendo and together we hoarsely howled,

> *Oer his white banes when they lie bare-o*
> *The wind sall blaw for ever mair-o.*

Pause. Wind-silence, then our ghost-voices echoed,

The winds shall blaw for evermair evermair ever mair.

The mandolin petered out. Last thud of cold knuckles on the guitar, then the wind and gulls repossessed Kellie Law.

We sat for ages in a silence that at first was part of the song, then the frame around it, and then the silence of reflection on what we had just done, and then the silence of the realisation we could never do it like that again.

We packed up and set off home.

In the cellar I cleaned up a cobwebby deer skull and antlers, brushed red household gloss down its cranium. George approved, brought along a thin green candle, stuck it on the top of the skull. We switched off the light and lit the candle.

Getting there.

'We need a fiddler.'

There were no fiddlers in our year. We found one in the class below us: Tommy Drysdale, whose dad owned the electrical shop and sold a few records, mostly K-tel's cheap cover versions.

'I play the violin,' he said. 'It's no the same.'

Tommy was long, thin and stooping, curly-haired, awkwardly blinking from behind big glasses. There was something pent-up about him, like a difficult screw-top bottle that would foam if loosened up.

'It's easy,' George assured him. 'All you have to do is play along behind us.'

'I'll need sheet music.'

I had the same problem with my mother and sister. They could play properly on the piano, but were helpless if you asked them to 'just play along.'

'It's in A minor,' I said. 'The only other chord is D minor.'

'So if you keep playing A and D, and the occasional C, it'll be okay,' George said.

'It's meant to be loose,' I added. 'If it's discordant, that's fine too.'

Tommy hesitated.

'Well . . .'

'Great!'

We enlisted two more pals for the performance. John Myles was popular but quiet, kept his head down, hid behind his fringe. But he said odd, funny and original things, sardonic and heartfelt. He had a good, accurate voice, a pleasing combination of broad Fife and mellow-throatedness.

We explained to John and Roddy what we wanted. They were up for it.

'I'll hae tae practice walking so I dinni fall on my face.'

We dress up in character as Sharpie and Hunch, a corvine-inflected take on our usual performing outfits. A black cloak, a drooping hat with feathers, black fingerless gloves. In my bedroom we swig vodka from the bottle, make ready to get into death, futility and the supernatural.

George and I meet Tommy at the side door into the school. He's wearing a long gold dressing gown, clutching his violin and looking pale.

'I can't do this,' he says. 'It's not on.'

We plead, we beg. He has a stubborn streak that is in danger of setting hard.

'Look, we'll just run through it once,' I suggest. 'If it doesn't work, you don't have to do it.'

I look at George, he nods, starts strumming A minor.

'Just keep playing A and D.'

We do the short version. To us the fiddle – sorry, violin – sounds great. Like we're a real band. It's ragged, but it should be. We finish, look at each other. We're on in ten minutes.

'That was really good, Tommy.'

'I don't know . . .' He looks dejected, woeful and nervous in his dressing gown and glasses.

'No, look, really,' George says. 'If anything, play looser and . . . weirder. It'll blow their minds.'

Tommy looks at the lino floor, scarred by a generation of Waiders.

'I'll need a go at your vodka.'

We ply him with raw voddy. He gags, passes it back to us. We take a last slug then cross to the temporary huts for our appointment with Burns.

Long tables, most of the fifth and sixth years seated along them, girls in their finery, the haggis dispatched. George feels the room has no atmosphere. It will take a lot to make this work. He concentrates on Kellie Law, holds that feeling.

A genial, witty Immortal Memory is proposed by Mr Leslie. Then the bawdy Toast to the Lassies, the scornful counter-toast to the Lads. Any alcohol has been drunk beforehand. The teachers relax. (In those days theirs was not a burn-out occupation. The good ones were good, others were lazy, eccentric, destructive. There was no management structure beyond the Headie and a secretary. You got what you got. We were fortunate.)

We slip out. Mr Leslie calls for the lights to be switched off. In the cleaning cupboard, John lights the candle on the deer skull. I fold away my glasses.

'Off we go!'

Roddy ceremoniously carries a stool into the near-black. Behind him John bears the deer skull with the flickering candle on its forehead. Behind John file Sharpie and Hunch and the Fiddler. Deer skull formally settled on stool, Sharpie and Hunch stand on either side with guitar and mandolin, the fiddler half-hidden. The candle flickers in the draft. An uneasy giggle, then silence.

The fiddler starts to drone a low A. Then the mandolin attempts rapid vibrato. A mercifully brief but intense randomly harmonised *Aaaah!*

Candle flame in my eyes, swirl of vodka in my head, audience invisible in the dark. I shut my eyes and go back to Kellie Law, the snell wind oozing through dyke and gorse, a body, two birds, a witness . . .

> *O'er his white bones when they lie bare⁄o*
> *The winds shall blaw for evermair⁄o*
> *The winds shall blaw for evermair.*

Still strumming A minor, we turn and stalk out. Last high squeal from the fiddle then we're through the door and stop playing. Stunned or baffled silence from inside.

Then applause, laughter, lights on. We come back in to take a bow, then head out across the playground, giggling, high on adrenalin. Tom the fiddler is flushed, his glasses hang skew-whiff.

'That was great, Tommy!'

'We're recording some new songs – can you come and add some fiddle?'

'It's a violin,' he says. 'Aye, sure!'

Track 11: *The Night Piece*

In a few months we would be ejected from school with its facilities, friendships and built-in audience. If we hadn't achieved enough – plays put on, poems published, songs, paid gigs and recording interest – come October we'd be conveyed into university. Then it would be too late to become who we could be.

Delusional on several counts, but that belief, along with trying to read the baffling demands and moods of Helen and Teri, made for the most intense, crammed, productive and mood-swinging weeks of that final year.

Bonded and emboldened by our Glencoe adventure, we resolved to send a gift package, along with our early songs, to the String Band and Joe Boyd. So we wrote some stories about Mike and Robin, Rose and Likky, taking the piss because that seemed in the spirit. George did sketches of Pan, and mocked up the cover for our first album (still in its early stages). Then we packaged it all up and sent it to the String Band and Joe Boyd.

No time to waste in waiting! In Commercial we poured out song lyrics, poems, stories and scripts. We used the piano and tape machine in the music room, increasingly recruited pals to act, play and record with. Who can play the whistle? That girl from Colinsburgh. We need a flute player! Try Cathy in fifth year. The minister's son can play the organ – get him in!

I sent off letters and scripts to Dennis Potter, John Hopkins, BBC Scotland. A selection tape of our Greatest Hits went to John Peel. Batches of poems went out and were duly returned. We knew no bounds or shame.

What were we after? Not really a career – that would have been banal and too like business. Fortune likewise. Like some ecstatic messianic cult, we believed we were in the last days of the old world, and the new one was rushing towards us like sunshine across a clouded field. What was the point in chasing money? Nor was fame our goal. As for girls, the ones we were with were quite enough, so long as Cherry remained unavailable.

We scarcely articulated what we wanted, but we hoped to make wonderful things.

The Headie agreed to a designated space in the school corridors where anyone could pin up anything creative they wanted others to see. Psychedelic posters for folk clubs, drawings of Pan, satyrs, sunsets. Others put up poems, rave reviews of new albums from Hendrix, the Moody Blues, John Martyn, Leonard Cohen. The mission was to turn each other on, *now.*

I read my hurried tiny scrawl in the one-inch space allotted to each day in my yellowed diary, and squirm, and wonder. A day then is a month now.

> *Sat 1 Feb '69 A hung-up day. Finished 'The Assassination' play, went over poems before sending off, wrote 2 new ones. G. phones, mentions Helen also hung-up. Call her, go and explain all. Meet her parents, she almost commits. Also Teri seen with Kirk! Send off 'Scotsman' piece.*

> *Mon 3 Feb BBC letter of acceptance for 'The Rain Poem of Jarvis Valley'. Too much! Five guineas! Practice with Tommy after school. Finish writing short play 'The Winner' for Jim A. and Vicki. Play piano in dark then write to Barbara Mullen, Dennis Potter and Alun Owen re scripts.*

> *Fri 7 Feb Boss in hospital with stomach ulcer. Re-wrote 'Apollinaire's Song' and experimented playing slide capo. All 13 batches of poems sent off. Chaotic at school with Teri and Helen. What's going on?*

George and I noticed each other's romantic problems. We sympathised, but silently. We never talked about it directly, any more than Mike and Robin discussed life with Rose and Likky (which we assumed to be entirely blissful and problem-free). We knew little of each other outside our collaboration and shared enthusiasms. This did not strike us as strange.

> *11–14 Feb Various Prelims – OK I think. Poems back from Horowitz and the Listener. Bastards. Snow everywhere. Letter from Rose! Amazing 5 pages. The Increds are in London, writing and arranging songs, recording, feeding ducks on a pond! Mike is in love with his psychedelic trousers, Robin is cooking lentils in*

an amazing shirt, and much more. We feel ridiculously high and smoke cinnamon sticks, then arrange 'You Get Brighter'. Frantic French revision.

Sat 15 Feb Poems back from 'Stand'. Merde! Hung up. Wrote 2nd Pan Song which is quite nice. Practice in afternoon. After George leaves, suddenly write 'The Night Piece'. All around later for Increds on Julie Felix – amazing!

'The Night Piece' is my only song from F & f days I still play. It came from an adolescent mood of satiety, fatigue and meaninglessness so duvet-soft and enveloping it felt like peace.

Tues 18 Feb Help Jim set up party, get vodka & cans, stash some. George and the girls come, we listen to Incredibles and play. All warms up considerably, 'Satisfaction' has everyone jumping. Out the pier with H, back to fudge-making behind sofa. She misses last bus, phones her dad. George, Jim and I finish booze stash, listening to Ravi.

Fri 21 Feb Set up Folk Club stage. Helen and Teri come. Do 'Log Cabin', 'Mountain', 'Air', 'All Too Much', 'Everything's fine' then 'You get brighter' and 'Painting Box' all together. Fab, but pass by Helen (specs off). Feel somewhat hung-up.

Things said and things not said, things done or things not done – all could get us into trouble.

Did these girls want more attention, or less? More kissing and canoodling, or less? They wouldn't say. We were supposed to know, but we were pinning the tail on a shape-shifting donkey, blindfold, in the dark.

Sat 22 Feb Send 'Inexplicable Events' to STV. Play 'Night Piece' with Fiddler, almost get it right. Go see Helen whose parents are out — lager, Josh White, Revolver. Explain. A very gentle relaxed fudging. Home to Thurber & Runyon.

Thus 27 Feb Went to 'Dr Zhivago' with Helen. Sat at back, without specs so we could snog. Saw lots of white — snow, I think. It sounded good.

Sun 2 March We play St Andrews folk club with Fiddler, H and T come. Go on at 9.25. Very funny indeed. Out to Sands with Helen, come back to warm smoky bar, harmonica player and Fiddler Tom going great guns.

George recalls the St Andrews gig as a disaster. Apparently we couldn't get in tune, played badly and forgot the words. Out of our comfort zone at the school folk club, our lack of experience was cruelly exposed. He resolved this must not happen again.

Was I unable to admit, even to my diary, the depth of my disappointment? Or was I so limited a musician I didn't realise how poor we had been?

Fri 14 March Very frenzied day. First 'Winner' rehearsal. We do our own songs at FC — Night Song, Moving Out, Night Piece, Jarvis Blues!

Sat 15 March Record in morn. Helen comes to Crail party and very nice too. Dance, drinks, then prolonged fudging behind sofa.

Mon 17 March Rehearse plays. Helen distant — overexposure?

Sat 22 March George ill, can't come to Boss's. Pity. Bit nervous what with Helen. Teri on bus — had won hockey, in good mood. H. looking great — new clothes. Great meal. Whisky, cider, Boss telling stories. Things seem OK with Helen though v. confused.

Wed 26 March Last ever rugby match (we lost). Send article to 'Scottish Field'. 'Assassination' better on second perf (ta, Mr Leslie!). Afterwards H and I talk and let each other go. Pack for London.

Only now does something emerge from the cave of the past like a half-mad hermit scratching his matted hair: Helen and I were probably never a couple in the first place.

I never asked if we were. She'd never said one way or another. Our time together amounted to several one-off evenings at the Boss's, the Elie disco, the St Andrews gig, a few parties, and going to see (or not see) *Doctor Zhivago*. How had she thought of us? No idea. What did she think I thought? Clueless.

The joke is I'd been 'hung-up' when I heard she'd been seen with someone else, when not only were we not really a couple, I was never passionate about the whole thing anyway. I just liked her and she was there. It was nice having lips to kiss, even if that kiss wasn't revelatory. It was exciting and memorable having a breast under one's palm (neither ejected nor encouraged, scarcely acknowledged by either), though it did not set off the 'Hallelujah Chorus'.

She was trying out elsewhere? Well, of course. I would have done the same. She may have wanted more time and commitment, though it's as likely she wanted less. But there were a couple of times I glimpsed that she was someone else, a world in herself, and that simple, extraordinary lesson was worth the painful learning.

Sitting in the shed with the diaries and winter's first light, 'The Night Piece' in my head, I feel an antique sense of loss, of something done poorly or not done at all, loosen its grip and vanish like a ghost at dawn.

> *And as I move closer*
> *To you on the floor*
> *I'm thinking that maybe*
> *We weren't made for more. ('Night Piece')*

Except we are.

Track 12: *Fish Lorry to Fame and Fortune*

A long phone call with George in London. It doesn't happen often, and we wonder why not. Each of us is the only other person who really shared this stuff that still matters to us. Busyness is why not. As our days to come get fewer, they go quicker. It seems unjust.

Then George's voice becomes more urgent and more nasally Pittenweem, like a burn compressed through the narrows.

'I've recently come to the conclusion I'm an atheist. I know all this and ourselves will disappear, completely and for ever.'

'Uh-huh,' I say, press the phone harder to my ear.

'Which means the ridiculousness and pointlessness of everything. Going to pick up the kids or get the potatoes peeled, and even all those songs we wrote – it all counts for nothing.'

I nod. Been there. Am I still there? Not quite.

I suggest to him the world, our lives, are not so much meaningless as have no given meaning. Meaning is something we make, otherwise we feel crap. But it's *our* meaning, not the world's. Maybe that's our job, the task of matter that has become aware of itself and creates meaning. Maybe that's what everything has been heading towards since the Big Bang. How should I know?

Silence at the other end in Great Missenden, where the light is starting to go.

'Remember when catching the fish lorry to London was everything?' George says. He sounds like a man grabbing a coal off the hearth rug. 'The world seemed to depend on it.'

Yes, I do remember.

James Fleming – *Jeek Fleeming* – owned the scampi factory off the Crail Road. He ran a daily lorry to London. '*Dinna be late. The driver will no wait for ye.*'

My diary says it was early Monday 31 March '69 when George materialised out of the salty dark. We had our Glencoe rucksacks, guitars, a little money, the scrawled address for Joe Boyd's Witch-season office, and a hard-won five-inch reel-to-reel demo of our first album *Tree Leaves*.

The driver flipped one of those truck-driver knots, got it over the metal peg, tugged hard and tied it off. Brylcreemed hair and sideburns, old suit jacket, battered winklepickers: Big Jim.

'You the boys for London?'

'Yes!' we chorused.

'Weel, hop in then.'

Tree Leaves by Fate & ferret

Side 1

    Moving Out (A)

    Mountain Song (G)

    Heads (G)

    Nab (A)

    Apollinaire's Song (A)

    Night Song (A)

    Fudge-Making Song (A)

    Balance & Turnover (G)

Side 2

    Green Gedde (A)

    Pan Song (G)

    The Porter (G)

    Discovery of Honey (G)

    The Original Jarvis Blues (A)

    Patterns (G)

    Easy/Go Slow Times (A)

    The Night Piece (A)

Of course the whole album wasn't on the tape. Some track-songs were largely aspirational. 'Odyssey' was a poem as yet without chords or melody. What on earth were 'Nab' and 'Heads'? 'Patterns' has completely unravelled.

We saw *Tree Leaves* as a calling card, then we'd hit Joe with the second album, already underway. We thought – rather too grand a word for our mental processes – that if you had some good songs, an album would result, as though the music business were another public service, like water, electricity and the Post Office. (The clue is in the word *business*).

The underpowered lorry shoogled and belched to some pick-up on the outskirts of Glasgow, then eventually ground on towards Carlisle. Another lengthy pick-up, then we laboured over Shap. It was cold in the cab, our feet became numb, but Big Jim told his stories, smoked Woodbine, and though the trip was wearisome, we were heading for our destiny.

A changeover truck stop somewhere in the night. We stumbled into a warm fug of tea and smoke, drivers with comfortable bellies hunched over pint mugs of tea. Piles of white bread along with fish and chips, tomato-shaped squeezy plastic bottles. Jim knew people, we joined a table of laughter and stories and cigarettes, stuffed ourselves and swilled away the grease with scalding tea.

Our new driver, Billy, was like Jim, but quieter and smoked Benson & Hedges, which we thought really flash. The cab handle imprinted itself into my side. The choice was smoky fug or window down and cold.

'Teri says you and Helen have split . . .' George murmured somewhere south of Scotch Corner.

'Yeah, seems thataway.'

The pause was so long I thought he'd gone back to sleep.

'You might get a song from it.'

'I hope to fill the second side of our next album with my plaintive cries.'

'It's all yours,' he said, then fell asleep.

I stared at Billy's stubbly profile in the green dashboard lights, thinking truck driver thoughts or perhaps nothing at all. He lit another cigarette and drew red arcs across the dark as he steered us through the night.

Mock-Tudor mansions then estates then council houses, then the river, glimpse of St Paul's. It was awesome and a little frightening. London was even bigger and dirtier than Dundee.

Billingsgate. Stiff as polystyrene we creaked down from the high cab. Knots untied, we helped drag back the big tarpaulin. Melted fishy ice streamed out over our jackets. Porters, crates, shouting, coughing, smoking. Laughter. Incomprehensible speech.

Ever polite, we thanked Billy. He scrawled down the place and time to pick up our return trip in four days, and George and I found a café where we could drop our rucksacks and guitars, get warm and eat egg and chips until it was light.

The Witchseason office in Charlotte Street was still locked at 9 a.m. Still locked at 10 a.m. It seemed the music scene did not operate normal office hours. We went across the road to a café toilet to change into halfway performing gear – I picture a paisley-patterned pyjama top, my dad's green silk scarf with dragons casually knotted round my throat, brown-and-gold reversible waistcoat, normalised by a corduroy jacket, jeans, my grandfather's sturdy brown shoes.

We saw two people go into Witchseason. Looked at each other, took a deep breath. We believed this meeting could change our lives.

Stranger things had been happening recently – 'All You Need Is Love' sung live on the world's first global broadcast while Vietnam peace talks began, *Apollo 10* orbiting, our teachers getting into Leonard Cohen, Pan running wild in Glencoe, five guineas for just one poem.

We picked up our sacks and guitars and pushed in.

The Witchseason office was not notably psychedelic, just a desk and a phone, and a dark-haired young woman sitting behind it. A few assorted seats, a couple of framed posters, others just pinned to the wall. Boxes, papers and some loose records. It did not look like the epicentre of hip London: the ISB and Fairport Convention, Pink Floyd and the UFO Club.

'We're Fate & ferret from Pittenweem. We've brought our tape for Joe.'

'You can leave it with me.'

George and I looked at each other. There were quite a few tapes of different sizes already on her desk. More piled up against the wall, some on the floor. The phone rang. As she talked on it, we conferred and decided to press our case.

'Joe asked us to see him when we brought our tape,' we claimed.

She glanced at the door to her left. 'He's with someone. Just leave the tape, or come back later.'

'We'll wait, if that's cool.'

We waited. A tall man in a dark jacket appeared silently from the street, glanced at us once – something vivid in that look – then studied the floor.

'Just go in, Nick – Joe's expecting you.'

The long black hair and averted face nodded and shuffled through to the inner sanctum. George and I looked at each other, shrugged.*
Five minutes later he emerged, raised his head fractionally to glance at us, then scuttled out.

We waited some more. Then an entrance as forceful as Nick Drake's had been near-invisible – very tall, her pale face all cheek-bones and long jaw, hungry-eyed and lean in black roll-neck sweater, black trousers. She had the longest black hair I'd ever seen, down to her hips. Morticia.

We had last seen her backstage at the ABC. From an aside in *Melody Maker* we had learned she was musicians' friend and Joe's right hand, Anthea Joseph.

She dropped her bags, greeted the receptionist, turned to us.

'So who are you boys?'

We reminded her about the Edinburgh concert, the address she had given us, the drawings, stories and poems we'd sent the String Band, the tape we had for Joe. We told her about Fate & ferret, Pittenweem and the importance of the lower case and the ampersand.

'Like e e cummings,' she said.

An ally! She made us coffee in a cafetière, something we'd never seen before. We talked about books and poets, Greek myths (Apollo, Pan), and moved on to the Regency bodice-rippers of Georgette Heyer, for whom Anthea had an unlikely passion.

'You must go to university!' she insisted. 'I never did.'

---

* Nick Drake, at that time recording his first album *Five Leaves Left* with Joe. Probably the most enduring cult among Joe's artists, due to the unarguable beauty of his recordings and early death. Sold very little at the time, and he seldom played in public due to acute shyness. No film of him remains, only the songs.

I thought she seemed a very good advert for not going to university. In time I would realise she always felt undereducated, especially in comparison to her parents, notable left-wing journalists from the Soho–Fitzrovia world. She'd grown up next door to the Freuds, said Clement had been a bit creepy – some incident in a tree – Lucian nasty but fun, the other brother Stephen everyone forgot, he was nice.

She produced biscuits and we wolfed them happily. We smelled of scampi and our feet ached, but any moment our lives could change. Perhaps they were changing now, while Anthea told us about being left alone by her mother to have afternoon tea with Tom Eliot in Aldeburgh, and how he had entertained her with children's poems, demonstrating cat's cradle, and tying false knots that pulled out to nothing.

She said he was *charming* and *great fun* – possibly the only person to have said that about T. S. Eliot. Yet it fits with his love of chocolate and musical hall, and *Old Possum's Book of Practical Cats*, and his struggles to play the mandolin. Like other hypersensitive people, Nick Drake, for instance he could relax with a child who expected nothing of him.

Then we were called in to see Joe Boyd. I got fair hair, longish and side-parted, a level, educated American voice. He was long and lean, unhurried, clean-shaven, *cool*. Engaged in a detached way. A natural onlooker, I thought, as we chatted and he assessed us, yet one who made things happen. Which is about right for being a record producer and manager.

'So, what have you got?'

He swung long legs up onto his desk and listened silently as we spread out our wares – the Pan drawings, poems, ISB stories, lyrics, the miniature LP sleeve George had mocked up. Then we put our tape on his desk.

He picked it up. Squinted at it.

'I don't know if I can play anything this slow,' he said.

He put it aside, on a pile of many other larger and grander tapes. He flicked through some of our writings, chuckled once. We waited. The warmth in Joe's office was releasing a distinct whiff of shellfish.

'Can I hang on to these?'

'Yeah sure, Joe. Far out.'

He shifted his boots off the desk.

'Come back tomorrow afternoon. I'll try to listen by then.'

He seemed very senior to us, but I know now he was just twenty-seven, near ages with the artists he was recording. They were all making it up as they went along.

Back in the outer office, Anthea was talking to a trio of waistcoats and furry jackets.

'This is Tim and Tim and Ivan. They're Dr Strangely Strange. This is Fate & ferret from Pittenweem.'

They did not look much older than us, but more authentically bohemian. Both Tims were Irish, Ivan was English, but they all lived in Dublin. They were chirpy, friendly and openly excited about their first LP. George and I looked at the cover. Three guys and a girl in weird clothes, one wearing a bird-beak mask, sitting on rocks in a mountain pool with assorted instruments.

We could do that.

We went to a pub and had a Guinness with the Strangelies. Mike and Robin appeared extraterrestrial, but these lads were clearly pals who laughed and took the piss out of each other. They had no side, were fun and easy to be with.

They seemed in no hurry and would carry on drinking, but George and I were short of money and had places to go. So we said we might see them at the Drury Lane Arts Lab that evening for a full-length version of *Magical Mystery Tour*, and hit the streets again.

Once back in Fife, we would buy their record, *Kip of the Serenes*, full of digressions and whims. We liked the humour of it, especially the song 'Strangely Strange but Oddly Normal' and 'Donnybrook Fair'. The effect was charming, stoned and cheering.

The vocals were uncertain. In fact they sounded like us, only better. This was encouraging. Give us a studio, we felt, some support and overdubbing and a bit of reverb on our voices, and we would sound like we did in our heads.

You could fairly call this delusional. But it's delusional in the way of two kids kicking a tennis ball against a wall, imagining the cup final, or the child scribbling stories in a school jotter, dreaming of being a Lady Writer like Enid Blyton, with three children. It's a fair bet that anyone who has actually played in a cup final once had the fantasy of doing just that: it's what kept them playing and training and playing, putting in their 10,000 hours. And the girl with her secret stories and her fierce, unrealistic desire? Her first eight novels raised her three children, then we met and we married, and she's still at it.

So I understand the necessity of dreams and delusions. Then again, most *are* delusions. Very few ever play football at the top level, very few write novels for a living, and Fate & ferret would never actually make any of their four albums.

Not getting what you once dreamed of is the story of most lives. What you *do* get is your actual life – which, looked at closely, may turn out to be what it is because of the manner in which your hopes, ideals and delusions did not come to pass.

At the end of Greek Street, George grabbed my arm. He pointed at a longhair in a donkey jacket, carrying a guitar case, coming our way.

'Hey, that's John Martyn!'

George had been playing Martyn's recent LP, *The Tumbler*. Great voice, astounding guitarist. Girls we knew liked him because he looked romantic, all dark curly hair and beard, yearning eyes with a hint of Lucifer.

George darted across the road to greet him. Surprised, I followed. Turned out he was our gym teacher's nephew – his real name the less romantic Iain McGeachy – and thus our schoolmate Kirk McGeachy's cousin. John/Iain had had the happiest times of his childhood visiting his relatives in Anstruther, and he and George had already met through Kirk.

We stood on the pavements grey, talking Fife. We talked about the fish and chip shop in Pittenweem, the foghorns, the summer haar and storms smashing over the pier. I had not realised how much Fife meant to me till I was away from it.

We began talking rugby, which was painful in a different way. John had been a keen rugby player at school – in the backs, judging by his build – and his face glowed as we talked about the recent brilliant defeat of France in Paris that raised hopes this would finally be our year. We set down our guitars so we could wave our arms, reliving the exploits of Laidlaw and Telfer, miming the charges of Alastair McHarg.

(Then, of course, the inevitable defeat to Wales, then to Ireland, scoring no points. Then we cruelly lost to England through two David Duckham tries. I'd watched the match on TV with my dad, the one time we could unselfconsciously be together.

Such was the cultural bond between three scruffy Scotsmen on the pavement in Greek Street – we knew triumph was an imposter, but suspected disaster was the real deal.)

'What are you guys doing here?'

We told him about F & f, our songs, our tape for Joe Boyd. He enthused about Joe, said he hoped to do the next album with him. (He would, the groundbreaking *Stormbringer.*)

Then he said he was playing at Les Cousins tomorrow night. Would we like to do a spot before him? Half an hour or so?

'Aye, sure.'

'Cool.'

We did not shake hands. That was for Americans and French people, or our parents' generation at funerals. We nodded, smiled, went our ways.

'Les Cousins – outta sight!'

'Wonder if we'll get paid.'

'I think I'm getting a cold.'

'I've got a sore throat too.'

We found a quiet corner of a park. Kensington, I think. All those Londons run together into hard pavements, heavy loads and resting sore feet in a park, then back lugging rucksack and guitar on the Underground, smelling of sweat and fish, running on excitement, exhaustion and hope, then sudden yearning to be home among familiar voices and proper beer, far from Watney's Red Barrel.

Cross-legged on the grass, we got the guitars out and tuned up. We agreed on two ISB covers, recently learned from the *Night Ride*. But which of our own songs? Because of the String Band and Joe, we had inadvertently become a recording band, with little gigging experience. What had worked on Kellie Law, or in front of our pals at the school Folk Club, seemed feeble in London.

And our head colds were coming on apace. Still, Les Cousins! Our first London performance!

That evening we were at the Drury Lane Arts Lab for a showing of the full-length version of the Beatles' *Magical Mystery Tour*. We had watched the TV version at my house on Boxing Day '67. It was a relief when my mother and father gave up and left the room without comment. We loved 'I Am the Walrus' and 'Fool on the Hill', but the rest of it was rather . . . silly.

Were the Beatles taking the piss? Were they all drunk, or on the drugs we were increasingly curious about? Of course we had to say it was great. But in our hearts we knew it wasn't.

Still, this was the full-length version. Maybe there'd be extra scenes that made sense of it, some amazing new songs or druggie stuff or nudity, things they'd had to cut out for the straights?

In a dim, cavernous yet stuffy space, many people were seated but more were slumped or lying against the walls. Some seemed asleep, a few wandered around talking to themselves. The air was thick and earthy-sweet.

The big difference from TV was the sound. It was LOUD, roaring from multiple speakers. Not having been to a rock concert before, I found it enthralling and a bit painful. 'I Am the Walrus' was mind-blowing. Even the most horizontally-inclined stirred themselves as the bass bludgeoned our guts and Lennon's papery voice delivered outrage, frustration, boredom transmuted into ecstasy, nonsense made sublime.

For the duration of that song it seemed true, that whole sixties thing: we were indeed all together, elevating through the fade-out as though rising to a higher plane somewhere beyond the police siren.

We finally exited into the night, ears ringing, guts churning from the monstrous sound-massage.

'Wow!'

'It, like, blew my mind!'

We had neglected to arrange anywhere to sleep the night. We had no crash pad, no hostel and very little money. We had come down here trusting to luck. Apparently our neocortices, so backward in Glencoe, still weren't fully developed.

We set off into the night to find the Golden Egg restaurant, where it was rumoured one could sit all night so long as you bought a coffee every hour.

Come morning, we groggily left the Golden Egg and returned to Witchseason. Anthea made us coffee and suggested we might want a wash. We brushed our teeth and changed our socks, then sat slumped like left luggage as she told us stories about Bobby.

Running the Troubadour in 1962, Anthea recognises a skinny kid in cowboy boots from the cover of his obscure first album. She says he can come in free if he plays for them the next night. Five quid, he got.

She said Bobby soaked up everything he heard, talked a blue streak when he was high. In those days he was funny and sweet and women wanted to look after him. He'd phone in the middle of the night:

Anthea, can you come and get me?

Where are you, Bobby?

Think I'm in a phone box.

Yes, but which phone box, where?

Gee, I don't know.

Well, if you look near the top of the box where you put your money in, it will give the address.

Pause. *Ain't no light in here.*

Have you got matches, Bobby?

Yeah, I guess.

If you light one, you'll be able to read the address.

Yeah, great idea, Anthea. Pause. *Giggle. My match keeps blowing out.*

Have you tried closing the door, Bobby?

Long pause. *I can't find the door.*

Joe arrived and took us into his office. He had set up an old tape recorder on the desk, opened our tape box and expertly threaded the tape onto the reel. We sat opposite him. He pressed *play*. A high-pitched gabble of chipmunk voices. *Catch me tomorrow and I'm called Big John*. He stopped it, rewound, silently adjusted the speed to the slowest setting in the world. Pressed *play*.

We'd had one wee plastic mic and no reverb. All single-track, without overdubs. To change instrumentation, we would pause the tape, pick up the mandolin or whatever, undo the pause, then hastily resume playing.

Joe put his boots up on the desk, gazed impassively out the window as the tape slurred and moaned through 'Mountain Song', 'Night Song', 'Balance & Turnover', 'The Night Piece'.

The fabulous bubbles we'd blown in Pittenweem burst in Joe's Soho office, leaving only soapy scum. My voice was often flat, the whistle was painfully sharp, the spontaneous *Aaahh* in the Robin Williamson manner was buttock-clenchingly inept. Our music made Dr Strangely Strange sound coherent.

George and I sat there as the evidence against us played on. We wanted to flee or to explain that these were just sketches of what the songs could be, should be, and that we had nearly an album's worth of new and better songs. You had to use imagination, a whole lot of imagination.

Eventually Joe swung his long legs off the desk and pressed *stop*.

'I kinda like the funny one,' he said at last.

Which one was that? One of the Pan songs? The fudge-making one?

Joe looked at us, sighed.

'I'm going for breakfast,' he said. 'Would you like some?'

I bless Joe Boyd for that breakfast in Mrs B's Pantry, for we were faint with hunger and lack of sleep. We wolfed the full English while Joe drank orange juice then coffee, had a cigarette and read the morning papers. Considering what he had been subjected to, he was very kind.

Perhaps he thought: *These boys are seventeen, they may someday produce the goods. Miracles happen.* Perhaps he saw something in the daft stories and sketches and the guileless fervour we had brought from Fife. Or perhaps it was just decency and the times.

On the pavement we talked about the next tape we would send, told him we were going to play Les Cousins that evening. He seemed mildly surprised.

'Well, good luck,' he said, and went back into Witchseason.

Time to go call on Robin Williamson. We had got his address from Anthea, and had a copy of the tape and some poems to give him. Doubtless he would be pleased to see us.

He seemed to be, in a slightly startled, cosmic way.

'Come in, man. I'm just making cakes.'

It was just a flat, quite bare. A good smell was coming from the oven. He made a pot of tea, didn't have any milk or sugar, had trouble locating mugs.

We sat on a bed, Robin pumping on a harmonium. George and I told him about our upcoming Cousins gig, enthused about 'Won't You Come See Me', which we intended to play there.

Robin looked pleased, but baffled.

'I don't really remember that one,' he said.

If we had written that one song – any one of Robin's songs – we would retire happily, feeling our work on earth done. And he couldn't remember it! Far out!

We took out our guitars.

'It starts on G7,' George said. 'Then it goes to D. Then the "Won't you come see me" chorus is in C.'

So we started playing it, at once self-conscious and immensely excited. He began joining in on the harmonium, and we sang it to the end.

'I remember it now,' Robin said. 'I wrote it when Likky and I weren't very together, and she doesn't like me playing it now, so we don't.'

'Wow,' we said, astounded on two counts.

He seemed a bit constrained. There was the odd sound from the room next door, a thump, a squeak of song. Robin got up and left. Low voices through the wall.

Robin came back in. We had a wee play at Mike's 'Air'. We would happily have stayed all afternoon, but he said 'Man – the cakes!' and hurried to the kitchen, found oven gloves and eased out a tray of rather lumpy and irregular little brown cakey things.

We stared down at them. They weren't so very burnt. A high, thin call from through the wall. It was time for us to leave.

On the pavement, George and I looked at each other.

'He put on oven gloves!'

'He burnt the cakes!'

'He couldn't remember the words!'

'It, like, blew my mind!' we chorused.

We went off to find a park to lie down in, still grappling with the revelation that Robin Williamson ever had to do something as mundane as cook or have trouble with girlfriends.

We sat in the little changing room at the back of Les Cousins, watching John Martyn glue on his fingernails. A lot of acoustic guitar players used fingerpicks to make the guitar ring louder, but his technique was so demanding he used glue-on nails, carefully trimmed to size.

He was sober, absorbed. We chatted about Joe ('a cool guy, great ears'), the String Band, Pittenweem. His girlfriend Beverley – a noted singer in her own right – came in, curly-haired, lively and friendly. We left them to it, went to the shadows at the back of the room to tune up.

It was early and not busy. A few dozen heads at most, draped by the bar or curled up in dim corners with a drink, smoking and mur-muring. Our colds had come on fast, with explosive sneezes, blocked sinuses and tightness in the chest. We'd bought a bottle of Benylin in the chemist, and drunk most of it, so we were feeling strange.

A short introduction, then we were on. We muttered something about who we were, apologised for our colds, and launched into the String Band's 'All too Much for Me'.

We sang through our Benylin haze, received a languid spatter of applause. Went onto the next number. I had backed out of doing any of my own songs except 'Night Piece', which we played at dirge pace, missing the violin.

I stood at the back as George did a solo of 'The Porter', a nifty piece of picking in open tuning. George was hoping that John

Martyn was still in the dressing room, for he knew the song was a blatant imitation of one of John's. I thought it sounded good. I could see he was nervous, but he played well.

We finished with 'Won't You Come See Me', then we were done, our London premiere performance (and our last). Slightly more applause, perhaps relieved the warm-up act was done. The place filled up when John Martyn began. We sat up against the wall and watched, listened and learned.

He was beautiful and young then – just three years older than us – with luminous dark eyes, red mouth, thick curly hair, and he played, my God, he played guitar in an original way.

We noted open tunings, effects pedals, tumblings and clusterings of chords. It was folk, jazz, blues, further morphed by an Echoplex. Instrumentally alone it would have been remarkable, but these were songs and his voice was fluent, tender and fearless. He slurred like honey uncurling from the spoon.

'I'm so glad we didn't go on after him,' George murmured.

In the changing room we watched John carefully strip off the plastic nails. He swept them into his hand and dropped them in a bucket. Someone passed him a bottle of wine and he necked it down. The room was crowded yet he seemed alone and inward now his work was done.

We had a bit of a chat with Beverley, said cheerio to the man who was trying to ride the twin horses of being John Martyn and Iain McGeachy. It was late, too late to take the Tube out to my sister's in High Barnet. Once again, our frontal cortices had failed to light up and plan where we were going to sleep that night.

As we stood dithering on the pavement, a youth approached us. He was skinny and tall, very long-haired and Glaswegian. Though East Coasters ourselves, when in London, Glasgow was near enough.

'Where did you get thae String Band songs?' he asked. 'I havni heard them.'

'Off John Peel's *Night Ride*,' we said.

'Far out, man.'

We told him about playing 'Won't You Come See Me' with Robin. He said he played guitar and sitar and acted, wanted to be a singer-songwriter. We liked him straight off. When he discovered we had nowhere to stay, he said we could crash at his.

We said *Yeah cool* and set off with him into the London night.

The flat was bare, but it had a floor. We sat up talking String Band, played a few songs together. He looked in the fridge and cupboards then cooked us what he had: porridge oats, salt and some golden syrup.

I think of that night as the essence of the sixties, when people with very little put up strangers on the basis of shared musical interests. It was all he had and it tasted great, though it could have done with some milk.

In the morning, more porridge, then we were on our way. Our host wrote his address on a scrap of paper, and handed it to George.

'If you lose that, I'm the only Allan J. Tall in the Glasgow phone book.'*

* In 2010, I found him on his website: still in Glasgow, he has spent his life as an actor, musician, director. When I contacted him, he replied to say he remembered that night and Fate & ferret. He'd read some of my books without making the connection. When we met up, I had the great pleasure of buying him lunch.

There was just time to return to Witchseason to let Joe know about the New Direction we were contemplating, and talk about our Second Album. He wasn't there – still recovering from an all-nighter at Sound Techniques. So we drank the coffees and wolfed the biscuits. The Strangelies showed up again and felt like old friends.

Anthea told her stories, about a very young Paul Simon ('in-turned but very polite') in England 1962, picking up songs and guitar techniques. She said Robin Williamson had been a really fine singer of traditional folk, while his pal Bert Jansch couldn't get a London gig on account of not being folk enough.

Above all, she talked about Fairport Convention. She emphasised – Anthea was always emphatic – we had to get the new album. Sandy Denny had a fabulous new song 'Who Knows Where the Time Goes?' The band was shifting towards a new interest in folk but with rock influences. They were fun and developing fast.

What we loved about Anthea was not so much her stories and name-dropping – she was entitled to drop them – but her lasting passion for music. ('The only human being in London CBS Records in the eighties,' Bruce Findlay – another lifelong ISB fan who also loved music from within the business – emailed me the other week.) Her pleasure and instinct was to look after musicians. She knew they were not machines; they were wayward, impulsive and problematic. They were to be treasured, not exploited.

We would happily have stayed for more biscuits and stories, but the scampi lorry waited for no man. We took our tape back, knowing we must do better, wished the Strangelies good luck. We hurried off with rucksacks and guitars to locate our driver at his digs, then get back to home ground to reconsider our future.

The elderly vehicle ground on through darkness lit by cat's eyes and our driver's glowing cigarette tip. George's head rolled on my shoulder. Somewhere in the night, around Scotch Corner, it became clear: to avoid being left behind before we had even arrived, Fate & ferret would have to *Go Electric*.

Track 13: Helping Mrs Monbirth

Time to resurrect an earlier interest in electronics. I ordered transistors, capacitors and diodes, got a soldering iron and built an amplifier – capable of a pulverising three watts. Our classmates Willie and Douglas – recently promoted through the streamed classes on account of outstanding mathematical ability – built us a fuzz box and a speaker cabinet. We attached a car battery with bulldog clips to the amplifier, which lived like a spider in its cardboard box.

It was a faff, this going electric. In Dundee we forked out for pick-ups, phono sockets and connecting leads for our acoustic guitars. We connected it all up in George's bedroom. The room hummed and squealed.

Then we strummed. It was LOUD. Coarse and painful, but LOUD. Was this what we wanted? We tried singing a few of our standards, then realised we would need a microphone to hear ourselves. And a stand to hold the microphone. Was there no end to this?

Still, we set about our second album, *Helping Mrs Monbirth*. Nothing of the title song remains beyond the opening line *Helping Mrs Monbirth in a two-birth world*, given to me on waking one morning. I have no idea what I meant, but it sounds promising.

Up to this point, George and I had missed out on the blues, only faintly aware that it underpinned most of the bands we loved. The blues puzzled us. Why keep singing about being unhappy? What was the point in that?

George borrowed a John Mayall LP. We listened reverently, then thoughtfully, and finally burst out laughing. It was so relentlessly, hilariously *down*. In the cover photo Mayall looked washed-out, drab in denim, longhaired but not in a psychedelic, joyous way. It seemed to be always raining in his world. Well, it rained a lot in our world too, but my new 'Rain Song' was not a blues:

> *Knock upon my door and then upon my windowpane*
> *I have long been expecting you, brother rain.*

If the rain so got on your nerves, why not move to Morocco or Greece, hang out with Pan and Apollo?

Even when electric, the Incredible String Band did not play the blues. We valued their songs as *anti-blues*, the musical equivalent of what our dads put in their radiators when winter came.

I think this sense of slightly forced conversion, our resentment at the hassle and expense of it all, gave a piss-taking edge to 'Pooby Blues', 'Electric Men', 'No Scratch Blues' and George's 'Unboltin' the Blues', which adorned the next album we started putting together for Joe to consider.

At that party we will have a ball
For Korner and Mayall tears will fall
We're all together and we're gonna start
Throwing our blues away . . .

George came into school on Monday, sleep-starved, eyes wide and head full of Eric Clapton, Ginger Baker and Jack Bruce. Heavy rock, man! Fifteen-minute drum solos!

After finishing a painting of our Glencoe adventure, with Cream's *Wheels of Fire* still thundering in the background, he had gone on to write a free-association prose poem titled 'HOOF'. An evocation of heavy rock, it took our Anster Town Hall dance nights and pushed them to mythic proportions, with the guitar hero morphing into an ecstatic sacrificial Dionysus as the amps caught fire and the dancing mob fought and the police burst in to find men and women dis int eg ra ti n g . . .

He was as excited about the writing as about the painting, and I thought both were fabulous.

Energised, slightly hysterical, at the end of the school day we set up with Fiddler Tom in my bedroom, the amp in its cardboard box, bongo drums (lacking a full drum kit), two acoustic guitars with their cheap pick-ups. The faithful Grundig recorder was loaded with a new tape, set to *record*.

We looked at each other. We would improvise a thrash, the heaviest thing ever. Not two chords but just *one*. E Major. We wanted the heaviest of the heavy, a *reductio ad absurdum* of rock, our response to the *White Album*'s 'Helter-Skelter', John Mayall, Cream, Deep Purple.

I started thrashing E on my twelve-string. Tommy erupted in bongo frenzy then picked up the violin and made cat-strangled screeches. George's guitar leapt screaming from the cardboard box with a monstrous two notes, over and over, distorted beyond music by feedback, fuzz box and overloading. Overexcited, Tommy began shrieking, jumped to a thunderous bongos outbreak, then back to violin. I began shouting *AAArrgh!* and indecipherable words. After some minutes of bedlam my wrist cramped. I slowed, paused . . . then George, sitting on the end of the bed, took it up again, still on E, thundering down the bass string. Revived, I followed with more E Major thrashing. A fade out . . . then a fade back in, still roaring, shrieking, thrashing . . . collapse.

We lay on the floor, across the bed, unable to breathe for laughter.

Parody, piss-take, enraged catharsis, Dionysiac and God-awful, 'GREAT MEAT THRASH' was probably, along with 'The Twa Corbies', the most authentic thing F & f ever did.*

Predating punk by seven years, it makes the Slits sound coherent, the Sex Pistols seem tasteful. Iggy and the Stooges are sensitive plants in comparison. The Velvet Underground free-forming 'Sister Ray' are sane and structured next to the mighty THRASH. One chord! Tuneless wordless howling! Bongos! Deranged Fiddler!

'GREAT MEAT THRASH' was our revenge on rock, on music itself, for being so far beyond us.

---

* Both proved unrepeatable, which enhanced their mythic status. Like Life itself, they were once and once only. For their duration, we abandoned any ideal of perfection, even of quality. It was strangely liberating.

The plans for building a bass guitar came by post. I went into Technical, traced the body shapes, then the teacher showed me how to use the bandsaw and cut the rough outlines. Then a lot of sanding. This took me back to winters spent building model gliders, another handy outgrown enthusiasm.

The neck was not so difficult, but the fretboard needed precision marking, then cutting grooves. I had failed technical drawing in school, partly because I struggle to draw a straight line with a ruler.

But I pressed on, went back into school in the evenings to glue and screw it all together. Cut out the pit for the pick-up, the groove for the wiring. Fitted the jack plug socket. Cut perspex (tricky) for the fingerboard.

The bridge and the end-nut on the neck are crucial to any stringed instrument. Their placing, height, material, angle are things that take as many years to master as it took Jack Bruce to learn to play bass.

Undeterred, I moved on to more sanding and varnishing. Two holes for the pegs that would take the strap. A lift from my dad over the hill to St Andrews – some talk about my lack of plans for next year, then silence – to the music shop to fork out for tuning pegs and bass guitar strings.

Is foolhardiness necessary, or a waste of energy? Is building a bass guitar that proved impossible to tune, whose strings buzzed against the inaccurate frets above the third, whose neck soon began to twist under the strain, in any way worthwhile? And all those misaimed flirtations, the kiss that establishes only its own pointlessness . . .

Are we right to abandon those projects, or right to press on? Are Fate & ferret a sweet-sad cautionary tale?

What connection, if any, runs between the life we attempt, and the life we get? Between the early objects of our romantic yearning, and our very real spouse?

I sit back from the keyboard in the shed, slightly breathless. The bamboo scrapes and rattles against the window. I am surrounded by books, some my own. A sketch of my long-gone father, a photo of my not-so-long-gone mother. A photo of dear departed Edwin Morgan with writer friends Ron Butlin and Ken McLeod, all squiffily beaming as they raise glasses towards my camera.

On the desk are timelines, a pile of diaries, scanned memorabilia and a photo of a String Band rehearsal outside Temple Cottage. Also, last summer's fishing reel draped in spider webs, a tiny photo of my mother's fiancé who died in the war.

It feels as if I have been moving along a Möbius strip, absorbed in a section marked 'Spring 1968', and then there is a twist and I raise my head in 'March 2015'. So far apart, so conjoined.

I sit back, winded, as anyone might who feels their past move, alive, within them. Something has just shifted, though I don't yet know what.

The bass was soon abandoned as a bass. I refitted it with old guitar strings. As a four-string guitar it was still badly out, but the thin metal strings buzzed in the too-wide grooves of the bridge, and whined in an interesting way.

Thinking of Richard's pink guitar, one wet afternoon I tuned three strings till they made a good drone chord, then detuned the top string till it sounded right, and played it up and down the inaccurate fretboard, learning to bend the notes into pitch.

It sounded like the distant cousin of the sitar Mike Heron and George Harrison were playing – a distant and rather dim cousin, but with a strange charm. I opened Apollinaire's *Selected Poems* at random, *It's raining women's voices as if they were dead even in memory*, and plucked the sitar/bass and began to sing and play, transforming boredom, the rain and missing Helen into some rapt ache.

'Apollinaire's Rain Song' does not appear on *Helping Mrs Monbirth*, or any other of F & f's never-recorded LPs, except as a title. Its ontological status is thinner than graphene.

I tried it the next day on George, but it never flew. It existed for only one afternoon, like kisses once exchanged by our town's abandoned tidal swimming pool. Such things come back from time to time, when we cannot remember the melody or the face, only that it happened, and it was everything at the time.

Track 14: Eric Plectrum Plays the Blues

We needed an electric guitarist who could play the blues, so we enlisted Brian Michie, aka *Eric Plectrum*. Though a year younger than us, he was proper rock 'n' roll. He drank heavily. He had had sex. He was into Led Zeppelin. He had been charged with GBH over an argument about a girl. He had a difficult relationship with his father, was sullen, angry-looking, gruff and quirkily funny. He wore skinhugging Levi's, T-shirt and leather waistcoat.

And he had an electric guitar, which he could play exceptionally well, after spending two years shut in his bedroom copying Hendrix note for note. His guitar had two tuning knobs missing, so he always carried a pair of pliers.

Eric P was emotional, highly romantic, with a yearning sweetness in him. And, unlike us, inherently stylish. He turned up in a dark suit to perform five Leonard Cohen songs at the school Folk Club after a girl had dropped him. He insisted on teaching us 'This Old Heart of Mine (Is Weak for You)' because another girl said she liked

Tamla Motown. At the school dance he – reluctantly – played 'Hey Joe' behind his back, then raised the guitar to his mouth and played the solo with his teeth, gaining more female fans in thirty seconds than Fate & ferret did in that entire year.

We didn't hold this against him. In fact we loved Eric P, despite him constantly being late for rehearsals and recording. He borrowed my new twelve-string acoustic and wrote yearning love songs – beautifully strummed and gruffly sung – with titles like 'Morna' and 'Lie Down, My Lady'.

One Sunday in early May, in the run-up to our final exams, we were all set up for a big recording session. We needed to nail electric versions of recent songs for our next Joe Boyd tape. It felt like our last chance, for, like a giant Hoover, university was heading our way, and Fate & ferret would soon be sucked into its lightless bag.

John Myles was there for extra vocals and guitar, Malcolm 'Cannonball' Campbell was on bongos, the Fiddler nervously fingered his violin. But no Eric Plectrum. This session was to be built round him, and with a one-track recorder, we couldn't do overdubs. The week before he had played a scorching lead on my new fast-shuffle song 'Levi Thighs'. He was the man.

Half an hour late. An hour. We phoned his dad and were gruffly told that Brian had set off on his bike from Colinsburgh an hour ago. George and I stood at the window, looking down the road. We had to finish this new tape and get it to Joe Boyd before music fashions changed yet again, but our electric saviour was lost in transit and the evening had been assigned to irregular French verbs.

'Oh Jesus, look!'

At the end of the road a youth on a bike wobbled past the Catholic church. He had an electric guitar tied across the handlebars. Perhaps that was affecting his steering, because he swung into the middle of the road, narrowly missed a car, then veered back to hit the pavement outside the house, toppled over and lay still.

We hurried out. Our lead guitarist was hopelessly drunk on a bottle of Old Tawny port. The guitar had lost another machine head. Eric P lay, eyes open but glassy, muttering curses.

We helped him in. George's mum fussed and made tea. We put him in the shower, got him out again. He drank the tea, wolfed some Tunnock's, then reached for his pliers.

'Aawright, boys . . . Whit are ye needin?'

A few bars to check the sound balance, two takes max at each song. Cannonball attacked the bongos, Johnny Myles crooned, Eric P unleashed a screaming volley of starshell notes. Outside, the fields of Fife inched towards harvest, the sea brimmed, gleamed and broke. With the window open to release perspiration, we could smell salt and seaweed. George's mum brought in a tray of tea and buttered gingerbread, and we took a break, cross-legged on the floor listening to the playbacks.

We were, I think, completely happy.

That last summer term glows in the memory like the Edwardian summer before the Great War, down to the cricket matches meticulously recorded in my diary.

Impending exams didn't rate much of a mention. There were a few parties, and barbecues along at Elie beach, with guitars, cider, vodka, new flirtations. Girls hinted at interest, then went off with someone else. I wasn't that bothered. Writing songs and poems about girls seemed more reliably rewarding than girls themselves.

George and I signed up for cookery, where we were the only boys, and learned to make brandy snaps, Scotch broth, macaroni cheese, omelettes, rhubarb tart and beef olives. On this basis, I could safely leave home.

We did our final Folk Clubs, spiced up with the amplifier in its cardboard box, with a helper solemnly lugging the car battery on stage. Eric P twirled his pliers then played his heart out. We assembled the *Mrs Monbirth* tape, drafted covering letters to Joe Boyd, the Incredible String Band, the Moody Blues and John Peel.

My mother presented me with *The Writers' & Artists' Year Book*, which suggested ways of converting writing into money. Encouraged, I reworked *Inexplicable Events Near Carstairs Wood* (the title was the best thing about it) as a stage play, then for radio, then as television. Maybe I would secure a commission that would let me live and write while carrying on with music. 'George Mackay Brown doesn't have a job' – that remained my ambition. I have followed it, falteringly yet ruthlessly, all my life.

The weekly production of poems slowed but, influenced by reading Norman MacCaig's poems in the *Weekend Scotsman*, they become shorter, clearer and acquired some spine. I sent them via the *Scotsman* to Mr MacCaig, with a note saying I loved his poems, especially the Lochinver ones, and I hoped he might enjoy these.

I was slightly appalled to get a note in return: *Come and see me.*

I have written about that visit in *At the Loch of the Green Corrie* because our meeting and subsequent friendship was, and remains, hugely important to me. What lasts is his wry observation that he quite liked my poems because they were quite like his – perhaps I should try to write some like my own? And read more.

His remarks were characteristically astringent, witty and true. And also generous. Norman had an ego and his vanities – what artist, what human being, does not? – but he was not looking for disciples. I can think of no better advice to an aspiring writer: *Write some like your own. Read more.*

We sat our final exams in hot classrooms with the windows open, breeze riffling our papers. I finished my dissertation on Absurdist Drama, then went slightly mad on my creative-writing section of sixth-year-study English, with a word-torrent called 'Waterfall', which towards the end started to stream down the page rather than across it.

I walked with George out into the brilliant light, free youths.

'I've decided I will go to Dundee Art College,' George said casually.

'Oh, right,' I said.

'We can keep writing songs separately, then get together in the holidays.'

'Sure,' I said. 'Right.'

He unlocked his Clubman from the bike sheds, slung his duffel bag over his shoulder then cycled off for Pittenweem. Not ready to go home, I wandered over to the sports field, where some of my pals were trying to make a discus fly. It seemed a wonderfully Greek thing to do. I never got the hang of it.

Dundee. George was a realist. He could see what was necessary. Everyone in our year was going on to university or college, to be town planners, doctors, teachers, engineers, accountants.

I picked up a stray javelin, wrapped my fingers round the grip.

It felt like I had been squared off and tied before being tipped off the school conveyer belt I had first been loaded onto, aged four and a half. The next conveyor belt awaited me at Stirling University. Its campus had been the grounds of Airthrey Castle, the former maternity hospital where my father had delivered me. A pleasing circularity, going back to where I had begun.

Then again, once that conveyor belt image had slipped into my head, it wouldn't go away.

I threw the javelin far enough to stick in the hard ground, quivering into stillness. Then I walked home for my lunch, which would be mince and tatties because it was a Thursday.

I found my father in the cool of the sitting room reading the *Scotsman*, and with a slight quaver announced I wouldn't be going to university in autumn.

He lowered the paper, the inside pages yellow-brown from the dottle flicked from his pipe.

'So, what are you going to do?'

'Write more plays and poems,' I said. 'I've had a couple of poems accepted, and I've suggested pieces for *The Scotsman*, and they want to see them.'

This was a slight exaggeration.

'Where and how do you propose to live?'

'Edinburgh,' I replied. 'Or Dundee. I'll get seasonal work, or in a bar, and write in the evenings.'

We had three grandfather clocks in the house, with slow and steady beats, a barometer and a baragraph. The carriage clock ticked fast and light. My father appreciated mechanisms that did their job reliably.

'Your mother once wanted to be a journalist,' he finally said.

'Yes, I know.'

Her brother had written sketches for *Punch*. My uncle Donald was a witty, elegant, sad-eyed man who became a director in his father's rail transport business. He didn't write any more.

My father cleared his throat then picked up the *Scotsman*.

'Put it to your mither, laddie,' he said from behind the paper. Sometimes his voice would slide into the Arbroath of his childhood, usually a good sign. 'She has the brains. I just had skeely hands.'

I got my mother alone with her feet up. I told her I wasn't ready to go to university. I didn't want to be on a conveyor belt. Maybe after a year writing and working, I would want to go.

She looked concerned. The concept of a gap year was some decades off.

'Why don't you do your degree, and then see if you want to take a year out?'

'No, I want to do this first and then see.'

'What does your father say?'

'That I should talk to you. And that I'll have to support myself.'

A hint of a smile?

'My father got me an interview with the editor of the *Newcastle Times*, who said I should do my degree first, then come back.'

'But you didn't go back.'

She shrugged. One could spend a lifetime trying to understand what lay behind our parents' shrugs.

'The war came, and after VE Day I ran away from the VAD to marry your father.'

I didn't regret being born, but her life story in brief inclined me towards doing what I wanted to do first up, not later. I was proud of my uncle's stories in *Punch*, but he didn't seem to have the life he wanted. It seemed most grown-ups didn't.

'This is what I want to do, Mum,' I said.

She got up and lifted some sheets from the clothes horse.

'Well, good luck,' she said, switched on the iron, and got on with it.

Cross-legged in my bedroom shrine, still a couple of months before my eighteenth birthday, I opened my father's copy of *Leaves of Grass* at the place where two blunt pencil lines down the margin marked a passage.

He had these Whitman poems in Penang in the twenties, long before he met my mother. I pictured a sultry tropical night outside, the young man reading alone by lamplight in his bamboo chair, maybe a whisky and soda on the rattan table. Struck by certain lines, he reaches for a pencil and marks them:

> *All goes onward and outward, nothing collapses.*
> *And to die is different from what anyone supposed,*
> *And luckier.*

I closed the book, slipped out the back gate onto the sandbar where the Dreel burn made its final turn towards the sea, then wandered one more time past seaweed tangle, along the dark skerry, marvelling at the surge. When I had gone as far out as possible, I turned to look back at the sleeping town that would soon not be where I lived.

Track 15: The Amazing Value Show

The Amazing Value Show was our sign-off to school and everything that the last year had been. George painted a psychedelic poster, we flyposted notices all around the school and the town. We and our pals were going public.

We used stage lighting, incense sticks and loads of cushions. Ravi Shankar played on the PA as the audience filled the Assembly Hall. The deer skull from 'The Twa Corbies' made a reappearance, along with some gold-sprayed giant hogweed along the back wall. The result blended Indian harem, Karol's garret, and the Kellie Law back country, as our parents, teachers and local worthies sat in expectant, or baffled, rows.

The programme's set list contained some familiar songs. An exuberant 'Cameron Loch' from Scobie and pals got a few shiny shoes tapping. Someone sang they would not be moved; another enquired where all the flowers had gone (though the hedgerows and gardens of Fife were thick with poppies, roses, fuchsia and laburnum hanging like yellow grapes).

But the community – back then it didn't need to be called that, it just was one – was exposed to strange developments. Their onstage children had sprouted peasant blouses and long, fringed skirts, with headscarves and beads their great-great-aunts might have worn. Others sported embroidered waistcoats, paisley pyjama tops, cloaks over flared jeans, quilted tea cosies as hats. Pheasant and peacock plumes were ubiquitous that year. The Fiddler glittered in a silver dressing gown.

No recording survives of The Amazing Value Show, so it can live burnished in the memories of those who were there. Two items are in mine still.

George had written a remarkable new song. He had gone off for a solitary sunset daunder in the back country, still shaken up from our encounter with Scientology in Edinburgh, thinking about Robert Graves, childhood holidays in the Highlands, passing the run-down chicken farm while wondering about God. When he sat down, the low red sun in his eyes, he felt the whole planet pulsing under his hands.

He stumbled home in a daze, picked up the red guitar and wrote 'The Hills of Kishorn'. It was our Western Highlands, our back country Fife, our pantheism and worrying away at death, sunsets, art and refuse bones, all in one song.

We arranged it then got Fiddler Tom along, and he played with an urgency and attack we hadn't heard from him before. George wasn't sure, but I insisted we had to perform it at The Amazing Value Show.

And this what I remember, sitting alongside George on our school stage, bathed in purple light. He wears the satin striped waistcoat and tan beret. I have my dad's deerstalker, my sister's green-and-gold velvet cloak from the childhood dressing-up-box. I set up a sustained strum in E, waiting for George to open up the song.

> *The hills of Kishorn, before their permanent home*
> *Are only the same*
> *The brine is their liquor*
> *They drink the waters of the West*

Then the fiddle comes in, a gate swinging on the hinge of two repeated notes:

> *Oh there's so much more*
> *Do it all.*

And that is it absolutely. *Do it all.* That is what we had heard in the String Band, in the sawing gimbri and Mike's from-the-heart vocals, and we have finally made our own:

> *I'll grant you Pan's own pipes*
> *If you play a mythical tune*

The fiddle turns dark, sawing insistently at a low note as Willie and Douglas in the lighting gallery bring up a brooding crimson:

> *I lay down and smelled the earth burning*
> *The yellow rose, the chicken run*
> *And the refuse bones.*

Our parents, the Headie, Alastair Mackie, Alastair Leslie and the Boss, the great and good, the salty, the dour and the downright peculiar of our town, sit staring back at us as we chant again: *Do it all.*

The song flows into a lyrical section (lit green and gold), then is dammed by three abrupt chords that widen in blue light:

> *The cruellest man you'll ever find*
> *Is the iron man who knows his mind*
> *The kindest man you'll ever know*
> *Is the travelling man who has to go.*

So far, so sweet, in almost-harmony, and Tommy fiddling. Then I drop out to leave George singing alone:

> *The strangest words I ever heard*
> *Were 'Silence. God is dead.'*

And we stop there; stop hard, with two ugly violin screeches. Silence. Darkness.

Hesitant applause.*

But this is '69 not '77, and we are not alienated. We feel profoundly attached to our family, friends, the East Neuk. We will not end on a downer.

---

* 'God is dead' was crucially qualified by 'the strangest words I ever heard', yet shock ran through the hall. Four years later I would read Nietzsche and come across the same phrase, then notice he had ascribed it to a madman ranting in the marketplace. I thought of George's lyric and Fate & ferret, high and exposed on the Waid stage.

All the pals we have played and recorded with come on stage to play piano, more guitars, rattles, to shake tambourines, parp the kazoos, blow whistle and flute as we sing Mike Heron's 'A Very Cellular Song'. The wobble-board goes *baa-woomp*, the piano bangs out the chords, over and over, and the massed voices sing ecstatically, ignoring the janitor signalling from the sidelines.

It is a leave-taking sung by everyone on stage to all the people in the audience who have made and shaped us and let us be.

The audience disperses into the summer night. Round the back we share vodka and cider and our excitement. Eric P lights up, blows smoke rings, releases a rare smile.

'Yon wis fuckin magic!'

The janitor straightened the chairs, switched off the lights and went home to put the kettle on.

A stern-faced man, not particularly fond of children, he is long dead. Practically all that grown-up audience are gone too: the provost, grave councillors, teachers, fishermen, farmers, chemists, mothers, policemen, grannies scolding and grannies kind. Eddie MacGeachy no longer patrols the touchlines exhorting us to ignore pain. The Boss, who gave us shelter, relationship advice, laughter and Drambuie, left her typewriter long ago.

And with them has gone the East Neuk I knew, so reassuring and confining, drab and magical.

The boatyard, where generations of youth went to snog and drink and smoke in the shadows below the timbers, is a vacant space. The fishing boats have been broken up, the harbour is filled with pleasure boats tied to pontoons. The outdoor swimming pools, where people once shrieked and swam, have long ceased to hold water. Kittlenaked Woods, where we once sat cross-legged and strummed by our little fires, have been erased.

Fife of the sixties still had much of the thirties and fifties about it. It was grey yet colourful, monocultural and busy. Neither impoverished nor well-to-do, it was narrow yet full of eccentricities.

Above all it was *personal*. It had farmers, fishermen, tradesmen and canny shopkeepers, and the women were down the street shopping six days a week, and they had all known each other all their lives – everyone had gone to the Waid. Nothing happened on Sundays except the Kirk and golf. It also contained Tahitian princesses, religious nutters, the inventor of the silicon diode, poetry-writing fishermen, a hollow-eyed outcast who painted exquisitely detailed paintings of long-vanished boats, several people who talked aloud as they walked alone. It had tiny shops lit by one faint bulb, where the bell pinged as you went in, and a kindly, weary fisherman's widow would shuffle through in baffies from her front room to ask *Whit can I dae ye for the day?*

The Amazing Value Show was nearly fifty years ago. Its echoes have long faded. Except they haven't, not in anyone who was young and there.

In his heavenly bungalow the janny blows on his tea, reaches for a celestial biscuit.

Track 16: A Country Dance

'Mum, can you give me five pounds?'

'Why?'

I'd never asked her for money before. I think we were both equally taken aback.

'Because I've just left school, and me and George are going to the Brownhills barn dance tonight.'

George and I stood sipping lager from plastic glasses, chuckling at the accordion-led band. Then he darted off towards two girls. Both had been in the class below us. One we called Likky because she had long, flat, straight black hair like Robin's girlfriend. The other I recognised from school prize-givings – frowning, strong-featured, wary.

Her name was Irene something, her dad was one of the Poles who had stayed on in Fife after the war. I had a notion something bad had happened. I had never talked to her before, though I'd been struck by the number of prizes she got.

George and 'Likky' entered the dancing crowd. Irene and I looked at each other. It was evident I hadn't suggested this, and her eyes were a dark, pained blue.

'Would you like to dance?'

'You're just trying to be polite.'

'I *am* polite,' I replied. 'But I would like you to dance.'

She almost smiled, and we did dance, shouting to each other over the accordion, bass and drums.

'You get a lot of prizes,' I shouted.

'So did you,' she yelled back.

The number ended. We stopped and looked at each other. She looked over where George and 'Likky' were still entwined, and pulled a face. She stepped away.

'Would you like another?' I asked.

'Why?'

'Well, you're clever and interesting – and very entertaining.'

She did smile at that. I sensed it wasn't something she did very often.

'Liar,' she said. 'All right.'

We danced together the rest of the evening. On a break outside she told me how to spell her surname, then muttered her father had been killed on his scooter. I caught her eyes, felt something dig in below my ribs.

'Yes,' I said. 'That must have been . . . horrible.'

'It is,' she said. 'It's getting better, though it will never be okay.'

I put my arm round her waist, and we went back into the barn to dance. What we would become is not something you can put on the scales of life to check the good against the bad. All you can do is feel the weight of it.

Summer of '69 was the time of getting to know the clever, hurt girl who had been pushed my way. I soon learned that, though born in Crail, she felt herself an outsider in the village and in her surviving family. Her intelligence, her name, her grief, all marked her out. People didn't know what to say and she didn't want to speak about it anyway, so she worked at her books and won the prizes. Her father had always hoped she would go to university.

We talked books, listened to Fairport Convention and Leonard Cohen. She liked the String Band, though not with my passion. We walked the back country behind Crail, out along the disused railway, the empty airfield. Along the way we tried to match our steps.

She lived in a council house that was supposed to have been rebuilt with better materials, but never had been. She had been very much her father's child, with his Polish nose, intelligence and emotionality. The house was faded and damp with unexpressed grief. Television and the radio were constantly on while Mrs P read the *Dundee Courier* and the *East Fife Mail* from cover to cover, including the small ads.

Mrs P echoed the country folk of my childhood. Her world was very small, and she was kind and poor. She liked to fuss and put out tea and pancakes, and I liked to eat them by the little coal fire and let the flow of her monologue mix in with the TV, always tuned to what my mother called *commercial television*.

Irene and I learned each other, slowly. Without the presumptions of Romance, we found each other interesting, peculiar, perhaps enjoyable. She was bright and curious, equally adept in maths, science and the arts. She had another year to go at the school; then she wanted away. I had no idea where I was going to be at summer's end.

On an early visit, she took me out to their garden shed, rummaged around in the dim interior, dragged out a battered suitcase, and opened it up.

She said these were the few remnants she had of her father. He had been the head of an art college in Kraków, escaped during the German and Russian invasions, walked across wartime Europe to a Channel port, and ended up in Fife. He got a job at the canteen on the airbase outside Crail. When the war ended, he worked as a waiter. He and the woman he had met at a dance married, had a baby, then another. They had very little money. He didn't like being a waiter.

Her voice was low and flat. She said it was the first time in years she had talked about him. My stomach clenched and my heart lurched. I was very aware nothing very bad had ever happened to me.

In the last years of her father's life, things looked up. He went to evening classes, which got him an administrative job with the council in Leven. He bought a scooter to get there. Then one day a van came round a corner too wide and swept him and his scooter out of the world. She'd been told the last thing he said was *Oh Jesus*. The driver was fined a few pounds.

She kept flipping through his art books. Her words sounded like they were being surgically removed from her throat. I put my hand on her shoulder. I didn't know what to say, so I said nothing. Her face was flushed but she didn't cry. She was resolute that way.

She pulled out a big scrapbook. I still see the drawings of butterflies stuck on its pages – very skilful, precise, painted butterflies. The paper had yellowed but the paint was bright, as in an Egyptian tomb. She said he would sometimes draw or paint in the evenings.

One of the drawings came unstuck, fluttered down onto the dust. She picked it up, handed it to me. It was gorgeous, alive with green and purple.

'It's lovely,' I said. 'I'm really sorry.'

She said nothing, but took the drawing and carefully placed it back in the book. She turned away from me, replaced her relics in the box, and we went inside for our tea.

Some time later – my birthday in late September, or that Christmas? – I opened a card and one of the butterfly drawings slid out, and I sensed we were in for the long haul.

Track 17: Friday Evening Blues

An evening in late summer finds me at the Boss's place in Lundin Links, telling traveller's tales from my impulsive hitch-hike to the Camargue. Then George walks in, glowing and ecstatic, just back from Belskavie Farm in deep Aberdeenshire – for him a spiritual home, where his mother had been brought up – with a clutch of West Coast albums under his arm.

He puts on *Crosby, Stills & Nash*. I like it a lot. I also register there is zero chance of me playing this stuff. The dazzling three-part harmonies, the precision-engineered guitars and vocals, all that forward velocity without even drums – it's fantastic, faultless, impossible.

In Pittenweem next day I play my new songs. They sound pretty thin after the West Coast Sound, but George likes 'Brother Rain', with the Scientology-referencing middle section, *Rain bringing Clear to me*. To go *Clear* is to have all one's hang-ups dissolved, which sounds desirable. It is also wincingly expensive. But in interviews Robin Williamson says it is transforming their lives.

When we record 'Brother Rain', George picks up my old Spanish guitar, and plays a slide-guitar accompaniment on nylon strings. The nylon slide has a soft, weeping sound that makes the song. The last chord fades, I lean forward to press *stop* and we look at each other. Perhaps we do still have something going.

Then George plays his new songs: 'Friday Evening Blues', 'Love Glove', a memorable instrumental called 'River Gnats', then 'I Left the Farm'. They're terrific, in a non-String Band way – well made, constructed, catchy. I sense they are songs for Teri, but don't ask.

George has a clear idea how he wants these done, and it will involve drums, piano and Eric Plectrum – ideally, a synthesis of Stephen Stills and *Nashville Skyline*.

The drums arrive – we can have them on weekdays. Eric P turns up, tanned and healthy-looking, pliers in the pocket of his leather waistcoat. We set up in the Pittenweem sitting room. I have been transcribing a guitar part to piano, Eric P eases onto the drum stool. We hang the sole microphone from the central lampshade and George sings his song for the golden girl who was being elusive again:

> *Friday evening I just spend within myself*
> *Tired on the outside, there's so much to say*
> *I haven't said it for weeks.*

The playback sounds good. The piano is slightly out of tune, and has a hollow echo, which conveys the song's ache. I keep stumbling on the little piano bridge between verses. George says I sometimes drop a beat.

I play it again.

'No,' George says. 'You did it again. Like *this*.'

He plays it on guitar. I listen, nod. Okay, got it.

We go for another take. And it's okay, though it seems I have still dropped a beat between the bridge and the last verse. Eric P drums the little fill for me, singing the notes.

Truth is, I can barely play the piano. I feel I'm doing pretty well just to stumble through the chord arpeggios, and that sudden jump to B flat is tricky, though it makes the song.

I want to live in simple harmony
Far from all the troubles that surround
And make a final study of the evening sun
And the peace of country sounds.

When George's mum brings in tea and Tunnock's, we take a break and listen to the playbacks. The piano has some duff notes, but Joe can sort it out in the studio.

Some dissatisfaction still unresolved, we move on to 'Love Glove'. I can't play bass or lead or drums, so Eric P stays behind the kit and starts happily swishing on the brushes. I'll have to try it on piano, without rehearsal time. And this song has a *lot* of chord changes, coming pretty fast.

While George waits, I transpose a tricky chord from the guitar onto keyboard.

'Can you do it, Andy?' Eric P asks gruffly.

'More or less,' I say, sweating.

I'm auditioning for a band I'm already in, and I'm playing an out-of-tune instrument I scarcely know. Still, we do it, and Eric swishes his wire brushes and the song swings nicely to its conclusion.

> *And if that would appear*
> *To be holding you too near*
> *Then show me how I can win.*

Piano and guitar run through the sign-off ('A total rip-off of "Nashville Skyline"' George says now), the drums do a wee muffled *ker-lump*, and we're done.

We listen to the playbacks, munching teacakes. George reckons they're not good enough for Joe (we assume Joe has a great imagination, but not that great). We can come back to them later. We have made demos of demos.

What became of Teri, the school's golden girl who, though she may not have realised it, tormented any boy unfortunate enough to want her, and gave rise to those yearning songs? She went to college, then, dropped off our map for ever.

Recently George sent me a photo he took of her long ago, on the sandy foreshore in front of the Anster sea wall. She sits askew on a wrecked chair. Her jeans are rolled up to show strong shins and large bare feet. Her hands project from an old denim jacket, her right fist grips her boots.

She is refusing to look at the camera; instead she stares down and sideways at something we can't see and probably never could. Her hair is centre-parted, blown back slightly from her powerful swimmer's shoulders. She looks older than the adolescent she was.

On her washed-up throne on the weed-strewn beach of our seaside town, she is slouched, withholding, preoccupied. She looks troubled and she looks like trouble.

I recently wrote a song, in part about her, but also about all the golden girls, for every school has an acknowledged one.

She may be out there somewhere
Maybe she's long gone
But I remember how dark she was
I remember how she shone.

Track 18: The Second Coming

On the first of November 1969, at the desk by my bedroom shrine, I finished typing up a TV version of *Inexplicable Events Near Carstairs Wood*; then went up to Waid to see Irene to tell her it was time I moved to Edinburgh.

We stood outside the school gates, very aware her classmates were looking. We hugged and kissed awkwardly, but when I stood back her eyes were wetly bright. It was then I understood that though we sometimes struggled with each other, she cared for me. It was a strange sensation. Her father had left her; I should not.

Back in Pittenweem from Dundee art college for the weekend, George finished off the cover of Fate & ferret's third album, *Skinnergate House*, our hasty semi-electric response to the changing times, then sat down to type out the track-listing.

Side 1

  Headstrong (G)

  Mr Carstairs (A)

  Trusting to Luck (G)

  Funky Cack Rack (Eric P)

  Poobly Blues Mk. 3 (A&G)

  Electric Men/Levi Thighs (A, Eric P)

  It Doesn't Matter (Do What You Wanna) (G)

Side 2

  No Scratch Blues (A&G)

  River Gnats (instrumental) (T&G)

  Barn Door (?)

  Skinnergate House (G)

  Sharpie & Hunch (A&G)

  The Hills of Kishorn (G)

  Friday Evening Blues (G)

  Love Glove (G)

  Unboltin' t' Blues (G)

George carefully made up the package of cover illustrations, song lyrics, photos of the band larking around on the West Pier. If this didn't clinch it for Fate & ferret, nothing would.

Our first String Band concert in August '68 was a triumphant home-coming after the international success of *The Hangman's Beautiful Daughter*. The Usher Hall on 4 November '69, following their double album, *Wee Tam and the Big Huge*, was something of a coronation.

The budding flowers had fully bloomed. Wizards mingled with mediaeval ploughmen, Afghan peasants in Turkish trousers, and the odd gaudy military man. Kohl lay thick around soulful eyes, glitter and ornaments spangled in tangled hair. Streaming into the grandeur of the Usher Hall, we were not so much an audience as a gathering of devotees.

We handed over our tickets and each of us received a simple pro-gramme. Beneath the flowery lettering – *Incredible String Band* – was a drawing. Our first thought was: cool, the String Band are still into Pan. Then we looked more closely.

'That's my drawing!' George whispered.

Then we looked at the contents, and found ourselves reading our stories about the String Band. We had last seen them on Joe Boyd's desk along with our first tape. I dimly remembered Joe saying, 'Do you mind if I keep these?' Now they comprised the entire programme.

Awestruck, we read the words *by Fate & Ferret from Pittenweem*; then hurried to our seats.

As we feverishly scanned the near-forgotten stories, done on a couple of wet afternoons to make up a gift package for the ISB, they seemed a bit juvenile. We had been sixteen then, we were so much older now.

In what we felt was the true ISB spirit, our stories were a kazoo rasped from the sidelines. Mike was being impulsive, horny and bouncy, while Robin floated ethereally and Likky was a sighing princess. Rose was practical, exasperated, coping with these idiot children. Our guesses, as always, were based on very little evidence – though they now seem not entirely inappropriate.

No one had told us this was going to happen. Now there would have to be permissions, an agreed, if nominal, payment. And we would have insisted on the correct lower case for *ferret*. But, at the time, we were gobsmacked and delighted.

Then the Incredible String Band appeared on the Usher Hall stage, each member in their own manner. Robin hovered, Mike was bouncy, Likky drifted in like incense, Rose glided on the castors of her smile. No dog. A great exhalation of approval rose from the audience as the band disposed themselves amid the carpets, lamps, microphones and shawls – a forest floor of instruments was strewn at their feet.

Grinning like the new moon, Mike selected the sitar. Percussion for Likky and her gap-toothed grin. A stir of excitement as Rose began tuning her bass. The last time we'd seen them, the String Band were two musicians onstage with their girlfriends and a dog. Now they looked like a four-piece.

Robin twiddled and fiddled, finally picked up a guitar, looked up, and seemed to register us for the first time.

'Hi,' he breathed.

'Hi!' we roared back.

Then he settled into prolonged tuning. Some things had not changed. The audience (a congregation, a supporting cast) waited. Eventually Robin looked up.

'Hi again,' he said.

(I wonder now if that absence of introductions and taking bows, of accepting applause and doing encores, if that *was* their routine. All I know is that more than forty years on and seen close-to, Mike still has the same near-complete absence of stagecraft, and I've come to the conclusion it is just him.)

Then Robin glanced over at Mike, then softly and precisely enunciated the opening lines of his epic 'Maya', and a sigh swept through the levitating Usher Hall.

My diary uses its limited space to record: *First half mostly John Peel sessions songs, and fantastic for us. Second half really weird stuff.*

This suggests that, though I couldn't quite face saying so, they were starting to lose us. One new Mike song 'This Moment' gave me the authentic shiver and wake-up. (It does to this day. Even if the gig is a bit flat, whenever Mike starts 'This Moment' he comes alive, and the world is present and precious again.) Mike was on a hot songwriting streak then, and the early electric songs 'The Letter' and 'All Writ Down' were a joy.

The 'really weird stuff' would probably have been Robin's fanciful meandering songs such as 'Pictures in a Mirror' and 'When You Find Out Who You Are', which had bombed at Woodstock. They brought us back with crowd-pleasers like Mike's 'Black Jack Davy' – essentially a jaunty reprise of 'Log Cabin Home in the Sky', one of the very few times he nearly repeated himself.*

Rose was playing more now, bass mostly, but she also played fiddle alongside Robin, plus some keyboards and mandolin. Likky sang in her strange high voice. The four of them manifested the ideal life:

---

* Being so eclectic and uncommitted to any one genre, the ISB songs were notably one-offs, rather than variations and elaborations on the same musical roots. When inspiration flagged, they couldn't fall back on blues work-outs or folk tropes.

love, friendship, artistic achievement and communal living. John Lennon and George Harrison had mansions in stockbroker land, but we knew our ISB were now living in the Glen, a row of cottages in the Borders, near Innerleithen.

We did not know that the chilly, damp and basic estate cottages were rented, not owned. We did not know that having a cottage apiece did not reflect financial and existential largesse, but was because they had ceased to be couples.

We could not conceive that Robin and Mike were anything other than soulmates, whereas in fact they had never been that close, apart from the near-miraculous things that happened when they brought their talents together.* And now, despite announcing their drug-free commitment to Scientology, and the band's improved communication skills, we sensed they were pulling in different directions.

Some absolute concurrence was passing or had passed. George was in Dundee. In a few days I'd be living alone in Edinburgh. Our classmates had scattered. Flicking through my dad's dottle-flecked *Scotsman*, it seemed not everything was getting better. The freedom movement in Czechoslovakia had been quashed by Soviet tanks. In Vietnam, something very nasty had happened in My Lai. The cartoon Archies' appalling 'Sugar, Sugar' was lodged in my head.

So, at moments during the concert, my attention drifted. Robin's whimsy seemed amusing rather than profound. I kept waiting for the old songs rather than being stunned by the new. Even as we laughed at 'Big Ted', the word *childish* drifted across my mind like a small, leaden cloud seeking companions.

---

* An open musical alliance, rather than a tightly fused gang in the manner of the Beatles, etc.

These were just hints and portents. Mostly George and I were swigging cream sherry from a bottle brought in under my tabard, and on some contact high from the rest of the audience. We had a new tape for Joe. Some of my poems were getting published. Governments might finally see what was obvious to us: apartheid, Vietnam, both capitalism and a communism that had to ban groovy music – all were wasted time and energy, and would surely end when our generation was in control. 'Sugar, Sugar' might finally slip out of the top twenty. All might yet be well.

So, a bit older but still very young, slightly chastened but hopeful, a little sceptical but still believing in the inevitable improvement of humankind and our own abilities, we stood to applaud what Robin announced as their last song.

This is the performance that remains most vividly from that night. Robin is on a high stool as he lifts a whistle to his lips. Mike is at the keyboard, face-splitting grin gleaming in the lights. Rose and Likky stand by. It is the sacred moment, an invocation to our togetherness. The song is austere and impersonal as pibroch. The tune sounds ancient, the shrill whistle scrapes and sparks like flint against the organ chords.

It is the true Incredible String Band, raising hairs along my young arm, binding us all as Robin sings 'The Circle Is Unbroken'. His clear, heraldic voice summons unchanging change, our scattering and our conjoining, the unending voyage towards our unsayable destination. My throat and chest swell, the entire audience stands, spellbound, to receive its affirmation.

The band drift offstage to tumultuous, grateful applause. They will not be back, encores being a show-biz convention. George and I are already heading for the wings, clutching sherry, our tape and our programme.

Backstage seems almost familiar. This time I talk with Mike and Rose as we hand over a copy of our tape and the latest *Inexplicable Events* for (we hope) their pleasure and safe-keeping. It seems Joe Boyd is busy in elsewhere, so he'll have to wait a few more days to have his mind blown.

We tell Robin and Likky that we have been into the Edinburgh Scientology place, had our free personality test, a lecture and an auditing session. Apparently we have fantastic creative personalities, plus some deep problems that need sorting. They approve. I've not seen Likky so animated and straightforward. I don't say the E-meter reminds me of a cod-gadget in *Doctor Who*, with its tin cans and mystery box round what is basically a galvanometer, a crude lie detector. And auditing seems very like the talking cure favoured by Scientology's bête noire, psychiatry.

They tell us they have been to Saint Hill, the British HQ of Scientology, and are looking to go *Clear* soon, and then on to the new, even higher, levels that L. Ron Hubbard has recently unveiled. As we talk, I am aware they are following the 'Communication Rundown' that George and I had been introduced to. Instead of making conversation easier and more natural, these procedures seem to make it more stilted and self-conscious. Perhaps we simply haven't practised enough?

In the past, the ISB playfully pilfered from Christianity, Buddhism, Hinduism and visionaries from Blake to Nietzsche to

Douglas Harding. Like busy bees they whizzed among mythologies, sucking the nectar and making new honey. That playfulness and its unexpected juxtapositions, interested in all and committed to none, seemed a glimpse of a new kind of modernity: the Joyful Player.

Now Robin and Likky in particular seem thirled to one truth, a message and a system. When the Beatles took up with the Maharishi, we had felt similarly felt intrigued and let down.

Outside the Usher we necked the last of the sherry then caught the bus back to George's sister's, talking all the way about the concert, Scientology, the future of our tape. Who knows where they would take us?

In the morning, still elevated, uncertain, tired, I scootered home through the cold leaf-strewn backroads of Fife. I watch that boy on his Vespa with trepidation, for the roads are strewn with wet leaves, and he has no idea of the treacherous slick of the world, the instability of his chosen transport, nor how far he still has to go.

Track 19: Real Life

It was a brutal adjustment.

Unawares, we had been cossetted for years. The house was always warm and clean, meals came three times a day. The fridge was full, the cupboards stacked. Afternoon tea and cake was part of the natural law. Clean clothes appeared. In return we did the dishes, made our beds, walked the dog when asked, brought up the coal, and largely left our parents alone to whatever they did when we weren't there.

We had very little spending money, but we were being completely looked after. Youthful energy apart, that was why we were able to do school and its exams, pursue golf, rugby and cricket, write, rehearse and record, read books and memorise records, go on back-country brouhahas, have difficulties with girls – and still complain of boredom.

The shopping, cooking and cleaning were done for us. We didn't read newspapers and there wasn't much to watch on television after

Top of the Pops, *Adam Adamant Lives!*, and *The Man from U.N.C.L.E.*
There was no social media to keep up with.

We had been time-wealthy in a way we would never be again,
except perhaps in some future care home.

With what I'd saved from late-summer hop-picking with my
now-scattered friends, I found a bedsit in 3 1 West Maitland Street –
the address still makes me flinch – between Edinburgh's Haymarket
and Princes Street. The high-ceilinged room had aged green-and-
brown wallpaper, sagging grey curtains, a narrow bed with blue
nylon sheets. The two-bar electric fire could never do more than
raise dampness out of the carpet and walls.

In one corner was a single-ring Belling cooker, a sink and a small
cupboard. That was the kitchen. My mother had given me *Cooking
in a Bedsitter*, a useful if sad volume. There was a small table, where
I hoped to write about this new world. I put my *Writer's & Artists'
Year Book* and new journal on it. The guitar, typewriter and some
more books and sweaters would be dropped off by my parents in
a few days.

The landlady had shown me how to operate the geyser. She
warned it could scald, and suggested I went to the pub to get plenty
of change for the gas and electricity. The lighting – one 60-watt
bulb, judging by the dimness – was included in the rent. There was
a communal bath in the hall, with hot water in limited supply at
certain hours I had already forgotten.

It seemed I had moved into one of the more depressing passages
of a T. S. Eliot poem. It was for this that I had forgone university,

a social life, a grant and heated halls of residence. Any point to this existence, beyond merely surviving it, would have to be made by me.

My father liked to say of a real or metaphorical heap of rubble: *Mak a kirk or a mill of it.* I dragged the sagging armchair closer into the arc of near-warmth, wrapped my gloved hands round a mug of tea and stared into the glow as the short day faded.

Next morning I got directions to the Labour Exchange. Brisk in name only, it smelled of cigarettes, sweat and damp. Men stood and shuffled forward in queues. The shorter queues of women were on the other side of the room. There was much coughing into fists. The older men wore bunnets, pulled low or held in hand. A low, urgent mutter of voices came from an opaque glassed cubicle. Yellow-and-green paint, everything else brown, faded, chipped. It might as well have still been the war.

For this middle-class country boy, brought up in small places where we had a few slightly shifty shabby men, acknowledged with raised eyebrows and a mutter of *ne'er do well*, but no actual un-employed, the Labour Exchange was as foreign and exotic as a brothel.

I located a board entitled *Men's Situations Vacant* and began to read the jobs on offer. Many involved a driving licence, which I didn't have, or trade skills. *Time served* was a recurring phrase. I didn't like the sound of that.

My eyes learned to skip over slaters, roofers, Ames tapers, short-hand typists, plumbing, bookkeeping, tractor/orraman, lathe operator. Experienced fork-lift drivers, carpenters and bricklayers were much in demand. Hotel waiting jobs insisted *silver service experience essential.*

I could parse sentences, translate *The Gallic Wars*, recite the inert gases from the Periodic Table and manipulate cosines. It was amazing how just little school had equipped me for.

Mortuary assistant. No experience required. Training given. It sounded like the kind of thing real writers had done before they became real writers, on the back flap of a book along with petrol-pump attendant, scallop-diver, office cleaner.

Then again, daily death up-close would probably be depressing. I might have to help at post-mortems, hold buckets and mop up and sponge down bloody slabs. That could be a bit too real.

I wrote down the reference number to think about it, then lingered over *Roofing work – head for heights essential*. I pictured scaffolding, heavy boots, thick gloves. I had enjoyed the hop-picking, and even the tattie-howking. An aching body was better than an aching mind.

Then again, heights scared me. I liked being in the hills, but looking down from my father's shoulders or the Wallace Monument, or even the windows of the train going over the Forth Bridge, made me feel ill. Just how high would these roofs be?

The man took my details while I registered as unemployed. He noted my school qualifications, raised an eyebrow and suggested I should be going to university or start training in a profession. I said I just wanted a job to earn money for a while. Casual labour, then? Seasonal?

I agreed, just so. *Casual* sounded fine. I watched him write down *No relevant skills*.

He suggested I keep looking, and check the *Evening News*. Come back tomorrow, son. I asked how I got unemployment benefit now

I was officially unemployed. My summer hop picking savings were dwindling in my Post Office deposit book.

'Have you got stamps?'

I had never heard of these stamps. It seemed I needed six months of them in a book before I could get unemployment benefit. No exceptions.

'Uh, okay. Thanks.'

Though I haunted that Labour Exchange for weeks, often going in twice a day to scan the *Men's Situations Vacant*, no one ever told me about supplementary benefit that needed no stamps, that was there to pay my rent and keep me from starving. And I was so green, so unworldly, I didn't know.

Across the hall, Allan had a gloom room like mine. A second-year engineering student at Napier, he had a grant. He also had practical skills. When I complained how the meter ate my money, he nodded.

'I'm going to show you something you mustn't tell anyone.'

Crouching by his fire, he showed me how his meter was lead-sealed. Apparently sealed. He had unpicked it, 'made a few adjustments', then crimped it with pliers. Now the wheel still went round but the money-eating mechanism didn't.

'She's set it at the top rate,' he said. 'I put in a few coins every so often so it doesn't look suspicious.'

'That's what they teach you at college?'

'One of the techy assistants did, yeah.'

In my room, he snipped the lead seal, opened the flap, then offered me his screwdriver.

'You'd better do this.'

Thrilled, uneasy, I gently poked with the screwdriver while he held the torch. A small cog slipped back and ceased to turn the one next to it. The wheel spun, the bars still glowed. It was as reality-changing as a String Band song, and in an oddly similar way.

Allan showed me how to twiddle the cog back into place for when the meter man came, then crimp the lead seal. To thank him I splurged on a Fray Bentos steak pie with mashed tatties with loads of butter and ketchup, which we shared with a bottle of McEwan's before he went back to his studies.

Alone again, I watched the fire glow, the wheel go round. I felt a bit guilty, but not very. Landladies were tight and we were skint.

When our elders talked of 'real life', it always came down to why you could not do what you wanted. In Scotland the facts we were told to face were invariably limiting and depressing. No parent or teacher ever said to us *Face the facts – just to be here is a delight!* Only the String Band had sung this heresy, and I still hoped it to be true.

I spent most days chasing jobs that had gone by the time I got there, or it turned out I wasn't qualified for. I went into the *Scotsman* offices and talked my way into meeting an editor. He told me they were running a couple of apprenticeships, the next intake would be in a few months.

Well, maybe. I grasped the distinction between being a staff journalist (steady money, but you had to write what they told you to, and for years that would be very small stuff) and freelance (write what you want, but you only get paid if they want it). This was emerging as a defining feature of Real Life: you could have freedom or you could have income security, but not both.

An elderly man ahead of me in the signing-on queue removed his bunnet, turned to his friend and said, as if pronouncing a profound and novel truth, 'Ah weel, life is whit you mak it.'

'Oh aye, right enough, Willie.'

It stayed with me for days, that casual exchange, and went into my journal. I noted how they passed one cigarette between them, received it with a nod of thanks, drew on it, had a good cough, then passed it back.

Could it be true, I wondered? Was life really what you make of it? They were not fit or well-nourished or young. The opposite seemed more true: those elderly, shabby, broken-down men were exactly what life had made them.

When not scootering around chasing phantom jobs, I went to the Central Library to write in the warmth. Writing was something I could carry on doing whatever the circumstances, whereas music depended on having other people around. I had been feeling increasingly musically inadequate in the face of George's new songs and Eric Plectrum's musicianship and John Myles' harmonious vocals.

I was working on two play scripts (one *gritty*, the other *Absurd*), an article about chasing employment in Edinburgh, poems and a new song from a morning in Princess Street Gardens, hoar frost dripping from bare trees, me dreaming of Irene, of Greece, of escape.

Provisionally titled 'Apart/Far & Near' (evidently still a fan of ampersands), Fate & ferret recorded the song back in Pittenweem along with retakes of George's recent songs, then we split, to see our respective girlfriends.

I took the Vespa to Anster, where my brother had moved into my old room. I ate a lot, washed my hair and clothes, lay in a hot bath, bagged up some supplies, assured my mother I was all right and my father that I expected to get paid work soon, had a good night's sleep then headed back to the fray.

I was living largely on porridge oats and fried bread. Fruit and vegetables (mashed tatties apart) did not pass my lips for days then weeks. I reverted to the core Scottish diet – salt, fats and sliced white. Most of the time my chest was bad, with a cough I couldn't shift. In the photos, my centre-parted hair is long and greasy, and I look pale, thin-faced. For weeks I scarcely took off my woolly hat and donkey jacket. Edinburgh seemed the darkest, dreichest, most dismal place on earth.

At any time I could have packed it in and gone home, but my father would be very unimpressed, and so would I. I did go home to refuel, see Irene for an awkward *Are we still going out?* exchange (unspoken, of course), go up to the school and see the Boss, liberate some more typing paper – but then it was back on the Vespa to Maitland Street and my dwindling Post Office savings book.

It was the first time I felt truly alone. At times, as I lay in bed through the afternoons still wearing woolly hat and gloves, coat spread over the coverlet for additional warmth, it felt downright unpleasant and wearing. At others it made me feel keen-edged and sharp, as if loneliness were a whetstone that might let me better harvest more songs and poems.

But mostly I was just cold, dribbling out the last of my summer savings, and achingly lonely. In those weeks in that city of smoke-blackened stone, chasing jobs that had just been taken, jobs for which I was unqualified, jobs for which I was overqualified, life resisted any attempt to remake it. The summery optimism of the songs I loved hit the wintry tombstone face of West Maitland Street, burst and slithered down like a Scotch pie thrown by a passing drunk.

I finally got a job. Following up a handwritten notice in the corner shop, I assembled with a bunch of other young unskilled hopefuls to be given an inspirational talk on how to sell Art Felt paintings round housing estates. The paintings were, even to my untrained eye, hideous, with the more vivid parts of the colour spectrum depicting puppies, huge-eyed children and near-naked exotic women.

Dozens of these were stacked in boxes. Our team leader explained our pitch was that we had painted them at art college, along with our friends, and we were selling these unique works to supplement our grants. We were talented, impoverished and *striving*, that was important. These people were striving too.

So Real Life was happy telling porkies? No need to apologise, our team leader said. If people believed they were buying a one-off original work, they would be happy to see it on their wall – and we would be happy to get our commission.

No, there was no wage. Only commission. That tempting sum on the advert was notional.

I learned some useful things from that job. Our leader, who clearly loved selling, told us to think of it as a game. Get a buzz from it. Make your enjoyment the buyer's enjoyment. Get the money and wave goodbye. For someone with this attitude, selling was easy and natural as breathing.

Our team leader gave us another valuable lesson. You see a sign by the doorbell *No salesmen. No hawkers*? Always ring on that door, for those people are frightened because they know they can be sold to. Once you get inside, they will buy just to get rid of you.

You go in boldly, make your pitch. You are the good news they have been waiting for. You show them the picture on the wall. *Here? Or maybe here, over the breakfast bar? Or do you prefer it above that lovely vase?* Ask open questions. Involve them. It's their home, after all! They want to add to it, to show their taste, to delight their spouse, surprise their teenage daughter with this lovely portrait of a dark-skinned, bare-breasted girl washing her hair by a moonlit stream with a fawn crouched at her feet.

Here is another thing I learned: the hardest person in the world to sell to is the one who says *Yes* all the way – *Yes I like it, yes I can afford it, yes there is room for it at the top of the stair* – but when asked to buy it, says *No*. No reason given, just *No*.

'Overcome an objection or hesitation,' our leader said, 'and you're on your way to a sale. You've got traction, yes? But someone who agrees with your pitch all the way then says, "No, I don't want it," is like a greased-up monkey – no purchase!'

We were driven through the night in a couple of vans, to a housing estate in Penicuik.

'Here's your paintings. Now go sell them!'

It was awful to be faced with irritation, anger, impatience, disbelief, at door after door. Horrible too were the few times my assumed bravado actually worked, and people let me in to their house, believed my struggling art-college student story, agreed this hideous thing on the wall looked grand right here – *Yes you've spotted the place for it!* – and finally bought it.

I remember the wave of exhilaration on making a sale – a tired woman who seemed happy at the surprise she would give her husband when he got back from his shift – and then the backwash of disgust as I shook on it and left to go on to the next house with another unique art work.

I sold two Art Felt paintings on the estates we hit that night, and I had to drop the price on one to make the sale. It was exhausting. It did not play to my strengths.

We met up to be debriefed. Our leader had sold ten without breaking sweat. *It's like rolling a log*, he said. *I just love it.* Two people had sold three, and showed some potential. I was given a pat on the back and a lesson on negotiating price-cutting. No one else had made a sale. One person never reappeared, having just legged it into the night with his paintings, which I felt showed initiative.

We drove back into Edinburgh. I pocketed my commission, then agreed on tomorrow evening's rendezvous, said goodnight. I wandered back to my digs through sleeping Edinburgh, sweat long turned cold under my shirt. I climbed the stairs, fitting aching feet into their foot-worn scoops, weary unto death. If this was Real Life, it was overrated.

I never went back. Discovering what is not for you is as valuable a lesson as finding what is. I still wince when I see *No Hawkers. No Salesmen.* I still think of the quiet hero who says *Yes* all down the line, then simply *No*.

One late afternoon, in misery, isolation and poor health, I looked up from my journal and saw my surroundings – the few books, the guitar propped just so, the feebly glowing electric fire – had all changed. Even my own hands in their fingerless mitts looked different. Everything was exactly the same, including me, but transformed into something glowing with – what?

It felt like abruptly living within a painting – perhaps a sombre Dutch interior – or a poem or a song. All these banal, depressing or irritating things revealed themselves to be dignified and right just as they were, because they were.

The rattle of hail on the window, the faint growl and zip of wet traffic and the distant moan of Mrs Hill vacuuming – taken together, they were astounding. Even my loneliness, the nausea-tinged yearning for the recent past and for future achievement, my self-doubt and lack of money, all seemed interesting truths about the extraordinary world.

I was fascinated by the ragged line where the dark wet on my desert boots became paler, drying as they lay by the fire. Meanwhile the wheel of the meter went round and round, recording zero usage.

Redeemed was the word. Redemption without a Redeemer, but redemption nevertheless.

It was as if unseen fingers had clicked in the space at the back of my head, and I had awoken from a hypnotised state. The cooling mug of instant coffee, the guitar propped slightly off-vertical, the rain-stained desert boots by the dull-barred fire, the aching, hungry, wheezing young man in the sagging armchair – how right and poignant, this moment in his history!

How ready to pass into memory.

How soon he will be leaving, and this room take on the next occupant.

How present he is, how fleeting. How just right.

During that Edinburgh winter, I began to notice and treasure this shift of perspective as it recurred – standing in Princess Street gardens, scootering round Arthur's Seat, scanning the job ads in the *Evening News*. Each occasion was different and short-lived, but had the same quality of transformation without changing or denying one detail.

It chimed with that electricity meter in my dismal bedsit: insert a long screwdriver, push a cog and decouple from the habitual clockwork of the world, and let the power come through. Let the wheel spin unencumbered.

It was also related to how some books, plays and some music – particularly the String Band – re-presented the world.

It was the opposite of absent-mindedness. It was present-mindedness.

I couldn't make this shift happen and I couldn't make it stay. Still, I began to look out for it, and it happened more often.*

One morning in early December I went to hang out in Bruce's Record Shop. It was warm and full of thin longhairs in greatcoats with headphones clamped on, nodding away. Bruce's stocked records no one else had, and they let you listen for ages without having to buy. I handled an LP, *Five Leaves Left*, by the silent Nick Drake, whom we'd seen in Joe's office. And here was Dr Strangely Strange's second album, *Heavy Petting*!

Maybe it was a sign. It had happened for them, it could still happen for Fate & ferret.

Someone pointed out Bruce himself, a skinny, wired, freak-hair, indistinguishable from his clientele. It seemed *our people* were taking over. He might know someone who would listen to our latest tape.

I edged closer, hearing the words *String Band*. It seemed he actually knew them. He mentioned Clive Palmer! I overheard mention of the Moody Blues coming in later for a signing party for *On the Threshold of a Dream*.

At that time the Moody Blues were big. Poppy yet experimental, melodic, dreamy, they were a bit far out, but not too far out. People were starting to call it progressive rock. They had been a

---

* I still alternate between understanding this recurrent phenomenon as essentially something initiated by an impromptu release of serotonin, and what it actually feels like – a glimpse of how things truly are.

Merseybeat-type band, then they made a concept album *Days of Future Passed*, played flute and sitar and went orchestral.

They were not my favourite band, being a bit earnest. They were good, if not life-changingly incredible, but they would always have 'Nights in White Satin'. I had read in *Melody Maker* they were starting a record label, looking for new or overlooked bands. We were certainly overlooked.

I returned at lunchtime to a shop bristling with Afghan coats and expansive moustaches. The day had been damp and the premises smelled strongly of animal hide. I scooped up fizzy wine, got a fistful of nibbles and approached the clean-shaven fair-haired Afghan I recognised as Justin Hayward. He seemed open, affable, nearly young. He apologised for being a bit glassy-eyed, on account of being just off the plane back from America. Infinite glamour! At the same time, I registered he was a well-spoken chap with a smelly coat that was collecting crumbs of cheese straws on its fringes.

The drummer Graeme Edge came over for some of Justin's cheese straws. He admitted he had written the poem 'In the Beginning', which opened the album, and the other spoken-word tracks on their earlier albums. I raved about Miroslav Holub, Cavafy and Keats, and how combining poetry and music was the way to go. Bubbles were bursting in my head. So many moustaches! Such vast and smelly coats!

Bruce came by. I said I was part of a band called Fate & ferret, doing String Band-type stuff but with our own poems and songs set in the East Neuk. The Moody who played keyboards and the spacey mellotron – a kind of electronic mind-expander – was Mike

Pinder. No relation of the Greek poet Pindar, but this didn't stop me recommending the Penguin *Four Greek Poets* to all and sundry.

I was a little overexcited, but still focused enough to get the name and address of their management, so I could send them our *Helping Mrs Monbirth* tape. A plump man from Decca started talking to me, which was fine and interesting, but he started stroking my hand while suggesting we might go for another drink at his hotel. I knocked back another glass of champagne, got a good fistful of peanuts and cheese straws, slipped away.

Still jobless, and down to the last of my savings, one morning I took my twelve-string to Princess Street Gardens, set down the cover and began to play. It was sunny but very cold, the strings stung my fingers. I had the harmonica in a rack alongside the kazoo, which saved my voice and drew a few smiles and a bit of small change.

It felt odd and exposed to be playing solo. My Incredible String Band songs drew some curious looks, and a grin from a couple of passing penniless longhairs. I went back to the early days at the Waid Folk Club to bellow 'Rosin the Bow'. Encouraged by some coins and loiterers, I tried 'Mingulay Boat Song', and followed it with 'Mhairi's Wedding', topped and tailed with a kazoo solo.

A few pieces of silver lay among the coppers. In those days Edinburgh was an international city for only a few festival weeks; for the rest of the year it reverted to smoke-blackened, stalwart, shivering locals. A couple of likely lads edged closer to my coins.

'Hey, son, ye'll hae to stop that richt noo!'

Two park keepers stood at my elbow, stout and uniformed like

Tweedledum and Tweedledee. The likely lads and small crowd melted away.

'You hae a licence to play music?' Tweedledum speired.

'Not really.'

'Ye'll hae tae apply tae the cooncil.'

'But ye'll no get wan,' Tweedledee said with satisfaction. 'Naebody gets wan but for yon auld codger up on North Brig.'

Right enough, the only busker I had seen in Edinburgh sat outside the *Scotsman* offices most days, rain or shine, playing accordion with grim efficiency behind dark glasses, white stick by his side. He had campaign ribbons and might have been crippled by the Great War.

My only disability being a tendency to sing flat, I scooped up the coins and put the guitar back in its case. The two wardens watched me as I sauntered down to the fountain at the west end of the gardens, in no hurry to go back to my bedsit.

Standing there waiting to see if the park wardens would go away to let me busk again, the breeze dragged fine fountain-spray onto my face – and there it is again, the world not so much stopped as remade.

I am witnessing it all as though looking down from above. Except I am not above but inside, more inside than I have been since age five.

This is reality, pressing on palms, moving equally within every cell of the body and the tight molecular structures of the Castle and its set volcanic rock, pulsing silently within these bare trees, sap-sunk, deep-rooted and enduring, as a young man stands in a wakeful dwam, at the centre and periphery of the whole shebang.

Shortly before Christmas, still jobless and with no money left in the Post Office savings book, I packed up my few belongings and a filled journal. Kneeling in the meter corner, I cajoled the little cog back into line, crimped the lead seal, and left Edinburgh with a new ploy in mind.

Track 20: Krysia Kocjan

Sitting near-defeated in the Labour Exchange a few days earlier, I had picked the *Daily Record* from the floor, opened it on a feature about a dynamic Scottish schoolgirl singer-songwriter with corkscrew hair. She was sixteen, apparently had an amazing singing voice, and wrote songs with guitarist partner Tom Hoy – long black hair parted in the centre, strikingly good-looking in the manner of James Taylor. They had a manager, lived in Glasgow, and were looking for a recording contract.

They called themselves the Natural Acoustic Band, and the interview confirmed they were huge Incredible String Band fans.

Her name was Krysia Kocjan, and I thought *Why not?*

Early January, I caught the bus to Glasgow, then the train to Milngavie, where Krysia Kocjan lived. We had exchanged letters, excited to find ourselves in the same groove: same heroes, similar dreams.

I carried my twelve-string guitar, and a tape of the latest F & f recordings.

George and I were already thinking: *supergroup*. Neither of us was much of a singer, we didn't look great, and neither yearned to be a front man; but sometimes we wrote good songs. The duo of Krysia and Tom as the Natural Acoustic Band could amalgamate with F & f, with maybe our Fiddler Tom and Eric P for some electric raunch if that's what folks wanted. Krysia would be the front singer, something like Sandy Denny in Fairport Convention, and we would all pool material. With their business manager to push and promote, we could get gigs then the elusive recording contract.

Perhaps call ourselves *Acoustic Ferret*?

The early F & f days had passed. Music had moved on too, mostly getting louder. *Heavy* was now good in music, if not in life, though we had loved lightness. Led Zeppelin and Deep Purple were Eric Plectrum's new obsessions. Apparently Fate & ferret's piss-take one-chord 'GREAT MEAT THRASH' was not the end of the line but the sound of things to come.

In photos in the music papers, the starry-eyed were being replaced by the blank-eyed. The Beatles had gone quiet, something was very wrong with them. Vietnam was getting uglier. Dylan wasn't saying much. The Stones did not look sexy so much as bleakly indifferent. A man had been stabbed to death at the Altamont festival.

In the face of this, the String Band had just released *Changing Horses*, their first Scientology album. It had a comic song, 'Big Ted', a very lengthy Robin song, 'Creation', and a big one by Mike, 'White

Bird', which had a lovely opening, passed through some kind of crisis (the bird is dead, frozen to the ice), then entered a musically mystifying passage of guitar jazz, before re-emerging into a communal resurrection chant: *White bird! White bird!*

We quite liked *Changing Horses*, but for the first time, 'White Bird' apart, we were faced with a String Band album that wasn't a revelation. It was just . . . interesting. On the sleeve photo they looked a bit improbable.

George and I had taken a long walk through the back country, through Crawhill, on to Kittlenaked Woods then up Kellie Law. We sat looking out over our Fife, and talked around the past and the present. Our practice and recording sessions increasingly depended on Eric P and John Myles. I liked but couldn't add much to George's new West Coast-influenced songs.

We tried to talk about it, but even with the Scientology Communication Rundowns we had been coached in, we couldn't. Still, Krysia and Tom might be the answer. Who knew what lay in wait in Milngavie? I might be smitten. We might form a joint band, or else just guest on each other's albums.

The hounds of aspiration were once more fleet-footing the imaginary trail.

She was at the bus stop, petite in a big Afghan coat. At sixteen, she looked very young to me. She said she'd just left school for music, something we'd not had the nerve to do. We shook hands, she laughingly corrected my pronunciation of her name, and of the leafy suburb she lived in – Milngavie with a silent v, like *Mill-guy*. For an

East Coaster, anything to do with Glasgow was exotic, threatening, exciting.

Krysia was tiny and weightless as a flea. Her eyes were huge, her hair long, curly, free. I thought she was fantastic.

In Tom's room we were nervous and self-conscious. I played a couple of our songs from the tape, not trusting my own voice. Then she and Tom sang a couple of theirs. It was immediately evident she had a great and big voice, neither wispy hippie nor po-faced folkie.

She sang clear, accurate, unaffected, like Sandy Denny with a hint of jazz. And Tom Hoy was a more than capable guitarist. At first hearing, their own songs were enjoyable but not amazing.

Then she sang 'Summertime', and that *was* astounding. I sat on the end of the bed, trying not to gape at the huge voice streaming from this scrap of a girl while Tom played all those jazz chords.

She was sweet as a linty, powerful as a sea eagle. She sang out her soul.

This is how I see us still. Tom is at one end of the single bed, wearing a blue denim shirt with sleeves rolled up, looking like James Taylor and deftly strumming, watching Krysia, his eyes alert. I am on the other end of the bed, tapping on my twelve-string, uplifted and amazed. And Krysia Kocjan is glowing in a gypsy dress, sitting cross-legged in an armchair singing, like a brass-lunged lark in Byzantium, of what is past, or passing, or to come.

I ended the evening at the house of their friends Brian and Jim (the grown-ups never appeared). We spent all our time in a big, dark, high-ceilinged communal room, where the curtains were always drawn.*

For me it has remained the archetypal hippy pad, at once bohemian and Victorian, stern and deranged. Mattresses on the floor, a strew of sleeping bags, LPs and guitars, incense and mugs of tea, and for the first time I saw fat joints being passed round.

I said I didn't smoke, sipped on my Newcastle Brown and watched to see if any of these friendly strangers tried to leap out the window or became generally strange. I had never met anyone in the East Neuk who had access to cannabis, let alone LSD. Even on our London adventure, no one had offered us any or smoked in front of us.† All I knew were coded mentions in songs, and the panic in my mother's *Daily Mail*. Drugs sounded alarming and interesting. Up to now we hadn't needed them.

There was a lot of laughter, giggling, strumming, long pauses and records played for hours. I finally fell asleep to Hendrix, curled on a mattress on the floor by several bottles of Newcastle Brown.

Sat 10 Jan '70 Wake round 11.0. Breakfast of Sugar Puffs, coffee and scrambled eggs. Great! All out for a walk in the country. It is mild and misty.

---

* Tom Hoy: a Never-Never wonderland, curiouser and curiouser, either side of the high mantle shelf, two Ostrich eggs were displayed framing an austere painting of a very stern-looking chap (no one knew who he was) – on each side of the fireplace, stereo speakers, balanced on a wobbly table on the left, a turntable that rolled on day and night, incense and smoke hung on the air, people came and went straight on till morning. At the weekends, if you got lost and wandered up the dark passageway and turned left, you could be lucky enough to stumble into one of Jim's grandparents' musical sing-songs, lots of cheap wine and happy faces, good times for all the family!
† We'd have done anything our heroes did, but we weren't ready. Maybe they could see that.

Feel very alive but ethereal. At Susan's house, meet their manager Mr Small.
He seems interested in F & f, asks us to play at a concert next week, which
is a groove. Play String Band songs with Tom, later Krysia and I work on a
middle bit for her 'Sweet Water'.

I added some lyrics and suggested a chord sequence for the middle section, then listened to Krysia sing it back. This could be our future. She was alive and light as a water-skater on a pond, seemingly composed of air and energy as she sang about the hollow of her womb.

Despite this womb stuff, she did not have the earthiness I found attractive, which was just as well. I felt I could elevate her with one hand, delighted by her talent, high spirits and self-belief. Though in some ways the embodiment of a young hippy, she was not fey and drifty. She was energetic, laughed a lot and seemed very clear what she wanted to do: sing, write, live creatively.

I found her life-enhancing, engaged yet self-possessed, charismatic; and her friends clearly thought the same. I had no doubt she was going somewhere, and the only question was how far and with whom.

A week later, I run for the bus, guitar in hand, overnight bag in the other. George gets on in Pittenweem.

'I feel terrible,' he croaks.

'Me too.'

We are both sweating and aching. He looks older, different. In its way Dundee has been as rough and lonely for him as Edinburgh was for me.

'Nothing prepares you for leaving home,' George comments. 'Whatever you think it's going to be, it's so much harder.'

Tom the fiddler gets on at Elie, sporting a nifty trilby. At Colinsburgh, Eric Plectrum comes lurching up the bus, sideburns like privet hedges. He clutches his electric guitar and leads in an old fertiliser sack.

In Leven, George and I buy aspirin, throat lozenges and a bottle each of Benylin, which we start swigging. No way are we not going to do this gig. It could be the next phase. We're now thinking a Scottish version of Fairport Convention.

On the train to Glasgow we get out guitars and fiddle, and subject the passengers to a much-needed practice. My ears are blocked and everything sounds odd and flat. Maybe it is. Our set is going to be a mix of String Band, our own more recent electric songs, and Eric P doing a couple of his own. I've stressed that Krysia and Tom are proper musicians, which is a bit of a concern.

Perhaps in this line-up we should call ourselves something different, say *Boiling Mud*?

We are met at Queen Street station by Mr Small. He is wearing a suit and tie! A grown-up. He says NAB are finishing the demo tape tomorrow for him to take round the record companies, and that he is sure Krysia is going to be a star.

We agree, groggily, and knock back more Benylin.

Then we are taken for lunch. This is the life we had imagined: managers, free lunches, recording contracts. We explain about Fate & ferret/Boiling Mud, the tapes and contacts we have with the String Band, Joe Boyd, the Moody Blues. Even John Peel has one of our tapes (to which he has not yet responded).

George abruptly collapses. Face down on the table, cheeks pale as dirty snow. After a few minutes he stirs and comes to. I've seen this once before, on a school trip when he just dropped. Low blood pressure, I think. Having the flu and the best part of a bottle of Benylin inside him has not helped.

As his eyes start to focus, we ask if he wants to go to hospital. He shakes his head, insists he just needs to lie down. He thinks he'll be able to play. He asks me to take care of the set-up and run-through. I say I will, and for a moment we are close again.

So he is taken away to a friend's house, and we are driven to the Kessington Hall in Bearsden. Tom and Krysia are already there. I do the introductions, explain about George. There's another musician, Robin Thyne, in waistcoat and striped shirt. We mumble *Hi* to each other. His position in the Natural Acoustic Band is unclear, but he'll be playing percussion, whistles, second guitar. This is probably not good news for the supergroup.

There is a drum kit, and Eric P immediately goes behind it and starts tapping and thumping like he was born for this. I meet the roadie-cum-sound engineer – F & f have never had one of those – and outline what we will need. *More on the fiddle! Less drums! I can't hear my guitar! Less fiddle! More guitar!*

It's my first experience of a sound-check run-through, that time of tension, arousal, frustration, boredom, all roiling together in the pit of the stomach. The lift of hearing your own voice bouncing back from the far wall, the dismay at how crap it sounds, the thrill at the anticipated audience that may or may not fill those empty seats, irritation at band members who won't stop playing while you're tuning. Everyone always wants to sound louder.

I'm worrying if George is going to make it. Hard to imagine what is left if he can't. My vocals are dependent on his, and I trust his songs more than mine. Eric P will be fine doing his own. Still, George is from Pittenweem, with a strong, salt-cured will. If at all possible, he'll do it.

He does, reappearing in his concert gear, the green crushed-velvet breeks and embroidered waistcoat, pale but upright, accompanied by Krysia's school friend Susan Reid, who has organised tonight's show. I go so far as to put my arm round his thin shoulder.

'You all right?'

'All right enough.' He shrugs. 'All set up?'

'We've got a sound engineer!'

'Far out!'

In my memory, the hall is pleasingly full of people our age and younger, sitting, standing, cross-legged on the floor. The surviving photos remind me I have slipped off my glasses as usual, making the experience ill-defined. I see I am wearing a black-and-silver metallic shirt bought in Dundee, loon pants, sealskin slippers and my dad's green silky neck scarf with tassels and dragons. Tommy is resplendent in a dressing gown of many colours, and tweed trilby. George has his green velvet trousers and a loose-sleeved, groovy shirt.

A lot of Tom and Krysia's friends and fans are there. They look like our pals in the East Neuk, a mixture of scruffs, freaks and straights, part-fledged from school.

A couple of very young local bands play covers, then we are announced as *'Fate and ferret's Boiling Mud!'*

Eric P has used his pliers to good effect, and he sounds and looks the real thing as he plays drums, electric guitar, then sings 'Morna' on my twelve-string. George manages to stay upright and croak through 'Unboltin' the Blues' and 'Friday Evening Blues'. I did my soulful 'Night Piece' and a mock-bucolic singalong 'Back Country Cider'.

Then the Natural Acoustic Band go on. Krysia sings sitting, holding a microphone that she sometimes dips towards the bowl of water she stirs on her lap. Between songs we listen to dabbled water – taken straight from the ISB's *Hangman*, just the kind of thing we do – then she starts humming, Tom picks guitar, Robin blows some woodwind. It is innocent, silly and mesmerising; then she opens her throat to sing 'Sweet Water'.

Whatever *it* is, Krysia Kocjan has it. We are stunned by her voice and charisma. She lifts their own songs above aspirational gesture. When they do 'Summertime', her manager's hopes seem entirely realistic: she is and will be a star. She has that capacity to give herself over completely, while remaining unknowable.

As the finale we join forces with Tom, Krysia and Robin, to do some String Band bankers – this audience all seem to know 'Log Cabin Home in the Sky' and 'How Happy I Am' – and finish with the altogether-now ending of 'Cellular Song'. In my astigmatic Benylin wooziness I look at the faces of my friends old and new, flushed and raised by the singing, and know this is what we came here for.

My diary notes that we were paid £9 by their manager, which was Fate & ferret's best-paid gig. In fact, probably our only paid one.

When we step outside, snow has fallen, is still falling in big white parachute flakes. The streets of Bearsden are unmarked and innocent again. Sound is muffled, our feet crimp and creak as we walk back to Susan Reid's. She – or perhaps her sister Pat? – is holding my arm in a companionable way. On her other side, George is silent, pale under streetlamps, faintly smiling. Eric P has disappeared with a woman – he was always more rock 'n' roll than us.

Tom Hoy walks in his Salvation Army greatcoat, with the collar high against the cold. Maureen, Krysia's friend, is talking at him in her Canadian accent, whilst he tries to block her out and evaluate the evening.

Fiddler Tom has flakes of snow sliding down his glasses, his trilby jauntily askew, still wearing his performing dressing gown, clutching his violin case and jerkily talking with a girl beside him.

And Krysia is on my right, snow collecting on her rainbow tam-o'-shanter. She starts singing the refrain of a song she and Tom and I had begun improvising the week before: *Ah ah ah, it's a good good life.**

We start joining in, and she ornaments it with harmonies. *Fate & ferret say it's a good life / Tom and Krysia say it's a good life / And you and me say it's a good, good life . . .*

And that's where I leave us, on that beyond-tired walk back to Susan's, with singing friends through snow-muffled streets, led by a young woman so light it is a wonder she leaves any prints at all.

---

* Tom: I remember very well singing with great joy in my room 'It's a good life' – we were all happy, till later George told us it was just like a Tyrannosaurus Rex song.

It came to nothing, of course, the supergroup. Months later we noticed NAB had signed to RCA, also medium-sized ads in the music papers for their gigs in cool places like the Marquee. They were touring with Ralph McTell. They made an LP, then another.

Times and music changed, my interests changed. Eventually I heard Krysia had left NAB,* then nothing. All that remained were some diary entries, a fragment of tape of Krysia, Tom and me singing 'Good Life' in Tom's room, and two photos of Boiling Mud on stage.

Then, in May 2007, for no apparent reason Krysia Kocjan's name bobbed to the surface like a marker buoy from a sunken vessel. I strongly wanted to contact her, see how and where she was. What had she done with those years during and after the Natural Acoustic Band?

Online searching told me she had made two NAB albums, *Learning to Live* and *Branching In* (how easily these could have been F & f titles!), then an obscure solo album as Krysia Kristianne Kocjan. After NAB she toured and recorded with Al Stewart, and worked with the Kinks, Robin Williamson and Mike Heron, as a backing singer. She moved to LA, and seemed to have lived as a session musician and singing teacher. And in Portland, Oregon, 21 February 2007, aged fifty-four, she died of lung cancer.

Oh Lord, that familiar contraction of the heart.

---

* Tom: Krysia came up to me and said, 'It's your band [news to me] so I thought I'd better tell you first – I'm leaving.' It was always on the cards – since the first day I met her. I never pleaded or begged with her to stay (though many others did) – I just wished her well – and that was that. We finished the tour and she was gone like snow on the water.

As long as computers thrum in vast air-conditioned sheds in Arizona, the internet will hold Krysia Kocjan's music and too-short life in its mesh. As it holds us all, virtually, from here on in. It's not immortality the way we want it, in the body, but it will have to do.

Yet it is not in the Net but in my head that the post-concert walk back to Susan's is still happening, as a happy, tired band of teen-agers carrying instruments stomp through falling snow, with Krysia leading us while we sing out our doomed, defiant credo: *It's a good life.*

Did she get what she wanted, even so?

'Do you remember a singer called Krysia Kocjan?' I asked Mike as we walked along the beach at Aberlady, east of Edinburgh. A brisk, sunny day, and we the living.

'Yes,' he said. 'She sang backing vocals on my *Reputation* album. Tiny woman. Fantastic voice!'

'I knew her at the end of the sixties,' I said. 'She was really into the String Band.'

'Well,' he said, part apologetically and part just stating fact, 'a lot of people were then.'

'She died five years ago, in Oregon.'

We walked on in silence.

'Really good singer,' he finally said.

Then we sat on the rocks in the sun eating biscuits, enjoying the waves breaking, and not being dead.

Track 21: U Too

April 1970 finds us heading for London in the scampi lorry, with new tapes for Joe Boyd and the Moody Blues. I have taken a week off my job netting salmon upriver from Perth; George is on his Easter vacation from Dundee Art College. We are back in the game. Squished together in the scampi lorry cab, comfortable, uncomfortable, we talk of how young we were last time we did this.

'This is our last throw of the dice,' George comments.

I hadn't quite thought of it like that. I nod, then stick my head out the window to stay awake, wondering about the fishing poems I had sent out to BBC radio that morning.

Joe has cut his hair! He looks straighter, yet worn and distracted. He accepts our tape and album material gingerly, apologises for not responding to our last one, says he'd be interested in using some of our material for the ISB's latest American tour.

'Hang around,' he says. 'I'll get Susie to give you tickets for the "U" opening. I'll listen to your tape when I can.'

We are dazzled by the radiant Susie Watson-Taylor, her leather boots and confidence. We hang around the Witchseason office, inspecting the posters for the forthcoming ISB show 'U'. It is to run at the Roundhouse for ten days, then go to the States.

It might be huge. It certainly sounds ambitious, involving a number of 'expressive dancers', complex lighting and staging, with the String Band playing throughout. As she gives us tickets, we ask Susie what it is about.

'I'm not sure,' she says brightly. 'But it'll be amazing – the next *Hair*!

The poster offers few clues. Against a virulent yellow-and-green background, two multicoloured sprites or pixies form a capital U. *Hair* had music we thought a bit banal, but it was also confrontational, angry and political, with full-frontal nudity. None of these were likely from the String Band.

'Janet drew these,' Susie says. Then, seeing our blank faces, adds 'Janet Shankman. Robin's girlfriend. She's from LA.'

We turn back to the poster to hide our astonishment. What is going on? Robin and Likky had been among the eternal verities. And LA sounds vulgar and crass.

'She's certainly not much of an artist,' George mutters.

Leaning elegantly against the filing cabinets, Joe's assistant Huw Price explains the scene is changing. We have to move to London if we want to make it. He says Joe is under a lot of pressure on many fronts. We feel he is trying to tell us something, but we aren't sure what.

Anthea Joseph lopes in, more cadaverous than ever. She remembers us, reminisces about being in Edinburgh with Bobby, maybe '63, while he wrote out lyrics for 'Masters of War' on paper napkins.

We boggle silently. I boggle still. Anthea Joseph had so many stories, well burnished in the telling for sure, but they were not counterfeit.

We start telling her about going into the Scientology centre in Edinburgh, and how they keep writing and phoning us. She listens for a while then abruptly holds up her hand like a policeman stopping excess traffic.

'Don't touch it, boys. It's fascism.'

We stare at her. She glares back. But surely the String Band are really into it?

'That's their business,' she says. 'You must never let *anyone* monitor your thoughts.'

I think of the E-meter that in fact just measures electrical resistance, and the box in the corner where we were invited to submit queries for L. Ron Hubbard as though he were sitting next door. We are still being pursued to sign up for auditing.

'If you join Scientology,' Anthea says, 'I will never speak to you again.'

Over her shoulder, I notice Susie twitch but she says nothing.

Sufism, Maoism, Divine Light, the Maharishi, TM, the Hare Krishnas, Scientology, anarchism, psychoanalysis, life-coaching and, in younger days, the Seaside Summer Mission – there has been much on offer in my lifetime. I have felt the pull of them all. Who does not wish to be saved, to be made whole? Who would not want to shed this burden?

But even the less preposterous precepts of humanism, Buddhism, the Quakers that my mother joined in her later years – in the end I've turned away from entirely signing up to any of them. Anthea Joseph was opinionated, loyal, generous and darkly troubled, but on this she was right. You must not hand over the burden of yourself to anyone else, not even to your beloved if you're fortunate enough to have one.

There's a handwritten sign by the A82 on the way to Fort William: *Bag your own manure*. Excellent advice.

John Martyn breezes in. He is mid-recording and seems in high spirits. My diary notes that he said Eddie McGeachy, our peppery, pint-sized gym teacher and John's uncle, was 'really beautiful', which was almost as boggling as Anthea's strictures.

He goes in to see Joe. I did not know they were increasingly in dispute about recording and would soon stop working together. It was improbable as the beautiful, curly-haired, effervescent Iain McGeachy becoming a swollen, brutally difficult, one-legged alcoholic.

Meanwhile Susie gasses about a friend whose 'old man is in Black Sabbath'. I think, *Blimey, I didn't know they were that old*, and fortunately don't say it. As always, we hadn't quite got hold of the lingo.

Joe is leaning over Susie's desk when a longhair drifts in – jeans, tie-dye, things dangling from his neck, sleeveless Afghan jacket, the usual. He hands Joe some photos. We understand he is involved in the 'U' production in some way.

'Hey man, I need a fiver for the taxi back.'

The expression on Joe's face combines irritation with deep weariness, as though this had been happening too often for too long.

'Take the bus,' Joe says curtly.

'I haven't the time, man. Need to get back there.' He sounds like a mosquito, whiny and persistent.

Joe turns and stares at him. There is a long pause, then Joe turns away.

'Susie, give him five pounds from petty cash, and make a note.'

'Thanks, man,' the longhair says, but Joe is already picking up the phone.

That scene was very short and must have happened every day at Witchseason, especially around the time of 'U'. It stayed with me, though, that playing out of the hassle, the pressure, the endless mosquito pinpricks, the hangers-on, money draining out and not coming back.

In our innocence we'd never thought of Witchseason as a business, a complex one combining recording sessions – Joe's true purpose on the planet – with management, tour organising, promotion, signing contracts, money coming in but mostly going out. All this while trying to deal with sharks, incompetents, wide-eyed wannabes from Fife, the delusional and the stoned, and, best and worst of all: musicians. Fragile people like Nick Drake and Sandy Denny, the hugely talented awkward squad like Richard Thompson and John Martyn, unworldly dreamers turned efficient Scientologists like the String Band – all needing to be nursed, cajoled, encouraged, diverted, produced and directed.

Joe had to operate in the real world while keeping it at bay; protecting the freedoms and talents that made the artists special so that they could flourish in that protected space. It must have been wondrous at times, but it can't have been easy, swatting away those mosquitos, giving out your life's blood from the petty cash.

Vaguely embarrassed, we leave Witchseason to go and hassle Zel Records.

That night we took up Joe's invitation to sit in on one of his recording sessions at Sound Techniques. We propped ourselves in the corner out of the way as gruff John Wood fussed over the controls of what looked to us like a vast flight deck (actually a small, eight-track analogue console that produced some of the finest UK recordings of the period).

He and Joe seemed at home but hassled. The Incredible String Band's psychedelic music–dance whimsy was opening in two days, and some of the music–was still being completed. In answer to John Wood's query, Joe said the show was something to do with an imaginary planet and Scientology. From his tone, he seemed no more impressed by Scientology than Anthea had been.

Joe explained that Mike's instrumental 'Overture' was to be played over the PA while the dancers and the ISB got into position. Mike and Robin had hastily recorded it in another studio while on tour. Now he had to make it work.

He played back the theme. It was basic piano plus Mike on a piercing electric lead-guitar, like a searchlight searching the night for bombers. It sounded wonderful. Joe pulled a face, conferred with John, who played back Mike's second take. And a third.

Apparently there was a problem. They all sounded great to us, but each take had a different glitch or fumble. It was also too short. It was too late to re-record.

Joe sat back. He looked tired, it was only ten o'clock and the Fairports were due in soon.

'Okay, here's what we're gonna try.'

He and John took the least-bad guitar track, combined it with the least-bad piano; tweaked it around. Then they repeated that adjusted take and on top of it laid the guitar part from the second take. The two guitars together, slightly out of sync, sounded great. More transcendental yearning.

Joe listened, frowning. Then they took the third-version guitar line, isolated and tweaked it, then laid that on top of what they already had.

'Lets hear the whole thing through.'

John Wood did deft stuff with a razor blade and sticky tape; then we listened to the playback.

If two guitars sounded good, three – each subtly and accidentally slightly different – lifted the top of our heads off. Joe said if they'd recorded it properly in the first place, he wouldn't have had to do this. John Wood muttered something, and Joe laughed.

And that was it. The 'Overture' theme now ran three times, building on each run through: one guitar, two guitars, then three electric guitars complexly not-quite integrated. We sat amazed at this rescue job. Imagine what Joe could do with our tapes!

Time for another coffee as John Wood copied, saved and labelled the tape. While we waited, Joe enthused about how much he enjoyed working with the Fairports: so professional, so competent.

They stumbled in an hour late, round midnight and extremely beery, boisterous and giggling. Joe said little, but sent them down into the studio. After trying a number of mic positions, it was decided to have all four of them sing into the one mic, old-school style. It should give the kind of naturalness and intimacy Joe prized.

Whenever I hear the jaunty 'Walk Awhile' or the lugubrious 'Sloth' (both on *Full House*), I feel a deep-rooted headache, and very, very tired from dehydration, too much coffee, and umpteen passive cigarettes. The Fairports who had come to do the vocals arsed about at the microphone, pulling faces till one cracked and the giggles exploded into laughter. It was somewhere between high spirits and sabotage. Mattacks and Swarbrick seemed to be the ringleaders.

Joe sighed. 'Again.'

And they'd do it again, and would corpse again. Around four in the morning, Joe gave up. He suggested they might be able to splice together the acceptable verses on different versions. John Wood muttered a simple profanity.

Joe drove us through silent, empty London to drop us off at the Golden Egg, where we drank tea till the Underground opened.

A day spent around and in the British Museum, buying fancy waistcoats, incense sticks, a printed silk scarf for Irene, something for Teri. We went through the Egyptian and Abyssinian rooms, then came to the Grecian for the first time.

We stood transfixed by the archaic torsos, the vibrating stillness of flesh made marble. The Elgin Marbles frieze. Nike forever bending to adjust her sandal. A vast head of Apollo that had been dredged up by fishermen – Apollo god of music and reason, rider of dolphins, the merciless flayer of Marsyas.*

I had to get to the source of this art – who'd have thought there was a point in sculpture? – with its wild, noble, petty gods, and its passion for reasoned argument, ritualistic plays, poetry and democratic governance. I was already saving my salmon-netting wages to go there, lying awake in my bothy bunk teaching myself basic Greek by torchlight. While my workmates played cards or slept, I dreamed of Delos and Delphi and the unparalleled light flashing over the Ionian Sea.

We stared at carvings of randy centaurs, the low-life Dionysus and his disruptive, pleasure-loving cousin Pan. Soon enough I would sleep out in the woods of Arcadia in Peloponnesus, share coarse cigarettes at dawn in a fishing boat off Cape Sounion, drink from the Castalian Spring on a moonlit night in Delphi, both believing and not believing it would bring me the gift of poetry.

It had been a long, cold, lonely winter, and now I yearned for the South. George would be in art college, Irene sitting her Highers, so I would have to go alone.

---

* One night in Crawhill Woods, as we'd crouched for shelter in a moonlit gale, we had glimpsed – conjured up, surely? – Apollo the shining one, striding thirty foot high amid the thrashing branches. Just a glimpse of appalling power, cross-lit by silver in the night, then gone. We never dared even speak of it.

Outside Joe's office we saw Susie sitting in a Mini. We were about to wave when we realised the man next to her was Mike Heron, and the way they were entwined left us in no doubt. Impossible! Mike was with Rose. Hadn't he written 'You Get Brighter' to her?

Yet he was getting it on with the lovely Susie Watson-Taylor.

It seemed everything was changing. Only later did we find out Mike and Rose had already ceased to be a couple, and years after that learned Mike and Susie were an item for a fair while. Unlike the ISB, Susie stayed with Scientology to enter the upper echelons, dying in 2008 of cancer. Once in a while Mike mentions her name, then moves on.

Susie came back into the Witchseason office looking flushed, told us Joe was out at the Roundhouse for a run-through of 'U'. So we went off to find the Moody Blues' office and drop off a copy of our tape. Another radiant receptionist in a cut-down Afghan waistcoat said the lads were just back from an American tour and were too exhausted to come in. She thought they had listened to our last tape. She took our new one and said they'd be in touch.

So we wandered around Soho. *Went to feelthy peectures, which were insufficiently feelthy for our purposes*, according to my diary. Then we went to see *John and Mary* because we were into Dustin Hoffman and Mia Farrow – short hair! Like a boy! Then we were cold, hungry and grubby, so caught the Tube out to High Barnet to have a bath, refuel and sleep on my sister's floor.

Along with delivering our latest tape, 'U' was the reason for this trip. A 'mystical pantomime' or 'a surreal parable in song and dance', it had originated in whimsical drawings of an imagined planet, El Wool, done by Janet Shankman.

Robin had taken these, added elements of Scientology plus songs in his spoof mode ('Robot Blues'), invocations to a golden age, a descent into darkness and programmed response, then an ascent through romantic love and spiritual union, crossing over The Bridge into a condition melding Scientology's Theta state and a good old hippy knees-up at the Glen. This would be interpreted by a largely amateur but enthusiastic dance troupe, Stone Monkey.

'It was very little to do with me,' Mike said forty-five years on, as we followed our partners through Edinburgh's Tollcross. 'It was Robin's kind of thing. I went along with it out of respect for his talents. He'd always wanted to do multimedia and storytelling on a big scale, and I thought he might pull it off.'

'The dancing was a bit rough,' I said tactfully.

'I had my back to it most of the time,' Mike said. 'I was just trying to keep up! We hadn't had enough rehearsal time.'

'It did seem . . . spontaneous,' I agreed.

'It did all right at the Roundhouse. But we were booked for these big venues in America that we couldn't call off. It completely cleaned us out.'

He laughed, shrugged. We went in to eat south Indian food. Sitar music buzzed quietly as we sipped our lagers and cracked our poppadoms.

'There were some good songs,' Mike added, then went back to studying the menu.

We got to the Roundhouse early. First thing we saw was Joe Boyd, striding about in cowboy boots. He had brief conversations with Rakis and Malcolm Le Maistre from the Stone Monkey dance troupe, then sat back impassively with his long legs stretched out and those fabulous stitched and dyed boots. He had reluctantly gambled on this show working, but he seemed cool again, or perhaps just tired of worrying.

In one corner of the dressing room we found Mike and Rose. He was teaching her a bass part. They sat, knees nearly touching. She played it, head down, hair obscuring her face.

'No. It goes like this.'

He took the bass, played the line while she watched, then handed it back. Rose played. He shook his head.

'No, that's not it. Like this.'

He hummed it out, she tried again. It wasn't the notes so much as the timing she wasn't getting. It was the kind of thing that happened increasingly between me and George.

'It'll have to do,' Mike said. 'I'll nod when you should come in.'

She played the part through again, her head down.

The show went on, and then on. We wanted to love it and we managed to like it. Afterwards we'd talk about Robin's 'Juggler's Song' and the bold inventiveness of 'Time'; how funny Janet Shankman was as 'Bad Sadie Lee'; the Williamson wit of the honky-tonk pastiche 'Robot Blues'.

It was great to hear the 'Overture' we had burned the midnight oil with Joe over. And, somewhere along the line, maybe around

'Bridge Song', I was briefly, genuinely, carried away, in the manner of old.

But the dancers, the expressive dancers. Not their fault that some were amateurs who made the East Neuk Operatic Society seem well-drilled and light-footed. It more or less worked on the pastiche numbers, but when they were required to be spiritual and emotionally convincing, we averted our eyes.

Perhaps it was our fault, to expect so much? The String Band – like the Beatles in *Magical Mystery Tour* – were just having fun with their pals, and inviting us along. It would have been fine, even magical, in a crammed cottage in the Glen, or a community hall in Innerleithen. But put on at the Roundhouse, after all the advertising and the build-up, with people paying good money, some with their critical faculties intact – it didn't quite work.

At best it was enjoyable in patches. At worst, it was indulgent and whimsical rather than inspired. Maybe El Wool was what it appeared to be in the illustrations: childish, not childlike.

I wonder now if that is too harsh, the harshness of love disappointed.

The String Band, like any true artists, had to follow their fancy. Sometimes it works, sometimes it doesn't. It's not a crime against humanity. Self-transcendence lives right next door to self-indulgence, in the way Robin, Mike, Rose and Likky and Stone Monkey all lived alongside each other in the Glen.

In common with the best of the String Band, 'U' celebrated non-mastery, spontaneity, fancy, mingling the high-minded and the absurd. Perhaps the crucial difference was an underlying sense that 'U' was intended as an allegory, that in the end it had designs on us.

And that can be laid at the door of a new enthusiasm, Scientology.

Or perhaps somewhere along the line the all-redeeming gift of melody had got mislaid.

Backstage, people were being jolly rather than ecstatic. George and I ligged like old hands, hoovering up drinks, nibbles and chat. Anthea whispered in my ear, 'My mother said Isadora Duncan was just as bad.'* She hailed John Martyn, looking like a lovely satyr with his curly hair and beard. Susie came by. Mike beamed, and Robin seemed more normal – maybe it was the Scientology – and less magical, as he talked to a reviewer from the *International Times*.

Meanwhile Anthea was drinking gin like lemonade while she and Beverley swapped stories of 'the early underground' and memories of Suze Rotolo in Greenwich Village. We sipped fizzy wine. No one offered us drugs.

I felt so tired. The crowd thinned out, heading elsewhere. We stepped outside for air, and somehow lost the party. So it was a taxi to the Golden Egg, where we eked out coffees with an old bag lady, who asked if we had any skins, and played 'Home on the Range' affectingly badly as we tried to stay awake so as not to be flung out.

* An aside effortlessly topped by her mother Tish who, years later, mentioned T. E. Lawrence used to come for afternoon tea, then motorbike back to his barracks. Did you ever go to his house, Clouds Hill? I asked. *I slept there once in an embroidered sleeping bag. In the morning he told me George Bernard Shaw and Robert Graves had both used it. I told him 'Next time I'll bring my own.'* They are all long gone, and I can't return to that from which I came without putting this vignette out there.

In Witchseason next morning, Joe's assistant Miriam had got in the papers with reviews, which were mixed – some good, some bad, some both. Few made 'U' sound like something you really had to see. There were still another nine nights to run. I hoped they had sold the seats in advance.

'Think I'd sprain an ankle,' George said.

'I did that once before a rugby match against Bell Baxter,' I confessed. 'The pitch was frozen and they were a right dirty bunch.'

Joe came in, looking tired. Today his short hair seemed a marker that he had separated himself from something. We went to Mrs B's Pantry, where he drank orange juice and coffee and read the reviews in silence. Even we could see it wasn't a good time to ask when he'd listen to our tape. We waited till the last moment then hurried off for the boarding house where our fish lorry driver Big Jim would be starting the run home.

During the long drive north, jammed uncomfortably between George and Big Jim, I replayed the trip.

'*Don't touch it, boys. It's fascism.*' Mike and Susie embracing in a Mini. The Fairports breaking down in laughter as they ruin another take. Joe's expression just before he authorised another fiver from the petty cash. Huw Price saying how the scene had changed and how we had to move to London to make it – and just his putting it that way made it clear something indeed had changed.

It was unlikely our tape featured high in Joe's to-do list. Some moment had passed.

Thurs 10 April Dropped paralytic with cold in Glasgow. Phone Reids' house, lunch with Susan and sister Pat, great. At Brian's, phone Stewart

Conn at BBC – incredible! Has accepted two fishing poems, wants me to record them soonest. So I groove on down there. He is a pleasant young guy, we talk ten a dozen, then record 'Notes while sketching a tree' and 'Auld Andrew'. Catch bus home at a run. Find 'Night Shift' accepted by Scotsman. Too much!

Meanwhile, George stayed on at the strange, crepuscular house in Bearsden where the heavy curtains were always drawn, sitting alone playing Captain Beefheart and Frank Zappa LPs, waiting for Susan to walk in – at which point they would fall into each other's arms and be together for ever. Somehow she didn't. She didn't because he hadn't told her he was there, or given her any indication of interest, and she had other reasons for avoiding the place.

He saw Tom and Krysia briefly, but was too distracted to bring up, or even hint towards, our notion of joining forces. On the third day he gave up and went back to art college to continue his course and think about his musical options.

The contrast between our complete lack of progress in London, and having my poems recorded on return to Scotland, must have been unmissable, even to me. I hadn't taken the poetry that seriously, not compared to our songs and the F & f project. Yet the poems were getting published and paid for, and the songs were not.

Something began to shift on the fish lorry home, as the cat's eyes lit up, flared, then faded behind us. Though heading north, back to the salmon netting, Irene and scrappy recording at the weekends, the ploy of a solo Greece adventure shifted gear from fantasy to firm intention.

While letters and urgent phone calls from Scientology piled up and Irene sat her exams, and George rehearsed with John and Eric

Plectrum, for me there would be the cool embrace of the Ionian Sea at dawn, cicadas falling silent under the blaze of noon, and the poems that might, with persistence, emerge alongside the early-evening stars.

Track 22: Moving On

We never did get a response from Joe Boyd or the Moody Blues about our last tape. A few months later we were aghast, but not entirely surprised, to hear Joe had abruptly disposed of Witchseason and returned to America to work for Warner Brothers. His excellent book *White Bicycles* gives a frank account of the disillusionments, changing scenes, difficulties with artists, which made Witchseason unsustainable. His time at the heart of psychedelic London was done. Not entirely coincidentally, so was an extraordinary musical and cultural period.

In late April '70, in Perth, on my day off the salmon netting, I cashed the BBC cheque for the two radio poems then walked thoughtfully back to the bothy. You start off pursuing what you want to do and be. In time you gravitate towards what you're actually some good at.

Two weeks later I applied for Edinburgh University. I would be paid – not much, but enough – to read books, learn to think better, and spend time with people who found the same things interesting, ideally people cleverer and better informed than me.

Manual labour had its satisfactions and vivid experiences, especially those owl-haunted night shifts on the River Tay, the nets glistening and tinkling with ice even as we hauled them in under the yellow hiss of the Tilley lamp, while moon and stars tracked across the sky. But it savaged your hands and back, and mostly left you too knackered to think or do much more than have a drink then sleep.

Soon enough, I dragged in nets for the last time, packed my few clothes, notebook and *Teach Yourself Greek*, then scootered away from Cleekum Bothy through the chill dawn. That night a bunch of old school mates met up at the Golf Tavern in Elie. Irene joined us, depressed after her Higher maths exam. She had a drunken argument with Tommy and decided she liked him. It was good to be back with old friends, but there was a nagging sense we were celebrating only our past.

After dropping off Irene in Crail, George and I sat in silence throughout the drive back to Anstruther. He stopped outside my house, turned off the ignition.

'This has gone stale,' he said.

A long pause as we sat in the darkness.

'Yes,' I replied. 'Yeah.'

We sat, unable to say more. I got out of the car, feeling very tired.

'Thanks for the lift,' I said.

'Sure.'

He drove off and I went in and up to bed.

It was the most important friendship of my youth. Though we did not know each other very well, in Fate & ferret George and I shared something that shaped us for life. We gave each other courage and conviction, no matter how unrealistic our hopes and hapless our productions.

Thanks for the lift indeed.

Four days later I hoisted an overloaded rucksack into the cab then climbed into the scampi lorry next to Wee Eck. I did not have a guitar, just a harmonica and a fresh journal. I was on my own, something I had long avoided and sought. I was on my way to Greece and whatever gods and home truths awaited there.

The ancient motor chugged and chuntered south through the night. Eck drew on his cigarette and whistled country songs. Above the green glow of the dashboard, the tip glowed on–off red, the ash drifting down onto my gym shoes.

As Wee Eck segued from 'King of the Road' to 'Careless Love', I wedged myself more comfortably into the oncoming dark.

Track 23: Banjo (2015)

"'A gentleman is someone who can play the banjo," Mark Twain said, "but doesn't."

'Fortunately, I am not a gentleman,' I add to the audience, settling the banjo strap across my shoulders. I glance at my musician friends, gather their nods and start the song.

I am almost used to this.

Dark-red antique sunburst mahogany, gleaming chrome, pearloid inlays on a rosewood fretboard, off-white skin drum and the fifth string's extra tuning peg like the flirt of a wren's tail – I loved the look, feel and heft of that Barnes & Mullins banjo.

Early in the twenty-first century, I had gone into the music shop in search of harmonicas for young Leo – now a teenager, my stepson was ready for the blues – but on impulse lifted the banjo off the stand. It was startlingly heavy, the product of a collision between cabinet-making and industrial machine.

I flicked the back of my nails across the strings. The open G chord with the characteristic high *ping* from the extra top string rang out through the shop, harsh and sweet. The few other music-grazers smiled. I smiled. The banjo makes people smile.

I thought, *It's an open chord – how hard can it be? Those years I spent learning to fingerpick could actually be useful.*

I tried the other banjos in the shop. Since the film *O Brother, Where Art Thou?* the banjo had been making a comeback, but none felt as good as the first one. I checked the price tag.

'I can't justify buying this,' I said to my beloved.

'If you play it sometimes at readings, you can claim it against earnings,' Lesley pointed out. 'You look so happy holding it.'

Some men buy a motorbike on turning fifty. I bought a banjo and it led to . . . this.

The banjo's flat crash cuts through pubs and crowded rooms. It survives fiddle and harmonica, guitars, even the accordion. Finger-picked, it adds bounce to stolid 4/4 time, and a swirl to 3/4. It can work with country, bring a lift or plaintiveness to folk. It cannot really take the blues, but works fine with R & B, Hank Williams, Dylan, Leonard Cohen, fifties pop and the American Songbook.

To quieten it down, I remove the back resonator and sometimes stuff a tea towel under the skin. People appreciate that.

Played fast, it makes us smile. Played slow, it makes a spare, plan-gent, accompaniment. It will animate 'The Twa Corbies' and refresh 'Perfect Day' when we round off an Orkney evening's music-making with friends.

It lifts the corners of the mouth, and the heart.

I can't play proper bluegrass, whose fingerpicking is quite different from the guitar style I painstakingly learned at sixteen. My stepson Leo, having rapidly mastered blues harp, found a banjo on a skip and went straight to clawhammer style.

Like me he loves the mountain music repertoire, how its musical plainness and corny religiosity are lifted by fervent harmonies, hair-raising virtuosity and that lonesome mountain tenor. It is white man's blues, haunted by hard times, guilt and salvation. Like the Gaelic psalm-singing George and I were transfixed by on a hung-over Sunday morning in Glencoe nearly half a century ago, it dirls to the bone.

When I bought that banjo in Sheffield, I had turned fifty and was for the first time living full-time with a woman and her children. After a near-fatal brain episode I stopped smoking and second-guessing my life. Writing books, family life with Lesley, Orkney summers and music sessions – all I asked for now was more of these.

I liked Sheffield a lot, but my sense of being in exile in England prompted a book about a Highland fishing quest undertaken in memory of my mentor and friend, Norman MacCaig.

I caught more than anticipated in the *At the Loch of the Green Corrie*. I found myself writing about old loves, dead friends, estranged friends, geology, Scotland, my father – and, briefly, about Fate & ferret in London.

A book is a small stone dropped in a big pool. Ripples go out, some bounce back and alter your life. This had happened before, when my first solo collection *Men On Ice* – itself a revisiting of *Inexplicable Events Near Carstairs Wood** – led to non-metaphorical Himalayan climbing, writing prose books, and making an honest living. Now it was about to happen again.

I was contacted by Adrian Whittaker, passionate editor of *Be Glad: An Incredible String Band Compendium*. He had read *Green Corrie* and wanted to know if the stories and drawings the ISB used in their 1969 concert programmes, credited to '*Fate & Ferret from Pittenweem*' were in fact by myself and a school friend.

I confessed. George and I had done them as a thank-you for the String Band, and left copies with Joe Boyd. We were Fate & ferret.

'Some people will be very interested to hear that,' he said. 'It solves a little mystery.'

He understood I had met Dr Strangely Strange back in the day, and that I played the banjo – would I like to play it on the track 'Mary Malone of Moscow' at the London concert marking the reissue of the Strangelies' second album *Heavy Petting*?

You bloody bet I would.

In late August 2011, still feeling myself a peasant in London, toting the banjo, I locate Camden then the Jazz Café. George is there, already talking to Ivan Pawle, Tim Booth and Tim Goulding. It is as though we had just left them in the pub in 1969, walked round the block and come back in again.

---

* A manuscript version, complete with incense and tea stains, sleeps largely unmolested in a cardboard box in the underground archives of the National Library of Scotland. My first reaction was to sniff it.

Still a bunch of old hippies, basically – goofy, generous, good company. Hair has turned grey or disappeared, but the levity and spark remain. The years have aged but not soured them.

We learn the Strangelies had played on after the second album, then, like a ramshackle VW micro-van, coughed a couple of times and petered out. They do a few reunion gigs, play at String Band conventions and the like. They all live in West Cork. I gather they have got by without doing things they hate, and still enjoy the things they love. By my lights, that is a good result.

George and I talk and catch up as the Strangelies rehearse. We don't get to see each other often, his life has long been in London. In 1979 I'd watched him onstage with the Headboys when they were touring their first album, and their fourth single 'The Shape of Things to Come' was well up in the charts. He'd taught himself bass, wrote and sang tight, witty power pop songs with Lou Lewis. Fate & ferret had been early apprentice work.

Had I felt *It could have been me*? No, because it couldn't.

Envious, then? Yes, in that theoretical, non-visceral way one might envy a fully occupied mother, a skilled picture restorer, or a good leg-spinner in action. In any case, in 1979 I was busy writing my 'divorce collection', the poems of *Surviving Passages*. I was twenty-eight, still writing and getting by without a Proper Job, in a new relationship, feeling like a bruised skinned peach lifted to the world's lips. It was what I'd wanted.

That night they closed with 'Money'. Changed times indeed. George came off stage, sweating and buzzing in his red suit.

'That was great,' I shouted in his ear.

'Too much top end,' George replied. 'Really glad you came.'

'Of course I did.' Our eyes met, then he was swirled away by fans.

For tonight the Strangelies have added a rhythm section, plus a fiddler, Joe Thoma, a quiet, sardonic Irishman in a tweed jacket. Joe brings a certain steadiness to the band, and plays a heart-melting solo air.

Someone is missing. Gary Moore was a brilliant sixteen-year-old guitarist who sprinkled rock magic over *Heavy Petting*, then went on to Skid Row, Thin Lizzy, Colosseum II. One of the great guitarists. But he died of a heart attack a few months earlier, and this concert is in part a memorial to him.

His youthful stand-in is Paul Simmons, who plays crunching, fluent lead guitar. At such moments, the Strangelies sound like a rock band in a way the ISB never did – then they cut to whistle and organ, some spacey harmonies, fiddle, snatch of country, a bit of baroque, then rock out again.

Time to run through 'Mary Malone of Moscow'. I start the lead-in my Orkney friend Mike Moldau had worked out for me. It opens, weirdly, on the third beat of the bar. Pesky hippy musicians! I stumble, lose it. Sweating, I apologise. Why do I put myself in these situations? I'm not really a musician and I'm not really a banjo player; any more than I was a proper mountaineer in the Himalayan years.

I try it again, get through it and the band take the song away. Standing in the wings, George gives the thumbs-up and a big grin. If he has regrets at packing in music after the Headboys broke up, not touching a guitar for years, he has never shown it.

The audience stream in; mostly grey-haired or no-haired, happy, buzzing. Lots of hugs, handshakes and reunions, introduction of grown-up children. A familiar herby smell clings to some sweaters and beards. Laughter, beer, red wine. Many missing faces, present by their painful absence. We're getting to that point in life when every celebration has an element of wake.

Adrian introduces the band to cheers and laughter as they sort themselves out. They start 'Ballad of the Wasps' at more or less the same time, and the evening takes off.

At our table off at the side, George and I check out the programme, and see that Mike Heron is going to sing 'Air'!* And there he is, just appeared in the wings. Forty-plus years on, the wide grin, beaky nose and stocky build are unmistakeable. His hair is still black. He is not carrying a guitar.

Mike comes onstage to be greeted with great enthusiasm by the standing audience. He looks pleased and surprised. A familiar Hawaiian melody ripples off the keyboard. My skin begins to prickle.

Mike takes his hands from his pockets, steps to the microphone. He leans in close and sings.

I look at Mike, at George smiling broadly beside me, then over the rapt faces. I'm thinking of Tennyson's 'Ulysses':

> *Tho' much is taken, much abides; and tho'*
> *We are not now that strength which in old days*
> *Moved earth and heaven, that which we are, we are . . .*

---

* Adrian says it was going to be his mate Green Gartside, but he cancelled late on, and Mike was in town and the Stranglies had played 'Air' at Joe Boyd's Barbican fest. Chance or synchronicity, without which we wouldn't have re-met, or written this.

Time for 'Mary Malone of Moscow'. Banjo neck slippery with sweat, I squeeze onto the crowded stage. Ivan at the keyboards gives me a wink. I can only hope the banjo is still in tune, because I can't hear much over the crowd noise.

I count myself in past the two missed beats, then begin. It's fun, loads of fun being with an amplified band, hoisted up in the net of bass, drums, keyboards. I come back in at the right place and then it's plain sailing, though I must keep counting bars. Always that balancing act of enjoying the moment, while anticipating what comes next.

What comes next is the pause, the cut out, the end. Applause and I'm off, flushed and heady, concentrating on not tripping over the cables.

I know what it's like having people coming and talking to you after a performance. You are still buzzing, a bit tired, already thinking of getting away. At the same time you have books or CDs to sell, and of course it is a lift to meet people who like what you do (fortunately, those who don't seldom come and talk to you afterwards). And then in front of you is a face you may know, who gives their name if you're lucky.

It is a privilege to have these encounters. But it is demanding, and you have already given what you came to give.

So these days I am hesitant in approaching people I admire after their performance. At seventeen, we just assumed that because we loved their music so much, the Incredible String Band would want to meet us. Now we meter out our social energy, and are more aware of other people's need to do the same.

But the pleasure of 'Air' and a powerful sense of gratitude impel me to go over with George to reintroduce ourselves after forty years. Mike grins and nods. His partner introduces herself and tells him I have written lots of books and poetry. He says 'Yes, great. Well done.' He pours wine. Pause. 'You're the ones who wrote those cheeky stories about us.'

We'd thought they were playful homages. We did take the piss a bit, but that seemed in the spirit of the age.

When a casual life-changing suggestion comes about, alcohol is often involved. In the post-gig ease at the Jazz Café, George is deep in conversation with Mike while I talk and drink with his partner. She tells me Mike is starting to play with a young alternative folk band called Trembling Bells, then asks about my doing book festivals and readings.

I tell her about finally coming to terms with performance. Readings are now not a promotional chore, but part of what I do. I've even started playing the occasional song when it fits and feels right. I add that I'm doing an opening reading set for the Strangelies at the Green Note Café tomorrow.

'Maybe you could do a gig together with Mike sometime.'

She suggests I could do my poetry thing and perhaps a song, then Mike does a set with the chamber version of the Bells, and I could join them on banjo at the end?

She repeats her brainwave to Mike.

'That might be fun,' he says. 'Why not?'

The Green Note café is tiny and packed out. George meets me there, exuberant.

'I've found an old letter from Rose to Fate & ferret! And some from Joe!'

I am holding a relic of 1969. Her five-page letter is in pencil, thanking us for our latest package. They are all staying at a friend's place in London. Mike has some psychedelic trousers he is very excited about. The boys are writing and arranging new songs. Robin has got an amazing shirt. Some afternoons they all go and feed the ducks on a nearby pond. Likky says hello.

The letter isn't trying to be amazing, it's just chatty and kind. Maybe that's why it touches me. Rose would have been in her early twenties when she wrote it. They were very young. They thought the world was changing, lastingly and for the better.

I hand back Rose's letter. Time to concentrate.

Better a small crammed room than a big empty one. I'm nervous of course – opening is always hard – but compared to playing banjo on a big stage on an unfamiliar song, this is home territory. I'm doing my own poetry and prose stuff, as I have for forty years.

I read from the *Loch of the Green Corrie*, flashbacks about Fate & ferret hanging around Witchseason with our terrible tapes, smelling of scampi, and meeting the young Dr Strangely Strange when their hair was still long and the grass still got you *into it*, not *out of it*.

Encouraged by the laughter of recognition, I decide to read from the letters from Joe that George handed me.

The Witchseason logo, the swirly lettering, the once-vivid green, the clunky manual typewritten text and the thick yellowed paper

– they're just another administrative chore by a hassled young man making it up as he goes along. Yet they glow with a lost age.

Joe's tactful *I confess I don't know what to make of these recordings* gets the laughs I'd anticipated. I get off, then the two Tims and Ivan and Joe Thoma squeeze onto the micro-stage. The club rather than the concert hall is their natural home, and tonight they're in great form. There are songs from *Kip of the Serenes* I haven't heard since 1970. Joe plays that heart aching air again, then lowers his fiddle and shrugs.

They make mistakes, at times sing differing words. 'Donnybrook Fair' reminds me how Irish they are, in the way loss and heart-break, history, piss-taking and death are all incorporated, accepted, celebrated. They are ramshackle then tight, erudite and innocent. When Ivan sings he must adjust his sense of timing, the rest of the band crack up.

When you drop perfection as an ideal, other possibilities present themselves. The String Band embodied that outlook, as did Dylan and the Velvet Underground. Accept no version of the song will be definitive; then it can be sung with the whole voice. Your life will not be judged but lived.

After the break I do some poems, without reading the book, but holding it for product placement. A poem is in essence a song that happens not to have a melody, though it has cadence, sound patterning, rhythm, tone, voice. The audience are mellow and my anxiety disorder has taken the night off. This comes from the well part of me.

At the end, George and I go on stage to join the Strangelies on Tim G's song 'So Young'. It's a joke among the grey hairs, and yet while we are singing, it feels true.

George and I part outside the Green Note with a twenty-first-century man-hug. He sets off to drive home to Mandy and the kids, and I head off for the Tube, toting the banjo case and my books. If Mike really does want to do that gig, I'll be up for that.

When the Headboys perished in a blizzard of illness, litigation and counter-litigation, George put his bass in the attic, moved to London and got a job in advertising.*

These last few years, we have become closer again. I send him parts of this for his comments, additions and corrections. He enthuses generously, and has been digging out old F & f material. In emails, his passing remarks sometimes startle me into wakefulness. *I look forward to reading more about someone I thought I knew.*

I replied *Me too.*

The last years have been hard. Mandy has been ill. He is now regarded as too old to work in advertising. He teaches a bit, does some storyboarding, has an improbable role as adviser on Alfa Romeo's UK publicity, which means he has to go to his beloved Italy and stroke beautiful cars. And he has started *painting like a bastard*, reawakening that early talent. With the kids grown up, at some point they hope to move back to the East Neuk.

Yesterday he emailed: *We never answered the half remarkable question, but at least we asked it, and that has to count for something.*

---

* Worthwhile finding the Headboys online. Judging by the threads, they are not forgotten. And *The Lost Album* has finally been released.

Track 24: A House Concert

Being here is as improbable as it is temporary. Look up at the night sky, fail to count the stars. Contemplate the million spermatozoa that didn't make it when the one that made you did. Not bloody likely, is it?

Before you there was as much time as there is Time. After you're gone, there'll be as much time again. And you worry about detail? Then again, what is there but the passing details?

The night air is cold but the banjo case grip is hot in your hand as you step into the venue for one of the more unlikely evenings of your life.

Edinburgh house concerts are held in Douglas and Jane-Ann Robertson's sitting room and photo gallery by Holyrood Park. No posters or flyers, just emails. No tickets, no box office, no security. No bar. The venue and the promoters take nothing. All the money, raised on the evening by voluntary donation, goes entirely to the musicians. No deductions, no fees. Now *that's* improbable.

The concept serves a scoop of sixties idealism, another of the do-it-yourself of the punk era, and a dollop of twenty-first-century recession sauce. Musicians value these house concerts for their intimacy and close-packed informality. And, because they pocket everything, such gigs can be better rewarded than much bigger club concerts.

Inside, I shake hands and go through the Robertsons' kitchen and up the stair to the gallery. Mike has not changed for the evening, still in shapeless jeans, denim shirt rolled up his muscular arms.

Hi to Mike's daughter Georgia Seddon, settling in at her keyboard, slight and shy as Mike is solid and relaxed.

Hi from Mike Hastings, the Trembling Bells guitarist who first suggested this venue for a joint show. He is another natural scruff, but a strikingly blue-eyed one, and his casual clothes, youth and beard only accentuate his good looks.

Hidden behind his long black hair, John 'Frogpocket' Wilson is fiddling with his fiddle, but murmurs hello.

This is the chamber version of the Trembling Bells. It allows Mike to do his String Band songs without changing arrangements. Frogpocket covers Robin's gimbri, fiddle and mandolin. Mike H. does second guitar, harmonica, kazoo, harmonies. Georgia's striking keyboard skills, percussion (she thumps a good drum, and shakes tambourine straight from 1968) and vocals, covers everything else.

I've had one rehearsal at the Glen with Mike and Georgia, where Mike made excellent soup from veg cut small and all the same size, then we had a run-through the songs I'll play banjo on. 'Greatest

Friend' has some idiosyncratic timing I had never noticed before, so I have to watch for the slight lift of the head just before he sings.

'Could you take the last verse, Andrew, so I can do my yowling?'

From Waid Folk Clubs to archaeological digs, to Orkney sessions and Glaister family weddings, for forty-five years I've been playing Mike's core repertoire. His songs are inscribed in me, as they are in so many others, as though cut into soft vinyl by a master stylus.

'I can do that.'

'And how about "Log Cabin"?'

'You still do it in G?'

The rest of the time I'd spent arranging a couple of my own songs with Georgia, who is so gifted it's a joy. Her only difficulty is with my inconsistent timing, which I've never had to sort out when playing solo, so she too has to watch for my trigger movements.

As people arrive, I line up my books. Check the vocal mic, the instrument mic, guitar and banjo on their stands.

Lesley waves from the sofa, glass already in hand. There's a buzz because it's been some years since Mike played in Edinburgh. Jim Hutcheson, long-time pal, illustrator, musician, is vibrant with excitement. Like me and George, and a thousand others in the latter sixties, he formed a band in the ISB spirit: the Great Deep. But he hasn't heard Mike play since the seventies.

The place is packed now, with some standing by the stair, others perched on the assorted sofas, the assorted chairs. Low stage, red curtain behind, a few lights, a simple PA. People have brought their own drink and nibbles. It's perfect. It's a *pad*.

Douglas Robertson does the intro for the evening. I look at the book in my hand, breathe deeply from the abdomen, hold my spontaneous opening remark in my head and trust the rest will follow.

As he introduces me, I'm still thinking about the innumerable stars over Holyrood Park, and about how weird this is, to be playing in front of and with Mike Heron.

A spatter of applause. The strangest thing is that though for the last couple of years I have lived with a generalised anxiety condition, I can do this. Despite all my intentions, I have become time-served.

I do my intro, get a chuckle, say how extraordinarily glad and honoured I am to be sharing the evening with Mike and the band. These poems are by way of a thank-you – the song he bears no responsibility for.

I glance at the first line of 'In the Tool Shed', close the book and begin:

> *'Hummingbirds', he said, and spat. Winged tongues hovered*
> *in the half-light of their names . . .*

A couple of hours later, we spill out into the night. Orion's Belt has shifted over the Crags. Sweat cools in the freezing air.

'That went well!' Mike Hastings exclaims. 'Let's do another soon!'

I glance at Lesley. She nods. It must have been okay.

The second half had been a shiver of joy, a sting of moisture in my eyes. Hearing and seeing Mike sing 'Chinese White', 'Painting Box' and 'You Get Brighter' again was to be reunited with part of myself. The hypnotic 'Douglas Traherne Harding' would stay with me for days.

You'll never enjoy the world aright till the sea itself floweth
In your veins, and you are clothed
With the heavens, and crowned with stars.

And to finish by playing banjo and singing alongside him, watching for his cues, feeling the songs fold around us all, was to be away with the fairies while trying to stay present with where the song is now. It would be fine to live that way more often.

Hugs and goodnights. That was great, Georgia. We'll meet tomorrow and divvy up the finances. Loved the mandolin! Goodnight all. Thanks, Mike. I'm glad, glad.

The voices fade, car doors shut. Holyrood Park is empty under the stars. The basalt sill of the Salisbury Crags is still arrested from its cooling 300 million years ago. Lesley yawns, smiles as she gets into our taxi. It's all improbable, so fleeting, real as it gets.

Inner Groove

At some point the overall shape and course of your life emerges like a distant ship sailing out of the mist. You will never captain your country at cricket, be awarded the Nobel Prize in Chemistry or anything else. You will not have children, or more children, not now. Adherents of the law of attraction say anything is possible if you will it enough, but this is delusional. It is clear you will not become a mathematician or a fine jazz pianist.

You get up a little stiffly, step off buses more carefully. You will probably not become much smarter, happier or morally better than you are now.

If you are very fortunate, the one that you yearn for is the one you are with.

At this point in life, when much of it is behind you, it becomes necessary to make an honest reckoning with how you feel about the distance between what you wanted and what you got.

Alastair Mackie retired early from teaching. He had hoped it would be a liberation, but his depressions grew like weeds in a cleared space. He began teaching himself Russian to better translate Pushkin. He wrote more poetry in Doric and English.

I would call in on him, sometimes with a new book by way of a thank-you. Medication made him put on weight and feel dull. But he persisted. His poetry embodies endurance, is thrawn, awkwardly-edged like granite chunks, and like granite has a near-invisible sparkle.

He died in 1994. Much of his life was spent in difficulty, resistance and distress. That was his nature and he lived with it. In 2012 another ex-pupil writer who owed a great deal to him, Christopher Rush, assembled a *Collected Poems*, larger and more varied than anyone could have guessed from the few slim collections Alastair published in his lifetime.

I like to think of Alastair Mackie not troubled but as I saw him one baking summer. Day after day as I played the Anster golf course, he was sitting in a deckchair in his back green, among billowing sheets snapping on the washing line, in shorts, stripped to the waist and turning browner each day as he read and wrote in a notebook on his lap, wearing dark glasses against the glare.

A couple of times he raised his hand as I went by. I waved back but didn't stop, for we were each preoccupied in our pursuit. In the blinding sun, in that garden amidst the washing, he seemed entirely happy. He was writing 'Lines to Mallarmé' and the magnificent 'Back-Green Odyssey', and whose life is not fulfilled who can do that?

And the Boss, who gave us sanctuary, our agony aunt and dating agency, passing around the Drambuie by the fire on wintry nights in Lundin Links – what did we give her, who listened mostly patiently to so much tosh? What became of her?

The Boss met Irene and approved. She believed a relationship with this intelligent, strong-willed, hurt girl might force me to grow up. She was overjoyed when we announced our engagement. She came to our wedding in summer 1977, and her presence there felt like an official blessing.

It was also the last time I saw her. When a couple of years later I had to tear the whole thing up and start again, I wrote but got no reply. I couldn't face her. I couldn't explain or apologise, and didn't want to.

She retired early in poor health – high blood pressure – and moved back to Crianlarich. She didn't get in touch and we were all busy in our new lives.

Years later I got her address, and wrote a short letter. I gave her a quick catch-up on what I'd been doing, the relationships, the books, the Himalayan trips. I told her Irene had married someone more like the person she had wanted me to be, had had two children, was back teaching and seemed much happier. I outlined what had become of the old gang. I said we had never forgotten her kindness and hospitality towards us.

She wrote back that she had not heard news from anyone in a long time, not even Helen. She said her health had improved since she stopped teaching and that it was good to be home. She wished me well.

She did not write *You must come and visit*. She did not say *You all used and then neglected me*. She did not say she was hurt, nor that she remembered those days with pleasure. She neither reproached nor forgave me.

It was on account of the things she did not say that I never quite got back in touch.

Eric Plectrum? The last we had heard he was in Glasgow, 1975, rumoured to be running a disco. Then he disappeared from our lives, uncontactable.

Last night I was parking my car, looked up and saw Eric Plectrum looking straight at me with a rueful grin. In a café he ordered bacon rolls and charmed the waitress with his low, gruff voice. He was elderly but looking good in a tan suede jacket, sideburns trimmed to manageable proportions.

This morning I emailed the dream to George, knowing it would entertain him. Half an hour later, his email response: *Eric P has been found!!*

Right enough, there's the photo on his recently created Facebook site. He is looking out scowling, sardonic, amused. The sideburns are no longer privet hedges, but his silvery hair and beard look good. Underneath he comments *I look like shit.* Same old Eric P, then. And there's a comment from Allan J. Tall! Turns out the sitar-playing hippy actor String Band fan, who put up George and me after Les Cousins and fed us on porridge and honey, is a long-time pal.

I can't wait.

John Myles stayed in the East Neuk of Fife. He married Margaret, a local girl, and they made the move from Pittenweem to Anstruther. With his brother, Dave, the Myles Bros played pubs, and in an augmented line-up played wedding receptions, anniversaries and general festivities throughout the East Neuk for over thirty years.*

John has kept it local because that is his nature. He still writes and sings new songs, and a vast range of old. He can play some of George's, and sing the String Band songs with me.

He was at my first wedding. He came to my father's funeral in March 1984, and shook my hand at the door. I could scarcely see him, but it meant a lot. Nearly thirty years later, he sat beside me at George's mother's funeral, and we whispered about the trays of tea and scones and cake through which she expressed her love. And there he was at my mother's funeral, to shake my hand again, formal and sincere.

When I meet with John back in Anster and he says, 'Aye, aye, Andy – how you doin?' I am back in a place and with people who knew and accepted me then. Our grey hair, facial lines and slight stiffness are surface detail. As we walk along Shore Street and out along the pier, what is striking isn't what has changed but what has not.

The girl I call Helen went to secretarial college, then became a PA. We bumped into each other in Edinburgh 1979. I was with my new, young girlfriend; Helen's eyes moved between us as we talked, she could see perfectly well what was going on.

---

* Had digital home-recording, which allowed the wonderful Fence Collective to create a fully-fledged music scene in the East Neuk, existed then, John would have been at the heart of it.

'Who was that?' my girlfriend asked as we walked on.

'Someone I went out with at school.'

'Really?'

Helen's grey eyes looking steadily at me, under a streetlamp in a haar in Lower Largo.

'Really. Not for long.'

When John organised a Waid thirtieth reunion, the only person I did not recognise was Helen. I looked down surreptitiously at her name badge, and even once I knew who she was, I couldn't see her. She was not in that assured, polished person in front of me, who lived in London, was doing well.

Perhaps I had never really seen her, bar once or twice. It takes a long, long time, if ever, to understand that the person looking back at you is as real as you are, that they too are the one to whom the world happens.

And Cherry, the fisherman's daughter, unattainable object of my longing? She met a man in the first week of her medical studies at St Andrews. They married during her hospital training years.

A few years later he developed lymphatic cancer. 'There are only miraculous recoveries from the kinds of cancer from which people have miraculous recoveries,' she said to me later. 'This wasn't one of them.'

We met up again a few years after his death. Loss had made a bonnie woman bonnier. I was still raw and aching myself, following the departure of my young lover.

That evening we drank too much, laughed, confessed, blurted out things, and I stayed. Which became a deep, healing friendship. Which was strange and lovely, but perhaps that vertiginous, overwhelming feeling had had its time in 1968.

We went out for years but never quite moved in together. In time, after many hills, many meals and a lot of companionable laughter and wine – we both knew the worth of being alive to eat and drink – we parted.

I went back for her father's funeral and sat with John Myles. The kirk was packed, though her dad had been no one illustrious, a deck-hand fisherman most of his life, someone who had taken the Scouts and been an unobtrusive kirk elder. The turnout for this modest, unassuming man made my eyes water. He embodied them and their virtues, and they were of a kind that passed with him.

We still meet up once in a while. Cherry smiles easily and warmly. She has retired, travels and spends a lot of time seeing family and friends. She still climbs hills and says she blesses me for introducing her to them. She has another non-live-in man.

'At this stage, they always have complications,' she laughs. 'I suppose I must have too.'

Krysia Kocjan's life had its successes, but never quite became the extraordinary one her fans, friends and she herself had anticipated. How do we reconcile, without bitterness, delusion, or self-accusation, the gap between what we once yearned for, and the life we actually got? I was aware it was my question, anyone's question at this point in life, even as I asked it through Krysia.

I went back to the Net and found a posting from shortly after her death.

> *Krysia and I, born two days apart, were solid childhood friends. Her vision, voice and visual artistry were beyond radiant — setting her apart from everyone at school. I spent many evenings at her home in Milngavie where she lived with her loving, sometimes nonplussed, parents. Her voice was like none I had ever heard, nor believe I ever will again. Susan xx*

Could this be the Susan in my diary? I had learned not to assume the writer was still alive. I wrote a hasty *I don't know if this means anything to you, but . . .* hit *send*.

> *Dear Andrew, I have to say that yours is one of the most uplifting e-mails I have received in a very long time — and yes, I think I might be the Susan you think I might be. I do actually often think of the time when Fate and Ferret came to Milngavie. George Boyter, at the time, seemed to be spun from a different dimension and almost elfin. You were all what would now be called cool and I was no doubt shy and in awe, even though I could simultaneously talk the hind legs off a donkey . . . Krysia really was a powerhouse, rich and deep and true and sweet — and far too unknown for someone so talented, imo. Susan*

Through Susan I was able to get in touch with Tom Hoy. He is very much alive and playing music. After the Natural Acoustic Band years, he played as part of Magna Carta, and now with his wife. He lives in Yorkshire, and has a son, Rory, who is highly successful as a DJ and music-maker, of whom he is very proud. His creative life, like that of Allan J. Tall, has been a version of what he'd hoped for.

He believes the very size of Krysia's voice, so remarkable in live concerts, was never captured properly in the recording studio. *She had this major talent, but no one ever worked out how to make it fit and present it.*

Between Susan and Tom I learned how after leaving NAB, Krysia made a solo album, *Krysia* under the name Krysia Kristianne, and worked as a session and backing singer, most notably with Al Stewart. She abruptly moved to Los Angeles, and circumstances and a few dubious choices made her life very difficult for some years.

She got very ill. Susan visited her. It was painful and at times they laughed a lot.

> *The last time I heard her sing we went to a hotel in LA for some odd reason and we found a piano. She sat down to play me a song she had just written – so there we were, just the two of us – Krysia's voice still making every hair tingle and me thinking how this mammoth voice housed in this tiny body was slowly disappearing from the world.*

But Krysia's life and health picked up. She met and married Robert and they moved on to happier times in Portland, Oregon, with Krysia teaching singing and making her own recordings. People who met her were struck by her humour, warmth and how at ease she seemed with herself, music and life as it had been and now was. Susan only learned of Krysia's death through the Net when, having lost touch, she thought she would try to find her again.

It's heart-reviving to be in touch again with people from so long ago, and feel a renewed sense of contact with their lives, and thus with one's own. Other people's memories can lodge in us as though they were ours. Through Susan, writing from a very isolated house in France where she lives alone with thirty-one cats (*I don't know how this has happened*), I picture Krysia Kocjan, already seriously ill, playing piano in an empty room to no audience but her childhood friend. And I think of how her life picked up, how even through illness she found a Buddhist perspective from which she could live gracefully and gratefully.

Krysia was I think one of those charismatic people who richly communicate yet remain ultimately unknowable, even as they sing out their song. In that, such people are like any of us, only more evidently. Perhaps that is why their voices and lives move us so.

It's raining women's voices as if they were dead even in memory and you too are raining oh marvellous encounters of my life

Our fantastical adolescent hopes don't come to nothing, though *Fate & ferret from Pittenweem* remain a footnote fallen through the hole in the lining of an ISB anorak's anorak. They lead to something else instead, something different from what we had imagined, yet connected to it.

Instead of a life in music, I have had a life in writing. Turned on by the String Band's vision of the Joyful Player, counselled by Alastair Mackie, influenced and encouraged by countless others, I have managed to live forty years without a Proper Job. That is hard work, and insecure on several fronts, but if my seventeen-year-old self had been offered that, he'd have grabbed it.

I show up in the shed most mornings, ready do my best. Some

days words are inert, and sentences aerodynamic as a leaden Zeppelin. On good days it is the best game in town, and I stumble out of the shed with very little idea of what has gone down, only that I can't wait to get back to it tomorrow.

By and large, good days are earned by persisting through the tough ones.

The aim is to make paper gliders that fly for a while across a crowded room, a correlative to the bird in Bede's *Ecclesiastical History* that flies out of the darkness, through the warm, lit, feasting hall, then back into the dark again. The hope is to make something of interest, pleasure and use to myself and my fellow mortals – values I took direct from the String Band.

There are plenty of people who can do things with words I can't, and even more who play much better than I do. That's not a reason to stop. When you cease pursuing perfection, it is possible to be more fluent, fearless and kind. Mike and Robin knew that in 1966, when they began to make the music they wanted to hear but didn't yet exist.

Through some unexpected, random yet inevitable connections, for a couple of years I have been doing gigs with one of the gods of my youth, who has also become a friend. Which is like wearing bifocals, and sometimes still makes me slightly giddy.

We never made those albums with Joe Boyd. The wonder is that he gave us any time at all.

Then again, our complete lack of success protected us from the grimmer realities and disappointments of the music business. As Tom Hoy remarked about his experience in the Natural Acoustic Band: *A shark wearing a kaftan is still a shark.*

As provincial schoolboys at the very fringe of things, we briefly met some people who made the sixties what they were. That was a scene where you could call in on Robin Williamson baking cakes while having a domestic stand-off, or sit in the corner of Sound Techniques studio while Joe Boyd tried to rescue 'U' and corral the drunken Fairports, or hang around in the Witchseason office gassing with whoever came in. And some jokey piss-take stories and Pan drawings sent as a homage would turn up in a concert programme.

We were too young and too geographically removed to catch the full blast of the sixties. Perhaps that saved us from being over-whelmed, over-influenced, or left burned out when it was over. The String Band affected us profoundly, but we had to invent our own local version. In this we were typical – silly, inspired, earnestly and laughingly aspiring, provincial. It is that common experience I have tried to explore, for though that time passed, it marks us to this day.

Recently Mike talked about how much easier it had been to get by in the bohemian world of the early sixties. A couple of coffee house or club gigs a week – solo acoustic guitar, no overheads – were enough to cover the essentials, with some left over for recreation. Before he joined the String Band, he was making about sixty quid a week, doing bottleneck folkie blues, Fats Domino and Dylan. Sixty quid, in 1965!

He smiles that same glad smile. 'I was quite well off, really! That's how I was able to leave home and move in with Michelle. When the String Band started playing bigger halls and making all these albums, there was more money, then there wasn't.'

At the very most, he is rueful about it. If they had played Wood-stock in the rain on that first magical downpouring folkie afternoon;

if Robin had been happy doing songs to plug the current LP and the back catalogue, instead of songs no one knew; if not for 'U'; if not for Scientology . . .

Then he grins, and that characteristic shrug. He just can't bring himself to worry or obsess about it, any more than he could have spent his life as a chartered accountant.

He is playing more than he was ten years ago. There are many grey-hairs and no-hairs when he looks out from the stage, but also a growing proportion of younger people curious about this strange, uncalculated, liberating music from a now mythical time, the sixties. To have played at Woodstock, the UFO club, Bill Graham's Fillmore West and East, and recorded with Pete Townsend, Keith Moon and John Cale – that makes you part of a legend. Not many people have responded to Eric Clapton's backstage offer at the Fillmore with 'Na, we don't jam, man.'

People want to come and hear and touch the multicoloured dreamcoat of the sixties. To those who were there at the time, it resonates with our early, truest selves. To another generation, it is a glimpse of a world that will not come again.

'If people want to hear my songs, I'm very happy to play them,' he says, and laughs.

In Ledbury, Edinburgh, London, Berlin, Aberdeen, Anstruther or Aviemore, Mike finally stops tuning his guitar, looks up at the audience – not vast but enough, an audience – and smiles that Joyful Player smile. He hitches up his jeans. He nods to Georgia at her keyboard, to Mike Hastings ready with guitar and kazoo, and

Frogpocket poised over his mandolin, then takes a deep breath and launches into 'Everything's Fine Right Now'.

Standing in the wings, clutching my banjo in preparation for the next number, I look on and feel tingly-glad because I can see that, yes, indeed it is all fine right now, because the song makes it so, and that is the point of singing it.

> *Come a little closer to my breast*
> *I'll tell you you're the only one I really love the best*
> *And you don't have to worry about any of the rest*
> *'Cos everything's fine right now.*

Acknowledgements

YOU KNOW WHAT YOU COULD BE

Many thanks to everyone who supported me.

For early encouragement and thoughtfulness: especially Corrina Seddon, Andrew Greig and Andrew Bicknell.

For helping to bring the days back and reminding me where I was: Atty Watson, Dave Clyne and Ian Ferguson.

For their parts in the story: Joe Boyd, Robin Williamson, John Wood, Mike Smith, Mary Stewart, Archie Fisher and Allan Coventry.

For generously giving their time and help on the way with lyrics, photos, tables, paper, pens, and assorted goodwill: Georgia Seddon, Dave Brown, John Schofield, Alan Danks, Nathan Osher, Ed Jones, Lindsay Levy, Vashti and Al, Adrian Whittaker, Lesley Glaister, Yonnie Fraser, Nick Pynn, Kate Daisy Grant, Roland Owsnitzki, Eva Gnatiuk, Alex Neilson, Vinnie, Mike, Simon and John.

For riverrun for their patience and trust: Jon Riley, Rose Tomaszewska and Josh Ireland, and literary agent Georgina Capel.

The following books were a great help: *White Bicycles*, by Joe Boyd; *Dazzling Stranger*, by Colin Harper; *Be Glad*, Edited by Adrian Whittaker; and *Empty Pocket Blues*, by Grahame Hood. Also the website www.wolfgangrostek.de, by Wolfgang Rostek.

Remembering Owen Hand, Hamish Imlach and Clive Palmer.

IN THE FOOTSTEPS OF THE HERON

My grateful acknowledgement and thanks to George and Richard and Eric Plectrum for their trust and enthusiasm in sharing their diaries and memories; to Atty Watson for his record-keeping and reflections; to Mary 'Spud' Stewart of Temple Cottage, for her generosity of spirit towards so many, then and now; to Susan Reid Ure, who filled me in on the Bearsden gig and her long friendship with Krysia; to Tom Hoy for his recollections, generous input and the crack about kaftans and sharks; to Adrian Whittaker for his invaluable *Be Glad: An Incredible String Band Compendium* (revised 2013 edition); and to Joe Boyd for *White Bicycles* and buying us breakfast at 'Mrs P's Pantry' when we were faint with hunger.

In memory of Alastair Mackie and Krysia Kocjan.

Photographs

YOU KNOW WHAT YOU COULD BE

Atty Watson © Allan Coventry

Backstage at Clive's Incredible Folk Club, courtesy Ian Ferguson

On stage at Clive's Incredible Folk Club, courtesy Ian Ferguson

Music shop © Joe Boyd

Temple Cottage, courtesy of Mary Stuart

Mike Heron and Robbie Stuart, courtesy of Mary Stuart

Publicity shot for the Incredible String Band © Michael Ochs Archive, Getty

Mike Heron playing Robin's guitar © Estate of Keith Morris, Redferns, Getty

Mike Heron, Georgia Seddon and Trembling Bells © Eva Gnatiuk

Mike Heron and Ashraf Sharif Khan © Roland Owsnitzki

IN THE FOOTSTEPS OF THE HERON

Kilconquhar Inn © P. Drahony
Back Country Brouhaha © P. Drahony
Kilconquhar '70 © P. Drahony
Bedroom Dream Corner © Andrew Greig
How to find Robin © F & f archive
Back country roof © P. Drahony
Electric Ferret © G. Boyter
To-Do List © F & f archive
Krysia and Susan © Susan Reid Ure
The Amazing Value Show © F & f archive
House Concert © Douglas Robertson
Strangely Young © Sean Kelly

Photographers otherwise unknown.

Songs

Lyrics reprinted in the book are from the following songs: